MEN

MONEY

and the MATRIARCH

Holly Gordon

To Janice,
Enjoy the road of my life! ♡ Holly/Morgan

Holly Gordon
Men, Money, and the Matriarch

First Edition

Softcover ISBN 978-1-0694040-2-2
Hardcover ISBN 978-1-0694040-0-8
eBook ISBN 978-1-0694040-1-5

Cover + Book Design | Angela Campbell
Editor | Judith Doyle
Publishing Management | TSPA The Self Publishing Agency, Inc.

"Being a female writer means taking what happens to you in life, processing it, and then putting it out in the world so you can turn your lessons into your legacy."
—Taylor Swift

"Everything is copy. Everything is from my life experience."
—Nora Ephron

The integrity and honesty of this book are dedicated to Courtney, the miracle and joy of my life.
I will always cherish the people who believed in me and granted me the freedom to be myself.
The individuals who betrayed or attempted to exert power over me were my primary motivation for writing my story.
Thank you.
This is our one life.
There is no dress rehearsal.

MY STORY IS MESSY,
RAW AND REAL.
IT'S FILLED WITH MOMENTS
I WISH I COULD ERASE.
BUT IT'S ALSO,
A STORY OF RESILIENCE,
FINDING PEACE
IN THE CHAOS, AND
DISCOVERING
A GRACE THAT
SAVED ME.

Contents

Prologue

My name is Morgan Ross. My life is a tale of risk, heartache, passion, trauma, betrayal, and learning to cope through laughter, love, impulsive behaviour, looking ahead, and, in many ways, not feeling. I keep moving. Dancing in the rain and singing to the red cedars has been my way of coping and experiencing the essence of life in its rawest form. Life is a wild ride, and this is mine. Others have persistently encouraged me to write my story, and now I am finally sharing with you, the reader, what life was like growing up as Morgan Cooper Ross.

One can only fully grasp a person's life by looking at the fabric of their youth.

Chapter One

Childhood Dreams

"Faster, Sally, faster!" My fingers grip the leather reins tightly as my body leans forward and my knees press into the saddle, galloping over the vast open pastures on my chestnut horse, clad in a cherry-red jacket and knee-high riding boots. With a smile, I feel the wind rushing against my face and experience the thrill of freedom.

Suddenly, a loud knock jolts me awake from the serenity of my perfect dream.

"It's time to get up, it's time to get up, it's time to get up this morning. Someday, I'm going to murder the bugler; someday, you're going to find him dead. It's time to wake up, it's time to wake up." I hear the familiar wake-up call of my father knocking on each of our doors, singing as loudly as he could.

It was his favourite way of rousing us and reminding us that the "secretary of war" was waiting for us downstairs in the kitchen. My mother never liked that nickname or the implication that she ran the household like an army boot camp, but it did hold for our family.

I am the eldest daughter, with three younger brothers: Charlie, who is just ten months younger; Henry, who is two years younger; and the youngest, Ben, who arrived twelve years later. My father often said Ben was the only one who was planned and my mother's favourite child. This has always unsettled me. My early years feel like time capsules filled with photos and reminders of life. However, with three energetic children born within three years, the predominant memory is chaos! The fact that Henry was an undiagnosed autistic child added a layer of complexity. The dinner table was always a gathering marked by dysfunction and unrestrained energy, devoid of calm and ordinary conversation.

As the only daughter, I had to help my mother with the cleaning. The boys were noisy and disruptive, so they were sent away to avoid causing distractions. While I wanted to support my mom, it felt unfair that my brothers didn't have to participate. "Like this!" my mom would huff at me, needing to control everything from what we wore and ate to how we spent our time after school and who we played with. I would tidy up swiftly and efficiently while watching the boys play hockey or wrestle in the living room.

It felt as if my mother viewed me merely as her third arm, a valuable extension of herself, rather than as someone who relished joining the boys outside on the baseball diamond my father built in our spacious backyard, where I insisted on playing first base. I wasn't just someone who enjoyed swimming to the farthest raft, skiing down our local hill to reach the gondola first or climbing trees the fastest. I sensed that I was more competitive than my mother; it wasn't her nature to participate in spelling bee competitions or strive for the highest marks in math. As the eldest, I wanted to be the first and the best at everything except cleaning up.

One day, I remember being fed up with my two brothers, angrily packing my porcelain ponies into a suitcase and running away from home. At just five years old, I stormed across the farmer's field to Granny's house, my little suitcase rattling and the sound of porcelain ponies clinking against each other, hoping not to break any of their legs.

I adored Granny and Gaga's home. Granny always greeted me with, "Hello, Sunshine," welcoming me because she knew I needed a break from the boys' constant fighting. I asked her if I could move in, and she said, of course, but I had to let my mother know I was there. Granny and Gaga's place felt calmer and kinder with Dickie, the little yellow bird in the cage with whom Granny often chatted, and he seemed to respond. "Doesn't Dickie want to fly free, Granny?" The thought began to upset me, so one day I let Dickie go by opening his little door and then the back door, hoping he would find his way to freedom. "Fly free, little yellow bird." Sadly, Dickie didn't leave the cage, even when offered a humbug from Gaga's bowl next to the big wingback chair he seemed permanently glued to. I tried everything to get Dickie to fly free and explore the world rather than simply listen to Granny's endless chatter all day and breathe in the room filled with Gaga's awful smoke. After one night with Granny and Gaga, I decided to trek home across the field when I couldn't stand the smoke from Gaga's chain-smoking, which turned his one finger yellow. It seemed he never went a minute without that little rolled-up piece of fire in his mouth. It made no sense that someone would want to take that awful little white stick, put it in their mouth, suck on it, and then blow out that dreadful-smelling smoke. Adults did strange things. His routine involved lighting the cigarette, inhaling it as if it were heaven, and then butting it into an ashtray full of other butts. That discouraged me from ever wanting to run away from home again. Mom was always so excited when I came in the door and would ask if I wanted to help make cookies because I think she felt bad that I wanted to move out at five.

My mother enjoyed routine. Every night at bedtime, after we brushed our teeth and put on our pyjamas, we knelt next to our beds, hands together, eyes closed and prayed. My prayer was always the same: Please, God, could you give me a pony? I would be so happy and kind to my brothers if I had a pony. I would treat the pony well and love you so much if you could do this for me. Thank you, God.

At nine years old, my life was happier than ever. I played on a baseball team with my best friends, and my dad and his good friend, Sharky Chapman, coached us. We wore striking, vivid red uniforms with bold yellow letters that proclaimed the Collins Bay Cardinals. I remember feeling proud to be a first base Cardinal, part of a team that gathered twice a week in the summer. The excitement of throwing the ball to home plate to get someone out, winning a game, and hitting a home run provided an adrenaline rush. After the games, my dad and Sharky would open the trunks of their Delta 88 cars so we could sit in the back with our feet dangling out as we drove to the corner store for ice cream cones on those humid summer nights. It might not have been the safest thing to do, but it was so much fun, and we laughed all the way, especially when Debbie ripped her shorts during the game while lunging for a ball as the catcher. Dad and Sharky loved coaching; it was a special time for me to spend with my dad.

My birthday falls in winter, five days before Christmas, and I remember waking up on my 10th birthday to the soft sounds of snow gently hitting my window, clinging to the pane in intricate patterns as I tried to see the six sides of each snowflake. Instead, I saw distinct angels with the morning sun streaming through. Magic always seems to happen on my birthday! The anticipation of Christmas blended with my eagerness for my birthday, accompanied by the twinkling Christmas tree lights, the music of "Joy to the World," a visit with Santa, and the crunch of snow beneath our feet when we went outside to build a snowman. For an entire month, I lived in a state of ecstasy. I felt fortunate to be born so close to Christmas, not focusing on the birth of Jesus Christ but rather on the arrival of Santa Claus.

After absorbing the angels flickering in the light on my window, I sat up to see so many beautifully wrapped presents with large, colourful bows at the end of my bed. I jumped out of bed and ran downstairs, embracing my mom in the kitchen, wearing her Christmas apron and making a big stack of pancakes.

"Happy Birthday, Mugs! Put on your warm clothes; we're heading out for a birthday ride in the snowstorm, so bundle up," Dad called out from the basement, where he was getting the boys organized with their goalie pads, sticks, pucks, nets in place, helmets, and usually a parent to referee for my brothers more than the others.

Finally, we climbed into the big Delta 88, an aquamarine blue car. I got to sit in the front seat for our secret destination. Bundled up in the snowstorm with my cozy coat, toque, and matching mittens, I felt ready for anything and anywhere Dad would take me. I always cherished one-on-one time with my father because he would surprise me or make me laugh until I cried. One never knew what the day might bring; it could involve chasing fire trucks to see if one was at a house he had built in the subdivision or meeting his buddies for pizza at Murphy's.

My father worked weekends and evenings in real estate and was often on the phone. He was funny and remarkable in his ability to make everyone laugh and feel good about themselves. However, I don't recall him joining us for many meals at the table, but I don't blame him.

He always felt proud of me and believed I could handle being around adults whenever we went out. Dad made me feel special and reminded me that I was the eldest, which meant I had the privilege and responsibility of experiencing life before the boys. My reactions to those firsts taught the boys how to respond.

As we drove through the streets in blinding snow, people were out shovelling, kids in boots and snowsuits hauling toboggans to any little hill or ditch to slide on, and cars moving slowly through the snow. My excitement was building as I wiped the condensation from my window. We approached a wooden fence I recognized as the farmer's field with cows and sheep. I hoped Oscar, their dog, was there so I could throw snowballs for him. We trudged through the deep snow towards the old wooden fences, and when I glanced at the red barn at the top of the hill, snowflakes kept getting into my eyes. Dad whistled loudly. He didn't usually do that when we visited the cows or Oscar, but the barn doors slowly opened, and three ponies galloped down the rolling hill, kicking up snow clouds. The smallest was a Shetland with a big red bow around her neck. They approached the fence, and he handed me cut-up carrots from his pocket to feed them. I placed the carrots on my mitten and eased my arm through the fence as they gently grabbed the carrots with their lips while I patted their noses and crunched down on them. Snorting through their nostrils and seeing their breath in the cold, desperately trying to get more carrots, I was smitten and overwhelmed by their beauty.

My father raised his camera just as I looked up. Amid the sound of crunching carrots, he shouted, "Happy Birthday, Mugs!"

As the little Shetland pony nibbled my glove, I was taken aback by the moment's significance. I shook my head at him.

He said, "All three ponies are yours because I bought the farmer's field, which came with the barn and the ponies. Their names are Judy, Debbie, and Smokey." My first thought was that I needed to change their names, but then I was shocked to realize my dream of owning a pony had come true, multiplied by three.

"Thank you so much, Dad, for this amazing birthday present, but how will I learn to ride them?"

He glanced at the nearby barn. A woman older than me emerged, walking towards us in riding boots, an oversized coat, and a cowboy hat.

She had long blonde hair and a big smile as she approached us. Dad quietly said, "Morgan, I want to introduce you to your new riding coach, Tabatha Winters."

She stood on the fence rail, leaned over to hug me, and whispered, "Happy 10th birthday, Morgan. You're one lucky girl, and I can't wait to teach you how to ride. Can you start after Christmas? We'll start you on Debbie and then move to the taller pony Smokey, a pinto and almost a horse."

It was all so exhilarating! I couldn't believe it, and I never took my eyes off those beautiful, gentle creatures. They resembled the porcelain ponies I had in my bedroom for so many years, covered in snow. I asked Tabatha if their feet were getting cold and how they stayed warm in the snow.

She said, "They are meant to be outside as their coats get thicker, and their feet have strong shoes to keep them protected and warm!" My dad and Tabatha chatted while I petted Judy, the beautiful black silky horse, and I realized they were all girls. With two brothers at home and their numerous male friends around, I was the only girl in the neighbourhood besides Carol, who lived next door.

Dad then said goodbye to Tabatha, made plans for me to come to the barn on Boxing Day, wished her a Merry Christmas, and petted each pony, saying, "Welcome to the Cooper family!" I have never felt giddier, more spoiled, or more bursting with joy than when I fed each of them another carrot.

As we bundled into the car after brushing the snow off our coats and toques, I leaned over and gave Dad the biggest hug ever. His cheek felt cold and damp. He wiped his face with his glove, wondering if he might be wiping away tears from this fairytale of mine. I looked straight ahead as the wipers struggled to clear the snow from the windshield with all their might. We sat quietly, believing this was the best day of our lives, unaware of what was coming our way.

Chapter Two

Broken Innocence

On our way home, the snow trucks were in front of us, making that loud grinding sound against the paved road. The snow was building up quickly, and kids were making snowmen with various hats and droopy smiles. I wondered if my friends could come to my birthday party that afternoon as I couldn't wait to tell them about my fantastic birthday presents. I was still shocked when I bolted into our house, yelling, "I got three ponies for my birthday!"

My mother was in the kitchen and asked me if I was surprised and what their names were. Charlie came bolting into the kitchen with a bloody nose from someone's hockey stick and didn't care about my news. He wanted Mom to see if his nose needed stitches and that Robby Thomson should get a penalty for high sticking. Does he realize he's not an NHL hockey player but 9 years old and in our backyard? That was my moment to run upstairs to my bedroom to carry my presents downstairs and open them at the kitchen table.

The first gift, all wrapped in beautiful pink flowered paper, was a riding jacket. Then the following gifts were riding boots, a crop, jodhpurs with leather patches on the inside of the leg, and an incredible black velvet helmet that fit perfectly. Mom knew the surprise and kept it a secret for a long time. I tried on everything and went to my parents' bedroom to look in the full-length mirror, and there, staring back at me, was the rider I had always dreamed of being. I loved watching the horse shows with the jumpers wearing poppy red jackets and riding their strong athletic horses over jumps so gracefully and effortlessly. In awe, I couldn't believe that at 10 years old, I would be a rider with three ponies. It was almost too much to take in. I asked my mother if I could wear my riding outfit to my birthday party, but she said, "No, they are only to be used when you are riding, and you don't need to brag to your friends about your ponies today. They will find out in time." It was exuding out of me, so how could I lie about my over-the-top joy? I told them everything with glee, and they were thrilled for me and couldn't wait to visit the ponies and maybe get to ride them.

After the chaos of my birthday, Christmas was filled with opening more gifts, stuffed stockings, my grandparents coming all dressed up for the turkey dinner, Gaga smelling like smoke, pumpkin pie with whipping cream, snapping crackers with mini toys and hats to wear, and always followed by playing the hockey game on the floor with Charlie and Henry. Tradition meant family with both sets of grandparents; my mother always rose to the occasion with the most fantastic meal.

Waking up on Boxing Day, after enjoying my hot oatmeal with maple syrup, I put on my warm coat, thick pants, and boots because my mother didn't want me to wear my beautiful riding outfit, which was only for shows and special occasions. She wanted to meet the ponies and Tabatha, so we drove in her little white with navy blue interior B2002 BMW. My parents loved their cars and always seemed to have the latest version of what was cool. This car, of course, could have performed better in the snow, but off we went. As we approached the barn, my mother stopped the car and said she had something to tell me. I feared something had happened to one of the ponies, which would be my greatest nightmare. Instead, it was another nightmare: she was pregnant and expecting a baby in the spring.

My only response was, "I pray it will be a sister. We can't have more boys in our family; we just can't." I don't remember feeling excited; I only recall dreading the idea of a baby in the house, contributing to the chaos.

My first riding lessons involved learning to put on a saddle and bridle and shovelling out the stalls filled with manure. We would walk around the field with Tabatha, ensuring that I could stay in the saddle when she started Debbie trotting. Posting posed the most significant challenge, but moving in rhythm with the pony beneath you felt sensational, as if you were one with such a fantastic animal when done correctly. The most exhilarating thrill was using your body and thighs to direct the horse where you wanted her to go. No words needed to be exchanged, no tugging on the bit in her mouth—just a movement of your legs and body to signal how you wanted to move and at what speed. When I got home, stinking of manure, I wasn't very popular as I walked through the door, but I felt so happy after spending hours with the ponies and Tabatha. My mother would send me straight to the laundry room, and the boys headed to the garage with their stinky hockey uniforms. The scents of sweaty hockey gear and horse manure filled our home—no wonder my mother felt constantly nauseous during her pregnancy.

In spring, my friends Kimmy and Phoebe invited me to go skiing for a weekend in Vermont. My mother was happy to have me spend the weekend with other girls instead of all the boys or the ponies I typically spent my time with. The snow was slushy, and many patches of mud were barely visible. Although the conditions weren't ideal, it was clear and sunny, and we loved having the freedom to ski wherever we wanted. At the top of the mountain, the French fries and milkshakes tasted the best, and then we skied down for our last run of the day. I tried to beat Kimmy down the most challenging run and get to the bottom ahead of her, but I hit some mud that I didn't see and fell. My ski didn't come off, and I could feel my leg twist and heard the cracking sound that I knew had to be my leg. Kimmy came up behind me and asked if I could get up, but I was in so much pain that I couldn't move. The ski patrol arrived and lifted me into the sleigh, knowing this was serious. They took me to a doctor at the First Aid station, who used a stethoscope and tapped my shin right where the break was. When I screamed, he said, "Looks like you have a break and will need a cast." Kimmy's parents decided I should have a cast put on back in my hometown in Canada rather than in Vermont, so we all piled into the car with me lying in the backseat. At the same time, poor Kimmy and Phoebe sat on the floor, handing me M&Ms throughout the trip, thinking that would help with the pain. Every bump and movement hurt. At the hospital in Kingston, my very pregnant mother stood there with my father, waiting at the emergency door as they placed me on a stretcher and took me for X-rays. The hardest part was when they took off my ski boots. Another scream! The diagnosis was a spiral fracture of the tibia, and I would need a full cast up to the top of my leg for six weeks, followed by a half cast for three more weeks. It felt like that meant no riding for a lifetime.

They kept me in the hospital until I could use my crutches, which was quite depressing. I was in pain and couldn't sleep. The cast was so heavy that I needed a nurse to assist me to the bathroom. All I wanted was to go home and curl up in front of the TV. Instead, I was told that my mother was in labour, and I needed to stay in the hospital because my father couldn't look after me at home with the two other boys. The next day, a nurse entered the TV room and said my mother had her baby, and that my father would bring the baby down for me to see. I began to pray that it would be a girl, and when my father walked into the room, he asked me to hold my new baby brother, Ben. I instantly started to cry. This can't be happening. He gently placed the tightly wrapped baby on my lap and said he would return. That was when I melted as our eyes met, and he looked so fragile and precious.

That year was a mix of double Dutch skipping; I was an ever-ender, forever relegated to holding the ends of the skipping rope while the others skipped while getting used to a new baby. Hobbling around school on crutches was humiliating, and I was also gaining weight, which my brothers noticed and nicknamed me Tubs, doing nothing for my spirits. My mother was often too busy to pick me up from school, so she sent Gaga in his red Ford pickup truck, which reeked of smoke. I watched him as he simultaneously managed the wheel and his cigarette, hoping the ashes would land in the little ashtray, but often, they fell onto his winter coat. I would plead with him to let me visit the ponies, as I was anxious to get riding again.

Every night, after I put on my flannelette nightie and turned off the light, I would lie in bed with my hands in a prayer position, my eyes closed in the dark stillness, whispering:

"Now I lay me down to sleep and pray to the Lord for my soul to keep. May His love be with me through the night and wake me with the morning light. And if I die before I wake, I pray the Lord my soul to take. In Jesus' name, Amen. And God, could You please make this cast come off very soon so I can ride my ponies, whom I love so much? Oh, God, thank You for my baby brother, Ben. I'm starting to like him a lot. Good night, God."

That year was a blur of blisters under my arms from the crutches, feeling sorry for myself, sitting for hours, giving a bottle to baby Ben, and watching him grow into a living human being. To top it off, I got my period, and no one spoke about it; only pads and pins appeared at the end of my bed one morning, so I had to figure it out quickly. With two boys using the same bathroom, I had to keep it all a secret, leading to much hiding in shame about the fact that I was now becoming a woman and was terrified about it. The lovely nicknames began with Charlie calling me "Bra" or "Tubs," so welcome to the world of puberty. When you can't run and jump around, you might tend to get a bit chubby, and it's just another thing that makes me feel self-conscious and aware that I am different from my brothers, but perhaps that's a good thing.

Chapter Three

Grow Up

Sweet children, I must warn you.
That by this time next morn
Something will be lost inside
As something else is born.

You'll forget about your fairytales
And worlds of make-believe.
Tonight, while you are slumbering
Your daydreams will unweave.

Reality will tip-toe in.
And by the new day's dawn
The little child that used to be
Inside of you is gone.
—Stefanie Anonymous, *Growing Up*

I was in the kitchen setting the table for dinner, walking on a boot cast, freed from that horrible full-length cast I had been wearing for the past two months. As the cast reached only my knee, I could finally bend and scratch my leg with my knitting needle if needed. Then, the landline phone rang.

My mother picked up and chatted with my father about his day when I heard her say, "Willy, are you there? What are you trying to say? Are you ok? What is happening?"

"What's happened?" I needed to know. Mom's face was white, and her mask of control was slipping.

"Um, your father just went quiet and hung up on me. Again. Three times this month." She shook her head.

"Does it have anything to do with his terrible headaches?" I rechecked to ensure all five and one baby plate were set.

"It must," she distantly uttered. Her nurse instincts seemed to kick in as she added, "I need to get him checked out."

One hour later, Dad tumbled through the door. He'd driven into a ditch, but the person behind him was kind enough to drive him home. Dad seemed confused but was speaking coherently now. My mother looked at him and said, "I'm calling Dr. Dinsdale." She was a nurse before I was born and knew all the doctors from socializing with them, so I wasn't sure what specialty Dr. Dinsdale had, but it felt urgent and severe.

The next day, my father went in for a CT scan. When the doctor called my mother that evening, she tapped my father on his shoulder to come upstairs so they could speak to the doctor privately. All private calls occurred in their master bedroom, which looked out over the golf course. I stumbled up our spiral staircase, sitting outside their door, hoping to hear what the doctor had to say and trying desperately to hear through the door.

I heard nothing but my mother crying. A sound I realized I had never heard before.

At dinner that night, we all gathered around the table with little Ben in his high chair. Dad broke the news to us, saying, "Alright, kids. I have some news to share with you, and it's not good, but you will need to be strong for your mother and support her when she needs it." I expected the boys to groan when asked to help, but even they could sense how serious Dad was.

"They found a brain tumour at the back of my head right here that needs to be removed." He patted his jet-black hair. "That's why I drove off the road. Look, kids, I may not be in great shape for a while, but I will fight with everything I have to be a good father for as long as possible. It would be best if you boys got along; no more fighting, and Morgan, you'll need to help your mother with Ben. We will get through this as a family." Dad was forty-three years old, and we sat at the table, each processing the news, but mainly we were just scared.

One week later, on the morning of his ten-hour operation, there was a light knock on my door. Dressed in a V-neck sweater and plaid tie, Dad came in and sat on my bed.

"I love you, Mugs." He patted my back. "I must tell you: you are stronger than the boys. You're only twelve but must be the pillar of strength now. If the operation is unsuccessful, I want you to know that you should take over my business. You and I are the same. Same personality. I know you will succeed. This may seem like a lot to tell you now, but you need to hear this from me, ok?" His piercing blue eyes radiated love and trust in me, something I felt deeply for him.

"You'll get better, Dad." I felt like I was giving him an order, but I couldn't picture my life without him; he had to recover. "Then we can visit the ponies together, like at Christmas. I prayed last night that they would remove this terrible tumour from your brain so you could laugh again without suffering from headaches. I love you, Dad." I wanted him to know that I could be responsible, and as we hugged, I promised to be as strong as ever, assuring him that Mom and I would take care of the home and the boys until he was all better. He got up and quietly left my room. I lay in bed, holding my pillows tightly, as I heard the garage door open and Mom's car drive away.

Mom told us when she got home at dinnertime that the surgery was successful and that they removed as much of the tumour as they could. Family friends came over, laden with casseroles, large pots of soup, homemade bread, cookies, and cakes, and hugged us all, though they knew not to stay for long. Seeing familiar, kind faces was a good distraction. My mother looked tired and rattled as she fed Ben while the boys had their dinner watching the Bruins hockey game in the family room. It was best not to ask any more questions to keep the home calm, to keep the boys busy, and to keep Ben entertained, fed, bathed, and off to bed. While I cleaned up the dishes, I asked Mom if the operation went well, if Dad was in pain, and when I could see him. She said, "Maybe in two days when the swelling has gone down."

Before crawling into bed, I kneeled against it, praying for my father that he was not in pain tonight and that he would come home soon. As I tried to drift off to sleep in the dark, all I could think of was my father's swollen head, what that must look like, and how much a knife cutting into your skull must hurt.

The day had arrived; I got to miss school so I could see my father. The scent of hospitals, the harsh sense of death, and the heavy burden of doctors and nurses tasked with the responsibility of saving lives while clad in their white coats, always with a stethoscope hanging around their necks, left me feeling suddenly weak at the knees as my mother held my hand. We wandered down a corridor with patients in glass-walled rooms, surrounded by large machines and numerous tubes.

I didn't know what to expect. I didn't want to see my father in pain, so I turned to face a room where a nurse opened the glass door, and then… darkness.

"Morgan, Morgan, wake up, wake up. Are you okay? Did you hit your head?"

A cold cloth was pressed against my face. I sat crumpled on the floor. Soft voices. White uniforms.

"I think I'm going to be sick." Waves of nausea crashed over me.

Finally, my mother, seated beside me, said, "Do you have any water? I'll assist her into the chair." As I slowly got onto my hands and knees, I noticed the small wheels on the metal legs and remembered where I was—the hospital.

In the chair, Mom wrapped me in a warm flannelette blanket and handed me a glass of water. That's when I noticed a man with a large white turban adorned with a huge purple brooch at the centre, his black and blue swollen eyes nearly shut, and a head twice the average size. Tubes emerged from his arms, poles flanked him on either side, and bags filled with pink and yellow fluids hung nearby. Machines surrounded him, with lights glowing on the walls behind his bed. My father, I recalled. We were at the hospital to visit this poor man, who wore a slight grin on his battered, unrecognizable face. I tentatively approached and laid my hand on his.

"Mu-uggs?" He squeezed my fingers.

"It's me, Dad."

Mom told me they had removed most of the tumour, but not all of it, as Dad didn't want to be left a vegetable or blind. I didn't fully understand what that meant or what it would signify moving forward.

He closed his bruised and battered eyes, trying to smile, but I noticed that one side of his face didn't move. Before I knew it, my mother said softly while taking Dad's hand, "It's time to go; see you tomorrow, Willy."

It had only been a month since he drove off the road.

Chapter Four

The New Game

"Always remember, you are braver than you believe, stronger than you think, and loved more than you know."
—Christopher Robin to Winnie-the-Pooh

Two years have passed since my father's surgery, and we knew it was only a matter of time before the tumour would grow back. It has been an adjustment for the family, as the home environment is heavily influenced by Dad's headaches and the amount of coffee he needs to stay awake. He continued working while I kept going to school and riding on weekends until, one day, Dad picked me up at the barn after I had been riding all day and practising my jumping. There was a horse fair in two weeks that Smokey and I were excited about, eager to show off how good we had become at jumping. I have only fallen off twice and, luckily, have had only one concussion.

From everyone's reactions when I come home from riding, it's clear that I smell like horse manure, but I don't notice it. My brothers cover their noses and dash to another room, while my mother always signals me to head to the laundry room.

When my father decided to swing by the golf club where he was the President, he looked at me and said, "You need to stay in the car, or you will empty the club with that smell."

I have always been proud of my smelly jodhpurs and riding jacket, so I never took it personally. While waiting in Dad's new Cadillac, I faced the driving range and watched boys around my age hitting golf balls. I'm almost fourteen, and these boys are super cute and seem to be having fun.

I don't recognize any of them from my school and wonder where they're from.

When Dad gets back in the car, wincing from the sudden hit of barn smell, I ask him, "Hey Dad, where's the girls' golf clinic?"

He looks out at the boys, then at me, and says, "That's a good question; we don't have one."

With that, I say without any hesitation, "Well, you need to have one, and I want to be part of it."

As we headed out of the club's roundabout, he was quiet and said, "If you can find twelve girls around your age who want to take lessons and whose parents are members, then you can have your girl's clinic."

I was excited about learning to play golf and meeting all those cute boys. However, riding by myself daily with a coach was lonely, and I realized I was desperate to socialize and belong to a group of friends with a common interest.

At dinner, I shared with Mom what Dad had said, and she immediately replied, "That all sounds great, but you can't look after three ponies, compete in riding shows, and take up the game of golf. You'll need to choose between riding and golfing."

My mother's approach was generally to tell me what I had to do rather than discuss the implications of each choice. I understand; she had four kids and a husband who could pass away any day from a brain tumour. We never knew when the tumour would start growing again and take him from us. That uncertainty loomed over our lives like a dark, ominous cloud, occasionally allowing the light in and then, without warning, erupting into a massive thunder and lightning storm, compelling us to seek shelter. My two brothers and I experienced this emotional cycle of fear of loss, fear of life without our father, and fear of disrupting the quiet rhythm of the house during our teen years, while Ben, being so much younger, didn't fully grasp the overwhelming dread like the rest of us.

Henry suffered the most. With his curly blonde hair and piercing blue eyes, he often banged his head against the wingback chair in the family room for hours while watching hockey. He hated loud noises, chaos, sudden changes, and conflicts. Aloof and labelled as shy by my parents,

Henry struggled with relationships. Unfortunately, he did not receive the professional help he needed for his undiagnosed autism. Teachers sent notes home stating that he had difficulty focusing in class and socializing with others during recess. Still, he was a phenomenal writer and a talented athlete.

My father worked hard daily acquiring commercial properties to generate an income that would support my mother and their four children without her needing to return to work as a nurse, all while maintaining their lifestyle. He consumed twenty cups of coffee each day to cope with the heavy doses of phenobarbital.

His encouragement to join the golf club and engage with a wonderful group of other kids was a gift. I loved learning to play golf, especially with those charming boys. It was incredibly emotional when I saw the three ponies being transported in a horse trailer to another farm, where a family had bought them for their children to ride. Visiting them at their new barn and meeting the two sisters who would care for them and ride them made me feel much better, although it did not stop the tears on my pillow that night.

I discovered some fun baseball hats to accommodate my blonde ponytail and swapped my riding outfits for new golf shoes, flirty skirts, and golf tops. My mother gave me a set of her old golf clubs but told Dad I needed a new set for Christmas since hers were too long and worn out. He replied, "When you break 100, you can get your own set of clubs." It felt so mature, and I was thrilled about this new world of golf etiquette, making new friends, and belonging to this membership. I love everything about golf: the morning scent of freshly cut grass, birds singing in the trees lining the beautiful, vibrant, lush fairways, and the perfectly manicured greens with a red flag centred in each one. The goal of striking that little white ball with the right club and achieving the perfect connection while keeping the target in mind was the most significant challenge. Though it was a solo sport, I played alongside others who competed against themselves, encouraging one another while trying to outdo each other. I felt happiest on the golf course, where the boys and the pro who worked with me admired my natural golf swing.

At fourteen, I envisioned my future in tournaments and playing on the LPGA. My confidence in my game helped me trust my swing and believe in the trajectory of each shot. Standing over the putt, I could see it going in and its path. It was the most incredible sound when the ball dropped into the hole. Nothing brought me more joy; the more I played, the more I wanted to compete. The golf club's junior championship was at the end of the summer, and every morning, I walked to the clubhouse to collect my new PING clubs and begin practising. I would set up little drills and then have my coach work with me to increase my yardage or improve my short game. Hours would pass as I hit bucket after bucket of balls beside the traps and the practice green, trying to get the balls as close to the hole as possible, oblivious to the others practising around me.

I played with Geoff, Jeff, and Cam daily throughout the summer. We would play eighteen holes, relax on the clubhouse deck, enjoy a burger and a milkshake, and then head out for another eighteen holes. Our home was a charming New England-style house with white siding and dark green shutters on the thirteenth fairway. I took pride in that home and its beauty, with window boxes overflowing with red geraniums and the exquisite garden my mother tended. It was a twenty-minute walk to the club each morning, and I would wander home, dodging golf balls on various holes while often waving to friends. It was a magical summer for me and my golfing friends.

I felt prepared and excited as the time for the club championship approached. It was a two-day event, and I was speechless when we teed off at the first hole. After my initial drive veered left—something I had never done before—I had to calm down, but it helped me focus. I finished third after the first day, and that night, my father said, "Mugs, if you want to win this, you can. It's up to you. You've got the best game of all the girls. I'll be there cheering you on."

By the ninth tee, a small crowd was gathering to follow my group, and I enjoyed the attention. The other girls were friends, so they appreciated the support as well. It all came down to the 18th hole, where Julie and I were tied as we made our way up the fairway. My approach to the green had to be precise to sink my putt for a birdie and win the tournament. Julie went first, and her second shot hit the edge of the green before bouncing past the pin. Someone yelled, "Go in, go in the hole." At that moment, I knew I had to be close. I glanced at my dad, who smiled and quietly said, "You got this." As the ball left my club, I reminded myself to follow through to the target; it took one hop and then ricocheted to the right side of the green, landing six feet from the pin. That's when I finally started to breathe. I sank my putt and clinched the club championship. Since my father was the president, he presented me with the trophy after a brief speech about Julie and my competitors, joking that I should give him strokes the next time we played together. That was an extraordinary moment with my father that I will always treasure.

The following summer, I entered any local tournaments I could and hoped my father or mother would drive me to them. I was desperate to get my driver's licence, but I was six months away from my 16th birthday, so I had to be patient.

My mother was never very supportive of my playing and would say, "Why can't you just play with the other members at the club? Why do you need to compete?" She golfed as a social member and didn't care about becoming exceptionally skilled. She loved chatting with her friends and walking on a beautiful course for four hours. It always amazed me how someone could take up a sport and not strive to be the best at it. We never played together, which seems strange now, so she never saw how good I was or how seriously I took the game.

At one of the tournaments, I placed second. As I walked off the green, a reporter from the local newspaper interviewed me about my game and whether I ever wanted to pursue a professional career. I said, "I'm only fifteen, but I would love to have that career more than anything. I'd freak out if I got to compete with those amazing pros."

After playing a game with my usual group of guys the next day, we sat on the patio, ordering cheeseburgers and thick milkshakes, when a member approached our table. At that moment, I had a massive crush on Geoff, which made me feel a bit giggly and excited to be around him. He was an impressive golfer, exuding great confidence with an incredible swing. His jet-black hair, deep blue eyes, and fit physique in Ralph Lauren-style golf attire made him quite attractive. The member was older than us and asked if he could speak with me briefly. He was a handsome man with blonde hair and a charismatic personality. I'd seen him around the club, where he always waved and commented on my golf outfit or the hat I was wearing. I sensed he was flirting, and I must admit, I liked it. How could you not? It was flattering, and I received plenty of attention in the cute little golf skirts I wore, with my long blonde ponytail pulled through the hole in the back of my golf hat. I now felt aware of my sex appeal for the first time, which gave me a sense of power.

I took my vanilla milkshake with me to sit with George at the bar at the Club, and he asked, "What are your plans in the next few years with your golf?"

I said I had no plans but to play lots and go to university after high school. "You should consider going pro, and I could get MacDonald's to sponsor you."

What? Sponsor? What does that all mean? He said it would mean living in Florida for the year, working full time on my game, playing in every tournament to lower my handicap and then trying out for the LPGA.

"I will need to talk to my father about it all, but I must finish high school, and that is two more years. Thanks so much, but I am not ready to do that at all and leave home."

As I thanked him and walked away, he said, "Think about it."

Sitting back with the boys, they all said at once, "Was he asking you out?"

"No, he thinks I should go pro at some point."

The boys said in unison, "He wants to date you!" I shook my head and thought they were all wrong and just jealous.

That night, I asked my parents to meet me in the sunroom because I had something to discuss with them. When I shared what had happened with George at the club, my mother shook her head and said, "I don't trust him."

My father smiled and responded, "Not yet, but I'll contact him tomorrow to find out what this is all about."

A few days later, George approached me while I was hitting balls at the range. I was unsure what to say, as my father hadn't followed up with me. As he got closer, I sensed his energy and felt excited to see him again. Leaning on my driver, he came closer to my face, whispering, "I have strict instructions from your father's good friend, Judge Henderson, to stay away from you."

"Why?"

"They believe I want to date you and that I'm too old for you."

I asked, "What could they do to you if we dated?"

"Run me out of town," he choked back. My first reaction was to rebel, my second was anger, and my third was how transfixed I was by his sea-blue eyes.

Then, as he walked away, I yelled, "I have a tee time tomorrow morning at 7:30 if you want to join me?"

He glanced back with a huge smile, tapping the peak of his Calloway baseball cap to say, "See you there."

Chapter Five

Unravelling Threads

George and I discovered that if we played early, not many of my parents' friends were around, allowing us to be discreet while sneaking behind trees for a bit of mischief. We would play golf right by my home on the 13th fairway, and I would wave, hoping my mother was looking out the window or gardening. One day, I made my longest drive on the 13th hole, thinking my mother wouldn't notice how far it went, but George did. Nothing else happened that summer except for kissing behind trees, mainly due to the fear of being caught and George's respect—or perhaps fear—of my father and his instructions. In September, I returned to high school to try out for the cheerleading team while George kept himself busy opening more McDonald's franchises in Toronto and Brockville. His world felt vast and sophisticated, and his wealth was impressive. Something was captivating about him owning a heritage mansion by the lake with a roundabout driveway, his thick blonde hair blowing freely in his stylish red convertible Porsche, and his thrilling career.

Yes, he was thirty-four, and everyone in town spoke of him with envy, jealousy, and curiosity. I remained silent about our secret golf games and flirtations, hoping to avoid causing any commotion.

I began grade 11 feeling excessively confident. My summer was filled with remarkable golfing: I won two tournaments, was featured in the local newspaper, and had a successful older man consider me extraordinary.

As I walked down the school hallways, I felt taller and cuter with my long, sun-kissed blonde hair, and my newfound confidence seemed to attract our head boy and star quarterback, Harry Steele. He was in his final year, two years older than me, and I used to have a crush on him. However, now that I was spending time with such a successful, good-looking older guy who had a house and a fancy car, Harry didn't seem to hold the same appeal. He lingered around my locker until, one day, he stood directly in front of it.

"Hi Harry, how's it going? Great game yesterday."

He looked at me nervously and quickly asked, "Would you like to go to prom with me next month?"

Going to prom was something I had always dreamed about. A prom involves wearing a stunning gown, doing my makeup, attending a pre-party, and enjoying a late night of dancing and celebrating with my graduating class. He was the star quarterback, so after processing the question and feeling my cheeks flush, I replied slowly, "I'd love to, Harry. Thank you."

While washing the dishes that night with my mother, I said, "Well, Mom, you'll be happy to know I'm going to the prom with Harry Steele next month."

Her response was what I expected. "Thank goodness you're finally interested in someone closer to your age, and his father, Dr. Steele is well-respected in the community. Dad and I won't worry now about you and that older man, George Cohen. He would only have caused you problems in your life."

I wondered if he would cause problems for me or you, Mom.

The prom was a magical night. My mother had a full-length dress made for me, and everyone was so excited about going. I was one of the lucky girls in my grade to attend. I had a fancy cocktail at the pre-party, which made me feel dizzy and odd. Harry was kind and said we had to dance to wear it off. He surprised me with his dance moves and made sure I met all his friends, which made me look at him differently.

Over the next few years, Harry and I became inseparable. He was romantic and kind and felt like part of the family. As my father's health began to decline and the tumour became more aggressive, I withdrew and sought emotional strength from Harry. He went off to university in the city, but we met every weekend and chatted on the phone every night. I was infatuated with him and wanted to attend the same university to be near him.

Our home was challenging since all three boys played hockey, which turned the garage into a storage area for their smelly hockey gear. One parent or both usually drove to or picked up from a game, making dinner together a rare occasion. I remember feeling the independence of building my own life while everyone pursued their paths without addressing the topic of death. We all thought about it, felt it, quietly feared it, and acted out impulsively, unsure of the reasons behind our actions. Tempers flared, boys shouted and swore, and teens tried to detach from their parents, but the idea of separating from a parent forever was overwhelming. We kept our feelings inside without therapy or discussion, repressing all emotions. That was the unspoken rule of the house to survive.

My brother, Henry, was getting in trouble at school, on the ice rink, with friends, and was struggling to understand his mental illness. No one was addressing the fact that Henry had a problem. He often sat in a chair with his hands over his ears, rocking back and forth. He was a talented athlete, but when anyone checked him too hard against the boards in hockey, he lost his temper and ended up in the penalty box many times each game. Henry was sensitive to bright lights and loud noises, which were overwhelming and stressful. He avoided social events by not showing up or leaving early. He could pick up languages quickly and had an excellent recall for song lyrics and dates. Henry was fragile and frightened about his father and life without his leading supporter.

My mother was overwhelmed and felt it was best to keep going, making decisions for us all, avoiding my brother's apparent illness, and not confronting her husband's impending death. Where does that leave her and all of us if the father, the breadwinner, the glue of the family, dies?

Chapter Six

Rocky Mountain High

"What are you planning to do this summer, Mugs?" was my mother's opening question at our Sunday night dinner.

We were all gathered around the table, and all I wanted was to play golf and compete. Harry was quite the romantic, and by this point, we were inseparable, so he tried to convince me to work near his summer job in northern Ontario so we could be together. My mother had other ideas.

"Your father and I have contacted Bill Henderson, who sits on the CP Rail board."

What? Then she mentioned that he sits on the board of CP Rail, which owns Jasper Park Lodge, and could help me find a summer job there. My first thought was, "Is that near Harry?" But no, as I was informed, it's in Alberta, which is 4,000 km away and has a two-hour time difference.

"When would I start, and what kind of job are you thinking of for me?" Part of me was excited about the opportunity to explore a new place, but I went numb when I heard I would start as a chambermaid.

My father looked up from his plate and quietly said, "You leave in two weeks, and we have a ticket booked for you. Many university students from across Canada work there for the summer. It should be fun. Think of all the new friends you will make."

I couldn't believe they had booked my ticket, which meant no golfing this summer and no Harry. "What day is my flight booked?"

At this point, my mother was clearing the table, the boys had dispersed, and Dad took a phone call from a partner, needing to leave the room to chat. In her apron and staring at the sink, my mother sheepishly said, "Dad booked a ticket for you on the train, which will be a great way to see the country. You'll be there in three days."

I stood up and yelled as loud as I could. "I'm not going. This is insane. You haven't even asked me if I want to go. I have golf booked and don't want to leave home for three months."

After running up to my room in tears, I felt a strange sense of excitement and curiosity about this adventure my parents had decided I should embark on. Somehow, I felt privileged that kids with unique connections to the board of CP Rail got to work there. I had never seen the Rocky Mountains before, and while I cried into my pillow, my mind went to two places simultaneously. One place was sad, and I was desperate to be with Harry and my family. The other was excited about change, new people my age from all over Canada, new challenges, and the fact that I could make a bed and clean a washroom. By the time my mother knocked on my door, my anger and fear of leaving home had transitioned into a turmoil of emotions. "Where do I sleep on the train?" I blurted out as I strutted around my room, sitting at my desk, rushing to my bed, and looking out the window as the questions and panic emerged.

"Where will I sleep at the Lodge? Will we wear uniforms? How much money will I make? Is anyone from Kingston going? How will I tell Harry that I won't see him for the whole summer when we can't even handle being apart for a week?" I finally sat down on my bed, holding my head in my hands, trying to quell the rising anxiety, unsure of how to cope with this unexpected situation created by my parents. There was no discussion: they had decided this was best for me.

My mother smiled and gently reassured me, "This will be good for you to gain independence from him and be free for the summer. Learn to enjoy your own company for a bit and meet all these new people. You will be in staff housing, sharing a room with three other girls your age, and you'll have some time off to play golf. I understand you can step into waitressing if a position opens, and then you could earn a lot of money in tips. Feel free to bring your clubs if you'd like. I wish I had had this opportunity when I was your age. It's an adventure, Morgan; embrace it. Trust me - have adventures while you can."

I did not sleep that night with the ping-pong game in my head, which caused me to switch from sadness to excitement. How do I break the news to Harry?

While packing and tearing up after saying goodbye to Harry on the phone, my mother came into my room with a gift for the train trip. I still wondered why I couldn't fly, but at this point, I was letting them dictate my plans and thought maybe they knew best. One week after graduation, I sat in the Purple Car of the train, waving to my mother and father as the train slowly left the station. I had that sensation that change was about to happen.

As the other passengers and I settled into our little compartments, I pulled out my needlepoint, which Mom had given me to keep my hands busy and started the new project. My stomach fluttered with anticipation of my first solo journey. As the whistle blew, the train jolted slowly, gathering momentum down the tracks toward the Rocky Mountains.

Three days on a train is exceptionally long and tedious, and the people in my car started to irritate me, being so much older, but I woke up early on our last morning and pushed the button to open the blind. The clouds looked like they were shining, but then the mountains became focused, and the shining clouds were glimmering snow peaks. Seeing grand, majestic, and powerfully stoic mountains made me start waking everyone enthusiastically, crying out, "Look, look out, look at these incredible mountains. They are massive and so beautiful. You must wake up and see them."

After some growling, grumping, and coughing, the blinds started rising, with my car mates rubbing their eyes and muttering, "Wow. Stunning. Beautiful. We must be there soon."

I packed up quickly and couldn't wait to arrive in Jasper. I wanted to get out, smell the mountain air, and be surrounded by these towering, bold pieces of rock. I was captivated.

I was the last to arrive in Jasper and ended up in the top bunk in the staff housing. Colleen was from Ottawa, Whitney was from Newfoundland, and Annie was from Toronto. We were all new, the same age, and so nervous and excited to be experiencing the same thing together. Whitney had a funny Newfie accent, which I loved.

On my bed was an orange uniform with a black checkered apron, and thankfully, I brought my own down pillow and stuffed teddy bear from

Harry to sit on my bed. Colleen gave me a tour of the communal showers, which proved to be my greatest nightmare, as I have always had privacy in my bathroom, being the only girl in my family. Luckily, I packed a big towel and a cozy housecoat. We went through the Staff House and met many new girls from all over Canada and from different universities. They all seemed so cool, and I couldn't wait to get to know them.

As we left the Staff housing, Colleen said, "You are going to love the Bean, our cafeteria, and this is the Quad where we hang out. Over there are the boys' quarters, where curfew is midnight. The ones I have seen are cute and are mainly from Calgary. There are 442 guest rooms and a golf course, and we must stay long enough for the Texas Conference at the end of August, where we make huge tips."

I needed a shower and decided to have one after getting unpacked. Maybe no other girls would be there, which was clear, so I was relieved. Whitney opens the door and yells as I dry my hair, "Morgan, we are all going for dinner. Will you be much longer? We're starved."

The head Char (chambermaid) was named Muriel, and she was like an army sergeant. Muriel checked everything with her clipboard, and the secret was getting into the room before she arrived to eat or steal anything left on their room service trays. That was my first and last experience with Caviar.

All the Chars were excited about the Sadie Hawkins gala the following weekend. The girls got to ask the boys, and I was excited about asking Bert East, hoping someone would not beat me to it. He had thick blonde hair, hazel eyes, and a fantastic golf swing. Luckily, I wore my favourite pink silk halter gown and striped pastels, perfect for the occasion.

Every night at midnight, there was a warden-style checkup to ensure we were in our beds, but we got a pass the night of the Sadie Hawkins. All I remember that night was Bert looking so stunning, a young Robert Redford, and he bought me a Harvey Wallbanger, which was so delicious. I remember having a couple, lots of dancing and laughing, then crawling across the Quad, a green space of long grass and trying desperately not to pass out in my pink silk gown that had arrived just in time. Why am I crawling on the grass? What happened to Bert? Why can't I walk? Where is my bed? Keep going, keep crawling; you are almost there. I made it to the toilet just in time to throw up; there was so much orange colour, and when I sat on the cold tile floor, my dress had green grass stains and mud all over it. My head hurt, my body hurt, and I needed to get into bed, or I might die.

I heard the girls come in, laughing and telling stories about the night, asking if I was still alive, but I couldn't speak, which concerned me. The splitting headache woke me up the next day, and I begged Whitney to call in sick for me. Before heading to work, she brought me a large bottle of ginger ale and potato chips loaded with salt. Slowly making my way to the shower down the hall, I stood under the hottest water, cleaning every part of my body, which felt like it had been hit by a bus. I never wanted to touch alcohol again and wanted to avoid running into Bert out of pure embarrassment. Being that drunk with messy hair and slurring my words, I must have looked terrible. It's just not a good look for all the vanity reasons, plus the pain in my head. It's frightening to think I remember little from over two hours when I usually prefer to be in control. While the water ran over my face, I thought, Alcohol equals NO control. Therefore, NO alcohol!

A few weeks later, as we lay in our beds one night, anticipating Warden Maureen's roll call, Whitney suggested that we sneak out on our day off and hitchhike to Banff, about four hours away. At first, I thought she was crazy, but as she laid out the game plan, I started to get excited about how much fun it would be to see Banff.

I whispered, "What about the warden check? How do we avoid that?"

Whitney quietly said, "We stuff our beds with our clothes, and she won't know the difference."

"Oh my god, that sounds wild, but what's the worst thing that could happen? Let's go!" uttered Colleen from beneath my bed. We all giggled in the affirmation that it was a plan!!

Hitchhiking with two other eighteen-year-old girls was reckless, but we made a pact not to get into any car or truck unless a woman was in the car. If a guy seemed weird, then don't get in. Off we went with our backpacks, stuffing our beds in positions that looked somewhat real. Out the window we crawled, and Annie had to stay behind to work and be our cover. It was light until ten at night, so we had time to hitch a ride. Trevor from Valet knew of our plan and volunteered to drive us into town in one of the guests' cars, which turned out to be a beautiful Bentley.

He left us on the side of the road, and we looked at each other, thinking, now what? Okay, let's put out our thumbs; let's see who's heading to Banff. We started walking, and as we came around a corner, we spotted four longhorn sheep on the road, prompting us to get our cameras out for photos. The beautiful animals against the stunning backdrop of the snow-peaked mountains were exhilarating. We forgot we were on a highway and around a corner, so when a pickup truck came barreling towards us, we froze with the longhorn sheep, hoping it would stop in time. Bert and Tommy screeched to a halt, rolling down their windows to shout at us, but then recognized it was the Chars from the Lodge. I hadn't seen Bert since that diabolical night of Harvey Wallbangers, which made me feel sick. I recalled hanging over the toilet in my gorgeous silk gown, covered in grass stains, mud, and bare feet. Where did those shoes ever end up?

They motioned to jump in the back of their black Ram pickup truck, and then Bert said, "But Morgan, you sit up front."

Tommy hopped out, and I climbed in with my backpack, squeezing between the two boys. Bert, who was driving, glanced at me and said, "Well, you look much better than the last time I saw you." Tommy laughed.

I sheepishly said, "I'm so sorry. I will never have another Harvey Wallbanger for as long as I live. What happened, Bert? Why didn't you make sure I got home safely that night? I crawled across the Quad, trying to get my bearings. It was scary. Where did you end up?"

Now, he looked sheepish when Tommy started giggling. He said apprehensively. "We returned to my room, but you passed out, so I left you to sleep. You had vanished by the time I returned with some aspirin and soda water."

I blurted out without thinking, "Did we go back to your room and have sex?" I started to recall some vague memory of being in his room, but then again, how would I know about his room? His face turned red, and I understood. My head drooped, and tears filled my eyes.

I asked again, "Did we have sex or not?"

He remained quiet, and when we stopped at a red light, his hazel eyes met mine. He said, "I wanted to, and you wanted to, but you were too wrecked, so I let you sleep on my bed while I went back to the dance. You passed out on my bed, and I wanted you to be safe there."

"So, you left me in your room passed out?"

"Yes."

"We didn't have sex?"

"Not really."

Three weeks later, after we got caught leaving the Lodge without permission, receiving demerit points, and having our parents notified, I missed my period. It came like clockwork, but perhaps it was late due to all the hard work in the dining hall after being promoted to waitress. I carried trays with up to ten meals during the breakfast and dinner shifts. The tips were incredible, and after one week, I earned more in tips than I did in an entire month as a chambermaid. I loved meeting all these wonderful guests worldwide and having fun bantering with them. It showed how much I enjoyed connecting with new people with unique stories.

What was happening to me? I woke up feeling nauseous, and my breasts were sore and painful. Colleen looked at me oddly that morning when I emerged from the cubicle after throwing up for the second time that week. "Morgan, could you be pregnant?"

I looked at her and said, "How could I be? I haven't had sex for months." Her face started to change, her eyes tearing up, and her hands began to shake as she put them to her face. "Bert. Sadie Hawkins. Did you have sex that night?"

I instantly collapsed on the floor, yelling, "Oh my God, Colleen. Fucking Bert. Seriously? Oh my God, No. This can't be happening. He told me we didn't, Colleen, because I blacked out, and all I remember is crawling home. He said he left me on his bed, though. Oh Shit! I need to see a doctor right away, Colleen."

My mind went into business mode. I can't have a baby now. I'm starting University in September and taking the Commerce program to take over my father's business after he dies. This does not fit into my plan or my life.

After receiving confirmation of my pregnancy that day,, I went to the Pro Shop at the Lodge and saw Bert chatting with two guests. God, he's cute, but what a fucking asshole. He lied to me, and I have the proof now. I was in a state of shock at the possibility of being pregnant, angry at myself more than anything for losing control, and saddened that this guy I liked had taken advantage of me.

He looked surprised to see me.

"I need to speak with you privately, Bert." He looked worried when he saw me. We stood behind the Pro Shop, where no one could see or hear us. I was strong and decisive. "What you did to me was wrong. Lying about it only makes things worse! We were both drunk, and I encouraged you in my Harvey Wallbanger haze. I'm pregnant from that night, and I'm getting an abortion next week. I never want you to mention this to anyone—not Tommy or anyone else—and I will never discuss it again. Do you understand? I'm taking responsibility, but you took advantage of me, and I'm equally mad at myself. Your father is the head of Atco in Calgary, and I know he wouldn't be happy about this. We're only 18 years old and need to live our lives. Promise me you will never do this to another woman for as long as you live." I was shaking as I spoke to him, saddened that he wasn't the person I believed him to be and angry that I was so foolish to let this happen.

"I promise. And, Morgan, I'm sorry. Please let me know if you're alright after your trip to Calgary. Do you want me to come with you? I never meant to hurt you. I was drunk that night as well, and I hope we've both learned our lesson about drinking too much. I think you're amazing, and please forgive me; if not today, then one day."

"You will be covering the cost of the abortion, Bert, and that is how we will proceed. You must clarify why you spent most of your summer earnings at Calgary General Hospital."

I walked away, knowing what I had to do now. I was sad and scared but resolved.

Chapter Seven

Dear Dad

Dearest Dad,

After graduating from Queen's, I didn't have much time to spend with you before Mom sent me on a flight to southern France. She wasn't keen on me spending time with Harry while he pursued his MBA in London and didn't want me to marry him. I'm only 22, so that would have been a bit silly.

I loved attending school in Aix-en-Provence and learning to speak French fluently. You would be impressed to hear me communicate now, especially when ordering a cappuccino or un vin rouge. My roommate, Rebecca Ram (pronounced Vibecaa), is from Norway; unfortunately, we spoke more English than French to each other. Madame Carlette often felt sad when her husband was away, so we tried to make her laugh with us. The French have a unique understanding of marriage in which men openly have histoires d'amour with their maîtresses. Now, Madame Carlette goes out on Wednesday nights, while Monsieur Carlette goes out on Thursdays. She seems much happier now.

After school ended, I took a train with Rebecca and Emma to Val d'Isère in the Alps and landed a job teaching skiing to British tourists. For some reason, the French don't seem particularly fond of the British, so they were keen to hire me for the position. The job includes a fantastic royal blue one-piece ski suit with an orange collar, and they provided me with Rossignol skis and my room in the main lodge, which I absolutely love. It's been an incredible experience, and the skiing is fantastic, featuring very steep runs and soft, light snow. Whiteout often occur here, and just the other day, I was using my poles to figure out which way was up or down, feeling as if I had six British lives in my hands. It was the scariest experience ever. At one point, I told them to sit in the snow because I had no idea which way was up or down.

Mom may have mentioned that Harry no longer wishes to wait for me, and I can't blame him for that. I planned to be in France for three months, yet it has now extended to nearly a year. It's time to come home, get my real estate licence, and start working with you and your business. I'm eager to dive in and learn as much as I can about the industry from the best. Thanks, Dad, for believing in me.

I plan to visit a friend from Queen's in Switzerland, whose aunt lives there. I'll enjoy fondue and chocolate before flying to meet you, Mom, and Ben in Marsh Harbour. It's going to be a challenge to wear that bathing suit.

Dad, I'm sorry for being away for so long. Mom mentioned that your tumour is worsening, which makes me feel sad. Your trip to the sun will be amazing, and I can't wait to spend time with you there. Thank you for encouraging me to spend time in France this year. I miss you more than ever, Dad, and I love you so much.

I look forward to seeing you on the beach soon.

Love, Mugs xoxo

After eight hours of flying back to Canada and then home to unpack my ski gear and repack for the hot weather and beach, I returned to the airport the next day to catch a flight to Nassau, followed by a small floatplane to Marsh Harbour in the Bahamas. With virtually no sleep, I felt the humidity and oppressive heat as I stepped out of the small plane onto the dock, struggling to cram my jacket and scarf into my bag. I scanned the area for a cab. What a shock it was after the snow and cold of Switzerland and the Alps! I missed the friends I had made during my three months of skiing in Val d'Isère. Jeremy, the Canadian mining executive, and his buddies from the gold mining company were charming and excellent skiers. We got to know each other through plenty of flirtation on the dance floor at the resort disco. Who cares if he was ten years older? He was very charming and attractive, I must admit.

The taxi slowed in front of a white, shuttered Colonial-style house on the beach as I grabbed my bag. Feeling hot, muggy, and exhausted, I walked onto the front porch and knocked on the door of what I hoped was my family's vacation home. The turquoise door opened, and my eleven-year-old brother Ben looked at me curiously through the screen door. He smiled and, squinting against the sun, looked up at my mother, who had arrived in her bathing suit, and asked, "What happened to Mugs?"

My mother opened the screen door and approached me, and I thought she would hug me. Instead, she grabbed my bag and walked into the kitchen, saying, "Mugs has eaten quite a bit of cheese and baguettes in France, by the looks of it."

Henry, who runs into the house from the beach all tanned, fit, and good-looking but still a little wired, said, "Mugs, welcome back. There's a Baskin-Robbins in town you may want to go to tomorrow," laughing and pointing at me.

Wow. I gained a little weight while living in France and eating yummy flan, camembert cheese, and baguettes. The ski suit was more oversized than I would typically wear, but everyone seemed to like me. While I figured out how to respond to my family's warm welcome, my mother looked over and said, "How much do you think you have gained, twenty pounds or so?" Her ideal number was 124 lbs.; therefore, that needed to be my number, even though I was an inch taller.

Mom showed me the room I was in, asking how my trip was and what the weather was like back home. I sat on the edge of the bed, wishing I was back in Switzerland, back with my new friends who loved me for exactly who I was and what I looked like. I could feel my eyes stinging and the tears inching down my cheeks. I took a deep breath and thought Dad would be excited to see me when he returned from fishing.

At dinner that night, after hugging my father and noticing the slight limp on his left side and the numbness on his face, he said, "Happy you are back now, and we can chat about real estate on the beach tomorrow." Everyone ordered crab, and while they were asking me so many questions about France and Switzerland, I was looking at Henry when I noticed my father's hand taking the potatoes off my plate. I quickly turned my face to his, and he quietly said, "You won't need potatoes for a while."

Pulling on my one-piece red and white striped bathing suit was a stark reality check as I hesitated to glance at my reflection in the full-length mirror in my Bahamian turquoise room. After wearing my stretchy ski instructor's suit for the past four months, I hadn't realized the twenty extra pounds I'd gained, but I also didn't feel judged for it in France. They seemed to love me for who I was and my size. I won't indulge in French food anymore, but I will miss those scrumptious croissants with unsalted butter, washed down with a smooth, silky cappuccino. Oh yes, and the camembert cheese after lunch and dinner with a baguette. Maybe the Toblerone chocolate wasn't the best nightly habit, but that creamy milk chocolate with bits of nougat that melted in your mouth was bliss! Sitting on the bed and looking at the rolls in my bathing suit while dreaming of my French indulgences was a significant moment of living my dream life; eating what I wanted and not thinking of anyone but myself abruptly stopped. Dad was noticeably worse, slurring his words, needing a cane to walk to the beach, with one side of his face drooping. The tumour was growing, and we had only so much time. Escaping to France from the impending loss of my incredible father was more than I could handle.

While we sat on beach chairs under a large blue and white striped umbrella, my father, looking straight ahead at the rhythm of the waves crashing on the white sand, said quietly, "I am happy you had a great adventure in France. I won't be here much longer, Mugs, and your mother will end up with Alan Coval when I am gone." This sentence was slow and slurred, but I heard Alan Coval.

"It's okay," he continued, the left side of his face unmoving, which made it difficult for him to pronounce certain words. "She's young and has her life ahead of her. He's a good man. He'll treat you kids well. I hope you're prepared to take on my business and shape it into the vision I have for it." I sat stunned by the weight of the realization that he knew who my mother would end up with and the reality of taking over his business at twenty-two.

All I could say was, "I'm so sorry, Dad, for what's happening to you." He reached over with his hand, touching the top of my sandy hand, and left it there until the screech of Ben echoed from further down the beach.

"Muggsy, come snorkel with me! You won't believe the variety of beautiful fish, some I've never seen before. I'll bring your snorkelling gear," my little brother Ben cried as he ran across the sand toward the water. He was so much taller and such a handsome kid. As I rushed to the shimmering water, my feet enjoying the sensation of that luscious, soft white sand, I realized how challenging it must be for him without his older siblings. He's alone every day with Mom and Dad, watching his father slowly deteriorate, knowing his dad won't be around for his teenage years. He won't teach him how to drive like Dad taught me and the other boys. I can't think about that; I must cherish this moment in paradise. Thank goodness the tears evaporated with the salt water when I plunged in, as I needed to revel in the sensation of being so buoyant in the turquoise sea.

I knew the next chapter of my life was going to be challenging, scary, and emotionally devastating.

Chapter Eight

Tonight's the Night

After being away from home for almost a year, I am back in my bedroom in our family home, where I haven't lived for five years since I spent four years at university. It felt strange because my mother had redecorated it with orange floral wallpaper that covered the ceiling and all the walls. When I lay in my bed, which is no longer my girly, pretty canape bed, I felt as if I were stuck inside a birthday present, which brought on a whirling headache that only faded when I closed my eyes. I had no idea what decorator had convinced her of this significant flaw, but I also knew she wasn't expecting me to ever live at home again. The message was clear.

Harry had called last night while we were unpacking and wanted to see me. He asked if we could meet at the steps of our high school to catch up, which I found odd, but I was glad to meet him there. It was a pleasant bike ride to my old school. Since none of my clothes fit, I quickly borrowed my brother's shorts and found a sweatshirt that made me look even larger. I wondered if Harry would notice since my weight had always been consistent during our dating years. Seeing Harry after so long brought back so many wonderful memories, but I also felt that I had moved on during my year in France. My inner voice said, "Trust your instincts when you see him, and don't overthink it." Regardless, I loved Harry deeply, but I wasn't sure if I still felt that same intensity of passion.

As I approached the roundabout by the school, I saw him sitting on the steps. When he noticed me, he stood up right away. He was even cuter than I remembered, and I realized I must have hurt him by being away for such a long time. We exchanged several postcards and the occasional phone call to stay in touch.

He ran down the steps, and as I set my bike down, he pulled me into his arms and said, "I've missed you more than you know. Your father needs you, and so do I. Thank God you're finally home." A sensation washed over me, making me want to run away again, overwhelmed by the intensity of his words and the guilt of being away from two men who needed me.

Smelling his shirt and nestling my nose into his neck felt comforting and wonderfully familiar. We chatted for over an hour, sitting in the sun looking out at the football field Harry used to play on as the all-star quarterback, and I was the cheerleader supporting the team at every game. He told me about his final year getting his MBA and how challenging it was but how excited he was about his new job in Toronto. A wave of envy and jealousy washed over me, knowing he had his life figured out, and I was at square one again, figuring out what I wanted to do and who I wanted to be. He had to leave to head back to the university to close his apartment and tidy up loose ends, but he wanted to see me when he returned the following week.

When I got home, I felt rattled by the emotions of seeing Harry, but I was also profoundly concerned about my next step. Should I follow Harry to Toronto? My mother was in the kitchen, wearing her half apron, which she constantly donned while cooking, and she wanted to know how things went with Harry. She and Dad loved Harry and hoped we would be moving forward and discussing marriage. There was a thought that maybe she desired a wedding so my father could walk me down the aisle, but it was never mentioned; only time was not on our side. More than anything, I wanted to bring joy and happiness to my family amid so much underlying sadness that none of us spoke about. The pressure to marry Harry was never addressed, but I knew it would have given my parents a sense of relief knowing I was with a good man they loved. I left it up to my mother to direct this movie and decide whether the topic of my father's impending death should be discussed together or with a therapist. She chose to smile and soldier on.

The next day, friends I hadn't seen since our university graduation a year ago invited me to the yacht club for the Friday night band that always played, and I thought about how wonderful that would be. Since I needed something nice to wear, I bought a dress that fit well, making me feel quite sexy as I had gained weight in my bust, which shifted the focus away from other areas. At least I was tanned from spending two weeks in the Bahamas. I met Betsy and Carol at the door of the yacht club. The number of people was overwhelming, and the energy in the club was exhilarating. The bar overlooked the sailboats, their lines constantly clanging against the masts, bringing back memories of sailing there as a junior. A balmy breeze wafted through the club, and everyone was in high spirits as it was grad week at Queens, with students celebrating their completion.

Betsy and I went to the bar, and she asked me questions about my year away. She ordered two beers for us, and while we were waiting, she turned to someone and said, "Oh, hi, Matt. How are you? My friend Morgan Cooper just returned from living in Europe for a year. Morgan, this is my friend Matt Jenkins, and he's graduating from med school next month."

I gazed into his sparkling, mischievous blue eyes and said, "Congratulations! That's a huge accomplishment. Where are you planning to intern now?"

He had a confident smile and inner security when he responded, "I'm heading to Vancouver in six weeks after doing some local rotations here in Kingston."

Impulsively, I remarked, "Has anyone ever told you that you resemble Harrison Ford?"

"All the time," he smiled, though he seemed bored by the compliment. Perhaps I insulted him, but I considered it a compliment.

Betsy recognized the awkwardness and stepped in to save the day, saying, "Morgan went to school in Aix-en-Provence and taught skiing in Val d'Isère, which is quite cool."

Matt appeared taken aback, touched my lower back, and pulled me closer. In a low voice, he remarked, "I'm impressed. It took courage to live alone in France for a year. Good for you. It's nice to meet a strong, independent woman."

Rod Stewart's song "Tonight's the Night" began to blare, and everyone got up to dance and sing, knowing every word.

Matt sang it to me as we danced, knowing every word as if he were the composer of the song and lyrics. He leaned in and shouted in my ear, "I couldn't have said it better than Rod." Then he flashed a beautiful, warm, sexy smile. I was smitten.

He grabbed me around the waist and pulled me closer as the dance floor got packed, pushing us closer together. He held my face and mouthed, "Where have you been?"

It felt like a lightning bolt; I couldn't stop staring at him. His turquoise eyes, intelligence, and confidence were magnetic. Within an hour, I realized I wouldn't leave this man tonight. He had me captivated. We danced, teased, flirted, kissed, and chatted on a sailboat until 3:00 in the morning about his studies in medicine, my teaching skiing, our families, and my dad, who has a brain tumour, holding us all hostage to the daily growth of cancer cells eating away at his brain like Pac-Man. He showed compassion for my father, but then he tried to make me laugh, and we got lost in the chemistry of discovering each other.

I felt no hesitation about going with him or what might happen in his bedroom. His desk was cluttered with books on dermatology, neurology, biochemistry, and gynecology. I was impressed by his status as a doctor, his intelligence, his dedication, and the notable accomplishment he had just achieved. While he was getting me a glass of water, I turned to him and asked, "Can I attend your graduation ceremony next week?"

He glanced over his shoulder and said, "It would be an honour if you came." He walked towards me, whispering, "Only if you are my girlfriend next week." With that, he shut the bedroom door, lit a candle, and undid the back of my dress.

Three hours later, as the sun rose, I realized I had borrowed my mother's little BMW 2002, which she would also be looking for since I had just returned home two days earlier from Marsh Harbour. I hadn't been in my bedroom for over a year and hadn't needed to inform my mother, but living at home wouldn't be ideal. I called her, and she said, "I need my car by 8:30 this morning," before hanging up.

When she saw me an hour later, looking somewhat dishevelled, she asked where I had been, lied, and said, "I had too much to drink and spent the night at Betsy's house."

Two days later, I moved in with Matt Jenkins. It was the most impulsive, rebellious thing I had ever done, and I never doubted my actions.

Matt and I were inseparable the month before he left to drive in his TR6 sports car across the country. I began to drink tea, eat salads, and spend time with my father, who was progressively deteriorating; he was randomly falling over, unable to feed himself, unable to speak coherently, and gradually disappearing like the magnificent Willy Cooper. My mother decided she could no longer care for him at home, so it was time to admit him to a palliative care hospital, a moment I'll never forget. The expression on my beautiful father's face was a mixture of sadness and fear, knowing that the time had come when he could no longer fight this evil in his head. The malignant tumour he had battled for eight years was now winning despite his efforts to outlive it, destroy it, ignore it, and conquer it. One side of his face drooped, and as I waved goodbye at the door of his new room after hugging him, I wept as I walked down the hall. My mother walked beside me, and I could not stop crying. How can life be so unfair to such a phenomenal man? He lost his dignity and pride as one of the most successful people in our community, the most gregarious of men, so beloved by his friends, to a man in a wheelchair, drooling from that numb side of his face, attempting to smile through the tears in his eyes. We walked away and left him there. I yelled back so he could hear, "We're going to the DQ tomorrow, Dad. See you soon. I love you."

While packing a few things to take to Vancouver, I stumbled upon a postcard from Henry after he finished high school and travelled to Greece and other countries, but we had no idea where he was. He didn't return for two years. My mother had a cousin at the Canadian embassy, and after a passport search, he informed her that Henry was in prison in Romania. He had been caught carrying marijuana, which was illegal in Romania but not in Copenhagen, where he purchased it. To cope with his anxiety, he began smoking marijuana, claiming it calmed his mind and was easy to get. He also developed an addiction to it. His postcard was so sad, and my mother never parted with it.

To my Dear Mother,

I humbly ask for your forgiveness for leading such a wasted life. I feel I have exhausted all my efforts worldwide, and my life has veered off course. I received a visa for Australia but was denied work in Singapore and Borneo. At this moment, I have jaundice (Hepatitis B) and feel that any moment I might die. I look in the mirror at my yellow eyes, reflecting a defeated individual with nowhere to go. Through this terrible suffering of endless vomiting, fatigue, and excruciating stomach pains, the evil turmoil within me has been revealed. I fear you have a manic-depressive son. It's only through my failure and shame that you haven't heard from me. But now I am retreating home like the Iraqi army in defeat and praying to God that He has mercy on my soul. Finally, after two years of travelling, I've realized it's not greener on the other side. I sense only death surrounding me. You're the only person I can turn to in this bottomless pit.

Your loving son,
Henry xoxo

Tears roll down my cheeks every time I read this. He felt the suffering and lack of hope when he wrote this to my mother. The combination of Henry's mental illness and addiction creates the perfect storm for a troubled life—a life of isolation, a life that struggles to fit into society, and one filled with shame and stigma. My mother didn't help the situation when she felt embarrassed about Henry ending up in a Romanian prison for carrying marijuana.

Status was crucial to my mother's position in our city. She would not want her image damaged. Henry was not someone she could mention with pride. Do you think Henry sensed her shame, her resentment over not having a successful son, not having someone to boast about, or not having a reflection of her stardom in the world? It somehow felt like a failure of her parenting, a failure of her family, and a failure compared to her friends who placed the same pressure on their children. Mental illness felt like a failure. The other children had to compensate for the shortcomings of her one son, and that pressure was immense. He needed help with his anxiety, depression, and autism, so he turned to self-medication with marijuana and alcohol. The perfect storm of mental illness collided with addiction, with no support from my mother or society. He ended up on the streets of Mexico, a child in crisis.

I gazed at the postcard, pondering what I should do. How can I help him? I'm only twenty-two years old, still trying to figure out my destiny and path to survival. How could I possibly know how to save him from his destructive ways? I concluded that my mother was responsible for her children, and one day, I would be accountable for myself and my children. The survival of the fittest is a biological imperative, and I need to be the director of my movie, which seems challenging enough.

Four weeks later, I arrived in Vancouver, eighteen pounds lighter, and Matt hardly recognized me at the airport. The excitement of starting my new life with Matt was mixed with the overwhelming sadness of saying goodbye to my father and the uncertainty of what I would do in Vancouver. Since Matt was working full-time as an intern at St. Paul's Hospital, I would have to explore the new city on my own, find a job and new friends, and let go of the guilt of leaving not only Dad but also Harry. I knew I had hurt him deeply and shocked him with my radical behaviour, but I could not stay in Kingston while watching my father die. This was my way of surviving and building a life without my mentor, role model, and loving father. It was unbearable, and my heart ached every day, all day. I was flying home for Christmas, unsure if he would make it, and privately, I prayed for him to find peace from the agony of dying such a slow, cruel death.

Matt was thrilled about skiing at Whistler, north of Vancouver, so he and a few other interns shared a cabin whenever they could. The skiing was challenging, with long mountain runs reminiscent of the Alps, though not as advanced, featuring huts along the trails. Matt felt frustrated that he wasn't as skilled as I was, but his determination and strong will soon propelled him toward his goal of matching or surpassing my ability. We were getting to know one another while living together since we had barely dated before he left.

One day in early December, we were skiing in a blizzard because we always skied, regardless of the weather. As we came over the ridge into the wind, sitting helplessly on the chairlift and pummelled by icy snowflakes stinging our cheeks, we spotted a large sign displaying the open runs, the time, and any emergency messages for skiers. A bold red message on that board stated: "Morgan Cooper, call home," dated December 5th, 1977.

The funeral occurred in our local Anglican church, and as we entered the warmth of this magnificent chapel, the bells chimed loudly. People gathered outside, embracing one another in their winter coats and hats. Harry was there to greet me at the door, his expression so sorrowful, with eyelashes frozen from tears and the winter cold. My mother, brothers, and I, along with my Granny, my father's mother, walked to the front pew and sat directly across from a mahogany coffin adorned with flowers. I couldn't stop staring at the coffin, wondering if I had made the right choice by not seeing my father after he had passed, even when it was offered upon my return home. There's a heavy burden of guilt for the loved ones left behind—feeling that we did not love enough, were not present enough, did not care enough, could not defeat the tumour, and did not tell him often enough just how much I loved him and how deeply I will miss his unconditional love and support. I will miss him on my wedding day. I will miss him when I have my first child. I will miss him with every achievement. I will miss him every day for the rest of my life. He was only fifty-three, and I was only twenty-three, turning twenty-four next week, just five days before Christmas.

Sharky Chapman, the current coach of the Boston Bruins and my former baseball coach, delivered a heartfelt and moving eulogy. He expressed gratitude to my father for introducing him to Don Cherry and nurturing his love and passion for hockey. After a service that honoured a man cherished by many, we proceeded in a line of black cars to Cataraqui Cemetery, where Dad would be laid to rest. I dreaded this part the most, as the weather was cold and bleak, the skies grey and overcast, with flurries greeting us as we exited the church, people sniffling and concealing their pain from broken hearts. As family and close friends gathered around the grave, I noticed the tombstones gradually covered by a soft blanket of white snow. A black tombstone stood behind the grave, bearing the inscription, William Newman Cooper, a man deeply adored by his family and community, with his dates of birth and death engraved below. I became fixated on the line below that read, His Beloved Wife, Maggie Dorothea Cooper, January 12th, 1930-.

My fur hat was incredibly warm, and I felt grateful for it at that moment when I had splurged on it during my trip to Switzerland. My mother stood beside me, leaning forward as my father's coffin was lowered into the dark, empty hole in the ground, whispering, "Look at Dr. Walker's coat." I shifted my gaze to the sea of black winter coats and spotted Dr. Walker's jacket, whose sleeves were far too short, resembling a child's jacket on him, making my mother and me giggle uncontrollably. I wanted to rein in my laughter, and I'm sure she did, too, but she couldn't contain the emotion of watching her husband of twenty-five years being placed in the frozen ground, so we laughed through our tears. People's eyes were on us, but nothing could halt our laughter and tears; that moment was ours to release him and find freedom. The love humans hold for one another can surpass what the heart can endure in times of loss; the thought of a body in a box buried in the cold, dark ground and the unknown—the unknown—eludes our understanding. Death is cloaked in mystery. No one knows what happens after we die or where we go. My Granny lost her son, my mother lost her husband, my brothers and I lost our father, and his friends lost a brave, courageous soldier who fought every day with humour and grace to stay alive: just one more year, one more month, one more day.

"Miss You."
Miss you, miss you, miss you!
Everything I do,
Echoes with the laughter
And the voice of you.
You're on every corner,
Every turn and twist
Every old familiar spot

Whispers how you're missed.
Miss you, miss you, miss you!
Everywhere I go
There are poignant memories.
Dancing in a row.
Silhouette and shadow
Of your form and face,
Substance and reality
Everywhere displace,
Oh, I miss you, miss you!
God! I miss you, Dad!
There's a strange, sad silence.
Amid the busy whirl,
Just as though the ordinary
Daily things I do
Wait with me, expectant
For a word from you.
Miss you, miss you, miss you!
Nothing now seems true,
Only that it was heaven,
To be with you.

Chapter Nine

Stockbroker

Matt and I returned to Kingston, where we met, grew up, and graduated from university. Queen's University boasts a stunning chapel on campus, located across from the soccer field and surrounded by towering oak trees, which we considered the perfect spot for our wedding. We envisioned a casual gathering with family and friends, hosting the reception in my family's backyard, overlooking the beautifully manicured golf course. Instead of a long white gown, I chose a lovely two-piece chiffon Giorgio Armani skirt paired with a feminine off-white peplum top. The emotions surprised me—the feelings of committing to someone for life, my father's absence as he would have walked me down the aisle, and the connections to my hometown from my years with Harry. The loss of Dad and Harry intertwined with the excitement and apprehension of the wedding. After my hair was braided with stephanotis and ivy, Charlie and I drove together to the church, and he graciously offered to walk me down the aisle. We arrived just in time and began climbing the limestone steps of the 150-year-old chapel. I felt its strength, safety, familiarity, and comfort as a pillar of this community, and Dad's presence enveloped me like a warm cloak. Charlie looked dashing in his suit, and as he extended his elbow for me to hold onto, he whispered, "We got this." I stepped slowly and nervously into the chapel, and the first person I locked eyes with, sitting in the back pew, was Harry. I hadn't seen him in three years. Oh my God, will he object? Why is he here? My thoughts weren't on the handsome man with blue eyes in the beautiful navy suit at the front of the chapel but on Harry, whose tearful, sorrowful eyes were fixed on me.

"Should anyone present know of any reason that this couple should not be joined in holy matrimony, speak now or forever hold your peace."

Everyone in the congregation, me included, looked back at Harry.

He was silent.

The ring was put on my finger.

I held tightly to my husband's arm as we walked down the aisle, friends and family clapping and wishing us well as we left the chapel. I glanced at the empty seat in the back pew. He was gone, and I would never know why he had come that day.

Returning to Vancouver was challenging, as Kingston had always felt like home but was now associated with the pain of loss. I had lost two remarkable men who had shaped my understanding of unconditional love and my initial trust in romantic, vulnerable love. They instilled in me the belief that love, in all its forms, is beautiful, tender, and painful when it ends.

Matt interned at St. Paul's Hospital for a year, so I needed to find something to keep me busy since we might return to Kingston. Earning a teaching certificate took a year at the University of British Columbia, and I thought that teaching would be enjoyable. We both loved Vancouver; Matt became a full-time Emergency Medicine doctor at Burnaby General, while I taught high school mathematics and physical education.

Teaching for two years had become a source of frustration. No matter how much effort I put into my classroom or my students, I earned the same as the beleaguered, burned-out teacher next door. The teacher who didn't decorate his classroom, didn't play music during art class, didn't take the students out for a quick run around the field when they grew bored with math, and didn't treat them to Dairy Queen Buster Bars at the end of the term. I knew it created a mess, but the kids loved DQ Day, and I always enjoyed spoiling them. The other teachers became frustrated because rumours circulated that Ms. Cooper's class received Dilly Bars and Buster Bars on Fridays. Instead of surprising their students with a treat, they grew annoyed with me and went to the principal to complain, which I ignored as I continued with DQ Day. I disliked being told what to do and refused to conform my teaching style to their dull, methodical, rule-oriented approach to educating young people children.

The teachers seemed more focused on battling the government for increased funding and advocating for their rights with the union rather than caring for the students—at least at the school where I taught. I loved teaching and cherished my students. It was my little world when the door closed, allowing us to collaborate in a productive, thriving environment. I believed I was a good teacher, but I wasn't fond of the restrictions imposed by the principal, who disapproved of playing opera music during art class and discouraged my class from doing star jumps when they were restless in math. Most evenings were spent marking homework and planning lessons, often leaving me to question why teachers were so poorly compensated. I enjoyed being the volleyball coach and was committed to creating a supportive, encouraging, and fun environment for the students. I loved learning and sought to pass that passion for curiosity on to them. "Ask questions, young minds; inquire without fear, without shame." Creating a safe space for them to learn, fail, and process life during the hours I had their attention was rewarding, as every child presented a unique challenge and responded individually to my enthusiasm. The problem was that my two-year contract was coming up in May, and I would not know until August whether a teaching position would be available. Sadly, this uncertainty had nothing to do with my teaching capabilities but rather with seniority. I felt deep sympathy for the kids stuck with old, passionless teachers and believed that private schools at least had the power to reward good teachers and dismiss poor ones.

That summer, I was invited to play with some old business school buddies who had also moved to Vancouver. I was excited to catch up since I hadn't played much because Matt didn't play golf, and I missed the game dearly. Cam Brown had become a stockbroker, and when he arrived at the golf club parking lot, I spotted his convertible BMW, which made me think things must be going well for him. He introduced me to his colleagues, and it felt just like old times, playing with the guys again. Thankfully, I played well, which surprised me, but I was grateful I had practised the day before since I hate not playing well. We had a blast competing in Bingo, Bango, and Bongo, a points game that keeps you focused as money is exchanged at the end of the game.

As Cam and I walked down the ninth hole after teeing off, I could smell the freshly cut grass and hear the cheerful, melodic songs of robins and distant lawnmowers. It was a delightful welcome to spring. I savoured the sensation of walking on a beautifully manicured golf course, focusing straight ahead on the target of the red flag in the centre of the green, contemplating my next shot and which club to choose.

After we both made our approach shots to the green, Cam glanced over at me and asked, "Why on earth are you not a stockbroker? You're like a guy: competitive, smart, comfortable taking risks, and eager to make a lot of money. They need women in the industry, and you would excel."

My mind raced with questions like, "Why can't I do what Cam does?" We received the same marks in school, enjoyed the same sports, and competed similarly. Women should be able to buy and sell stocks as effectively as men—perhaps even better. I grabbed my seven-iron and concentrated on the landing spot to the right of the pin, knowing it would break to the left and bring me close to the pin.

I heard three voices: "Great shot, Morgan." "Nice shot and good kick," and "You're solid with your irons." I placed my club back in the bag, realizing I was on the verge of changing careers to play with the boys and earn money like they do.

My inner self tried to remain calm, but as we approached the eighteenth green, I said, "Thanks for the suggestion. Who should I speak to, and what must I do to obtain my brokerage licence?"

He smiled, shook his head while glancing at the others, and replied, "Here we go; she's going to excel in the business and take all our clients. I'll call you tomorrow to arrange a meeting with Luke Ryan at Pemberton Securities. I understand they offer a year-long training program in the fall, and it's the only one based in Vancouver. The other brokers are all in Toronto. You'll need to complete your Securities Course this summer and get your licence, but that shouldn't be a problem. You're bright."

The universe was now guiding me in a new direction I had never considered or felt capable of pursuing. Having Cam's confidence in me meant so much, and I approached the long twenty-two-foot putt with renewed zeal, envisioning the ball going in before I struck it. Euphoric after my birdie and this newfound career path, I walked with purpose and a buzz I hadn't experienced in a while.

The following week, after Cam arranged a meeting for me with Luke Ryan, I entered the securities office of Pemberton's on the 34th floor of the Bentall Tower in beautiful downtown Vancouver, which juts into the Pacific Ocean and is sheltered by the mountains to the north. I felt nervous and excited, realizing I had never sold anything except while working as a waitress at Jasper Park Lodge, where I promoted the chicken parmesan over the dried-out mushroom risotto. My only skills were teaching with enthusiasm and my ability to learn quickly. I sat in a green leather chair in the mahogany-panelled reception area, noting its masculine and severe vibe. I noticed the pink tulips the receptionist must have purchased and wondered how many other female brokers they had employed. A woman with platinum blonde hair and a very short skirt came out to say hello and asked me to follow her to Mr. Ryan's office. As we walked through the bustling office filled with cubicles, each occupied by four men, I noticed the lively noise and energy. A small paper airplane landed at my feet while men shouted out earnings and cash flow figures, and Newmont shares were slipping. One guy stood up, leaning towards his cubicle buddies, saying, "Hey guys, it's time to buy back this sucker. Down 20% and a fucking great deal here at a 15 P/E ratio." Another handsome guy with sandy blonde hair in a white shirt and tie yelled from another cubicle, "Don't forget we tee off at 2:46 today, boys." He glanced at me as I walked by. I was staring at him, and he called out, "Hope we see you here again. Good luck with the boss." At that very moment, I knew I had found my tribe.

Loud, aggressive, confident, competitive, and bold were all character traits I admired and aspired to embody. The energy felt electric, intense, and risky, creating a dynamic, team-oriented atmosphere. That day, I opted to wear a royal blue suit I had splurged on, and I felt relief in that decision. It appeared businesslike, serious, innovative, and conservative, ultimately making me feel like I belonged. I noticed only two other women among the maze of cubicles, bobbing heads, and a predominance of young, assertive men. In another part of the space, I spotted desks occupied by women who must have been assistants, given their more feminine attire. I saw two of them chatting with one of the male brokers.

Carolyn knocked and opened the president's office door, leading me into a spacious area filled with books, family photos, and a sitting space the size of my living room. Mr. Ryan rose from behind an enormous antique oak desk and came over to shake my hand. I appreciated his smile; it instantly put me at ease. Once we sat down, he asked me about my education, experience, and interest in becoming a stockbroker. I was honest. "I first considered it while golfing with Cam and two of his friends last week."

Right away, he interrupted and asked, "You golf?"

"Yes, I have played since I was twelve and competed for three years on the amateur circuit back in Ontario."

"What's your handicap?"

"I currently have an eight handicap, but it was a four when I played regularly. I've been busy teaching, but I would love to get back to it." "Tell me about why you like playing golf."

This was an excellent question! I told him I did my final paper in marketing called The Game of Golf is Like the Game of Life. I went on about how, in golf, you need to pick your target and focus only on that target and then trust your swing to follow through on it. It's like life when you want to set a goal and visualize the outcome. You also play with other partners you enjoy competing against, but the game is against you. It came to me that the four men sitting around in a cubicle shared a similar scenario with Mr. Ryan.

"Not unlike your cubicles of four brokers who are friendly with each other but also want to make sure they keep up or beat the others in the number of clients or commission earned. It's pleasant, but it's still competitive gamesmanship. I love that scenario and thrive in it. I need to be in a competitive arena, setting goals, trying to be the best, and loving the camaraderie of the game."

He asked me where I grew up and what degree I got at university. I asked him, "Will women stockbrokers be treated equally here? I'm used to being one of the boys, growing up with the same amount of respect as the men in my life. I would hate not to be given the same opportunities."

He responded, "I believe you are rare, and we would welcome you into our sales program, which begins in September. You will need your CSC licence, and my assistant, Carolyn, will help you complete the paperwork. Congratulations: I know you will be a great success in the business."

I worked on the assignments and studied for the three-hour Canadian Securities Exam that summer. Strangely, I loved studying all the material outside at the picnic table, listening to the birds under an umbrella in the summer heat while learning about bonds, stocks, options, macroeconomics, and microeconomics. I was excited to grasp all the terminology. Still, I didn't enjoy memorizing the forty formulas I knew we would never use. I could start the training program with my CSC, which I completed and passed in September. When I walked into the classroom and met Ivan Muldown, our instructor, I immediately knew I was in the right place. I was relieved to see three other women around my age finding seats among the guys in their twenties and early thirties. There was a nervous giddiness in the room, along with a palpable excitement.

Mr. Ivan Muldown was a successful stockbroker who also loved to teach how to be a salesman and how he succeeded in his early days with the firm. I wore a summer dress that day with a jacket, but the other women wore suits that I noted. Do I imitate the men in navy suits, or do I lean into my femininity and be different from them? I decided to try both on and see which gave me the most success and what felt most like me.

The year flew by, and I cherished every day we came together for training. I got to know the others, learned much about selling, and built my clientele. I was eager to establish my book of business by attracting the kinds of clients I wanted to work with.

Every Thursday was pub night when we would go after class and have a beer together. I didn't love these nights, as drinking with colleagues who were men was not the best idea, and I could never even finish one beer before it was time to go and before they got silly and flirtatious. One night, one of the other female colleagues, Nelly, who was hysterical in class and made me laugh all the time, came to pub night with a mission to drink. I noticed that her words were starting to slur, so I approached her, said I was leaving and asked if I could give her a ride home.

She looked at me and yelled, "Oh, Miss Milk, who doesn't drink, wants to drive me home. I love this song. Do you want to dance with me?" She tossed her blonde hair, climbed onto a table, and started a striptease with her suit jacket and scarf.

I grabbed Stu and Alex and told them we needed to get her down and home.

We looked up at Nelly, and she was now throwing her business cards, which we just got today, all over the bar, yelling out, "Who wants to be my client?"

Oh, Christ, this isn't good. The guys and I tackled her to the ground, and then she dashed into the men's washroom. Someone knew her boyfriend, whom they called, and fortunately, he arrived to find her passed out, leaning against a urinal with her skirt hiked up, buttons undone on her white shirt, and no shoes in sight. It was a nasty mess and solidified my belief that no one looks good when drunk. Nelly was a gorgeous girl, but not now.

Watching her poor boyfriend struggle to carry her out of the pub was sad and embarrassing for him. I could tell by his expression that he had experienced this before, and she had an issue with alcohol. That was my last time going out for pub night, as nothing good could come from drinking with men in a bar after work. Sticking with the golf course would be better when socializing with colleagues; at least in that environment, I had CONTROL. I believe that is why I never tried smoking dope or taking drugs of any kind, why I put ginger ale in my beer bottle. To always maintain control!

The routine of being a broker began with a 5:30 am alarm clock, a hot shower, a quick blow-dry, a few strokes of mascara, throwing on whichever suit I had left out from the night before, hopping into my black BMW, and grabbing a cappuccino and a blueberry oatmeal muffin from the lobby coffee shop before heading up to the twenty-third floor. The elevator doors would open to the sounds of others settling into their days, accompanied by the usual morning chatter about hockey scores, golf games, and global news. I was eager to dive into my list of prospects and follow-ups for the day. Even if I cold-called thirty people a day and received twenty-five rejections, I would focus on the five positive calls of hope. It became a game of numbers, and I never took it personally; I was tenacious and determined that what our firm and I offered was far superior to anyone else on the street. I developed a strong work discipline, and I loved the game of trying to build my client base to ensure a steady flow of commissions and to continue achieving my goals. If I was outperforming some of the guys, that was the fun part.

My routine was established, and I loved being part of this dynamic group of people, mainly achievement-oriented men, sports enthusiasts, outgoing extroverts at heart, and eager for life's adventures. Young, courageous risk-takers were excited about the possibilities of what success in this business could offer them and how it would create their dream lifestyle of golf memberships, skiing at Whistler, travelling the world, and living in their spacious four-bedroom homes with the perfect partner and three to four children. We all perceived this in the senior men who worked at the firm. We heard about their weekends in their log cabins, summer flights to their island in the Gulf Islands, the pool where the kids played, and their trips to Maui every spring break. I wanted that lifestyle and could visualize it; I could see it and feel it. It was the life my father had built for me and wanted me to continue enjoying after he was gone.

My routine was established, but Matt's was chaotic. He worked twelve-hour shifts from eight at night to eight in the morning, which meant that when he woke up at 5:00 p.m. after a night shift at the hospital, he preferred breakfast to a full dinner before returning for the night shift. He worked four nights and then had four days off. We rarely saw each other and often disagreed about what to do during our time together. We loved skiing and hiking in the mountains around Vancouver.

Every September, we planned a BC holiday, aiming for adventures like hiking the West Coast Trail, a seven-day trek along the west side of Vancouver Island, where we camped on the beach every night while carrying all our food. My pack weighed about thirty-five pounds, while Matt's was nearly fifty. One morning, I woke up and peeked through the tent flap to see fishing boats in the morning mist, and then I realized it was a spectacular pod of whales breaching. The trek begins with a 200-foot climb up a rope ladder, followed by navigating streams and mud to sections built on walkways, resembling an obstacle course. Climbing up ropes and down onto beaches was exhilarating as we carefully read tide charts to avoid getting stuck in a surge channel. The ocean would rush into these channels, carved out over thousands of years by powerful storms, potentially pulling you into its depths if you got caught. You had to climb down, run about eight feet onto the sand, and climb back up before the water came rushing in with a vengeance.

Matt would tie a rope around my waist, making me do this without my pack in case I fell or got caught. Once, I felt the ocean's power hit my boot just as my foot stepped onto the beach, and I learned that I didn't want to make that mistake. Matt completed this climbing challenge twice with a backpack on, feeling that even with his waist secured by a rope, it wouldn't be enough to save him if the ocean surge came and swept him away. I couldn't entertain that possibility. We stayed focused, now on safe ground, and continued hiking to our next camping spot. The sun warmed my face, and I was relieved I had unpacked the homemade spaghetti sauce for tonight's dinner around the campfire. I took a deep breath, relishing the comfort of my pack and settling into its weight, absorbing the magnificence of West Coast magic—the ocean's power with every rolling wave crashing on the sand to nurture and destroy. There was energy, vitality, and an overwhelming sense of joy in being at one with nature, in harmony with my body's ability to carry this pack for seven hours a day, fully present in this magical moment.

Tears came to my eyes at the thought of my father and how much he would love to be alive, experiencing all that life has to offer. I will honour his enormous love of life and the loss I feel by never taking these breathtaking moments for granted. I looked at the brilliant blue sky and placed one hand over my heart, quietly whispering, "I love you, Dad, and miss you so much. I pray you are with me now, protecting me on this adventure." I closed my eyes for a moment to breathe him in, and when I opened them, a magnificent eagle flew above us, its mighty wings flapping against the breeze and its white head beautiful and proud. As I watched it disappear into the horizon, I knew then that miracles happen and that Dad is always with me in some spiritual form.

Matt and I walked in silence, constantly manoeuvring around the rocks and mud or, when on the beach, the challenge of not sinking with each footstep. Setting up camp every night next to a freshwater stream was the reward after a challenging day, and the sense of accomplishment was always the bonus as I prepared our dinner over the campfire Matt had made. Tonight's special delight was s'mores with graham wafers, chocolate, and the marshmallows we toasted over the fire. The sun was setting, casting crimson, pink, and orange wisps that reflected on the ocean as Matt poured a splash of Kahlúa into my hot chocolate. He looked over at me with his growing beard that made him look rugged and very handsome; the sun-touched cheeks and his blue eyes also caught the sunset in them. I loved him so much as we sat on the log next to the campfire bundled up in down jackets and cozy sweatpants, proud of our accomplishment, happy to be experiencing this incredible moment right now with each other, feeling safe, exhausted, and exhilarated all at the same time. "I'm so happy right now," was all the energy I could muster as a slight breeze swept over my face.

Chapter Ten

Fly Me to The Moon

I didn't start with the intention of cheating. I was in a happy marriage and enjoying my life with my Emergency Physician husband, even though we were heading in different directions. I always believed we would come home to each other and feel safe and secure after his shifts at the hospital and my rounds in the office with mainly men like me. We engaged with one another, competing, laughing, swearing, expressing ourselves, and acting like a team on a soccer pitch or a golf course. The bond that was forming was subconscious, but I felt I was in my element, part of a tribe of men that brought out the masculine traits connected to my upbringing, my DNA, and my comfort zone. I couldn't wait to get to work every day at six a.m., armed with my coffee, excited to see what was happening in the world on a macro level and what my world on a micro level was stirring up.

On a stunning autumn day, we received notice of a conference held at Qualicum Beach on Vancouver Island that we had to attend. The buzz was about how enjoyable it would be for all of us to go golfing, brainstorm about our client base, and, most importantly, spend time together without our spouses. Matt wasn't too keen on my group of merry, competitive, money-driven men, as he referred to them, so he was happy that I would be off for the weekend with them, allowing him to work. We carpooled on the ferry to Vancouver Island, where our welcome party was held at a magnificent country estate on the ocean. As we drove down the long winding driveway, past the tennis court, coach houses, and caretaker cabin, we arrived at the most beautiful home I had ever seen. We entered through the massive wood doors into the foyer and looked up at zebra, bear, and other animal skins hanging over the balcony above.

We continued into the living area, which featured an enormous twenty-foot fireplace made of local river rock, and I felt as though I were in Ralph Lauren's private home. The fabrics, rich in earthy colours, and the oriental carpets throughout the expansive living room were spectacular, while the view over the gardens to the beach was breathtaking. We were all in awe, and when I discovered the kitchen, I was officially blown away. It included a floor-to-ceiling fireplace with a built-in rotisserie, two long islands crafted from white marble, mahogany cabinetry along the walls, red cedar plank floors, an enormous antique table, and French doors inviting me onto a patio sheltered by purple wisteria cascading over the trellis. The frequent wafts of ocean air, the sound of seagulls mewing, and the beauty of this stunning country estate, which must have cost millions, captivated me with its lifestyle.

I ran from room to room uninvited, captivated by every detail, piece of art, and the quality of everything I observed. So, this is wealth. This is where one of our younger colleagues, Scottie Weston, who was five years my junior, grew up. He was twenty-five, charming with sandy blonde hair, blue-grey eyes, and a mischievous cockiness, as well as being a talented tennis player. He walked with purpose, always impeccably dressed, exuding confidence and self-assurance from an elite world of privilege. When we arrived at his summer estate, I was struck by his cherry-red Mercedes convertible, hair blowing in the wind, wearing Ray-Ban sunglasses, khakis, no socks, Sperry navy boat shoes, and a white cotton shirt, radiating style and charisma that both fascinated and unnerved me. He was twenty-five and married to the stunning daughter of a lumber tycoon, clearly having found his match. Was this feeling I had the twinge of envy? I had not yet seen or touched that world of the one percent, and it looked spectacular. Scottie significantly raised my estimation of him as the guy who worked in the cubicle next to mine, tossing the occasional paper airplane at me and teasing me with his gregarious personality. As we gathered and our manager ushered us into the living room to kick off the weekend conference, I was in a state of wonder, unable to take my eyes off him, Scottie.

The next day, we had a golf tournament after our morning meetings, and Scottie and I found ourselves in the same group. He mentioned he had never played with a woman before and was impressed by my game and natural swing. A good athlete captivates me every time, and I adore watching the power of a beautiful swing while witnessing someone's personality naturally shine on the golf course. You learn whether they possess golf etiquette, cheat when recording their score, display patience, can handle a bad shot, and care about their fellow playing partners. It's the best way to discover someone's true character. Scottie and I enjoyed playing together, creating a somewhat flirtatious back-and-forth that made our two teammates uneasy. I could feel the chemistry building when he leaned in on the eighteenth hole and quietly whispered, "Why don't you stay the night after everyone leaves, and I can drive you back tomorrow?" With everyone catching the six o'clock ferry, I had to think quickly. Matt was working the night shift, so he would head in around seven and sleep through the day.

Scottie and I could share dinner and get to know each other better. I knew it was reckless and risky, but I was hooked and couldn't muster the willpower or desire to say no. I longed to spend the night at that spectacular house by the ocean, just the two of us. I called Matt and told him we had missed the ferry and would stay one more night but would be back before he woke up tomorrow. He was understanding, and the pangs of guilt set in, but not enough to change my mind or the course of my deception. I didn't want to think about what this meant or what would happen. I only wanted to live in that moment with the freedom to explore this attraction, and the danger of it was intoxicating.

We waved goodbye to our colleagues, mentioning that I was driving with Scottie and would see everyone on the ferry, fully aware that we had no intention of catching it. He called out, "Hop in, and let's pick up some groceries for dinner. I make a fantastic linguine vongole, and we need some white wine to go with it."

As we drove off, with the wind whipping through our blonde hair and my sunglasses shielding my eyes from the strands, I laughed out loud, feeling freer and more exhilarated than I had in years—if ever. I felt so alive, and as I glanced at his radiant smile, I noticed him taking my hand while shifting gears as we sped faster onto the highway. We both embraced the thrill of freedom, doing precisely what we wanted without considering the repercussions of what we knew was about to happen. After seven years with Matt, I had now lied to him for the first time, and for some inexplicable reason, which I didn't want to ponder, I felt justified in my risk and my need to honour this intense chemistry. It was perplexing, yet it wasn't enough to halt the course of this new love affair. After Scottie ran around this cute little country store selling homemade local baking, the locals knew him and seemed to defer to him in a familiar way, which impressed me greatly.

We returned to the private estate with our groceries, and the sound of the heavy metal gates closing behind us offered a sense of complete privacy. I was captivated by the elegance and style of the estate at the end of the winding, tree-lined drive. My heart raced, and my face flushed as Scottie poured me a glass of white wine. We began discussing our lives, our marriages, our company, his family's business, and the origins of their wealth. He prepared a delicious pasta dish with steamed clams, and we carried it out to the patio by the outdoor fireplace, overlooking the ocean as the sun began to set in rich crimson reds and orange hues. My head buzzed from the wine, the golf game, the intoxication of infatuation, and the thrill of this moment as we propped our bare feet up on the stone wall, inhaling the essence of living in the present. I gazed into those deep blue eyes and softly said, "I feel so alive."

He got up and took my hand, guiding me up circular stairs, going past all the animal skins and into one of the bedrooms with a canopy bed. Then, pulling me in, the kiss, our first kiss, sent tingles throughout my body, and I could not get enough. Before I knew it, we were naked on the bear rug, laughing and could not stop for hours. I was smitten when I rolled over in the middle of the night with a bear head next to me and a blanket on top that Scottie must have brought for me. The chemistry between us was unlike anything I had ever experienced, a mutual thirst for each other's bodies and the way we harmonized. I adored his scent and touch and was overwhelmed by my desire for more. When we awoke, he guided me to his bedroom, which had a more comfortable mattress than the bear rug and tried to sleep. Sleep came reluctantly, but the morning light and chirping birds signalled that it was time to rise and return to our realities. After stepping out of the shower, I slipped into his white dress shirt and the white bobby socks I had worn while golfing. My hair was tied back in a high ponytail, my cheeks still flushed, and my body was digesting the night of lovemaking as I headed downstairs to find him in the kitchen. The morning light poured in, illuminating him in a pair of boxers and a white T-shirt, inhaling the aroma of fresh coffee while scrambling eggs.

"Good morning, Sunshine".

"My Granny used to call me Sunshine."

"Well, she and I see the same thing in you. You radiate from every pore of your body, which is sensational and in perfect proportions." He walked over and wrapped me in his arms, kissing my neck and saying, "What a night. I will never forget it. I love you in my white shirt and bobby socks. You are amazing."

"Yes, it was a crazy night, and I badly needed a coffee. Thank you for making it and the eggs. You have spoiled me, and I loved every minute with you."

I glanced at him as we ate our eggs and toast, sipping the most delicious cappuccino. We acknowledged that we would be at work tomorrow with our colleagues, who would likely figure out quickly that we missed the ferry. We needed a game plan that wouldn't reveal our truth to protect our spouses and our jobs at the firm. Following the fairytale night of romance and frivolity, it was a heavy reality, but it was a conversation we needed to have. We both understood that no one could find out.

Looking towards the ocean, he flatly stated, "My father would not be happy."

That wasn't my initial thought; it originated from him, coming from his world of wealth and influence. The power lay not with his wife but with his father.

As we left the magical estate behind in our rearview mirror, the future loomed over us both, raising questions about what this means for our future relationships and how we will handle this undeniable attraction.

Scottie dropped me off in front of my home and drove off as I entered the front door. I knew Matt would not be up but asleep from his night shift, so I immediately went to the laundry room, stripped down, put all my clothes in the wash, and hopped in the shower.

I felt like I had been drugged; the high from the night before and the withdrawals were setting in, but the craving for the drug again was real, even knowing I should not touch that drug again. Matt would be up soon, and I needed to remain calm and have my story about missing the ferry solid, as I didn't want to give him any reason to doubt or mistrust me. Even as I write this that sounds unbelievable, but I had to figure out what this meant. Was I not happy in my marriage? Were we drifting apart because of our careers and working different schedules? Was I no longer in love with Matt? What allowed me to take such a risk, knowing the devastation it could cause?

My thoughts were as scrambled as the eggs I made for Matt, which I spread with Swiss cheese to melt while I heard him showering. Brewing coffee at six in the evening always felt odd, and his going to work at eight o'clock also seemed unusual for our health and well-being. I admired and respected Matt, his work ethic, and his dedication to the patients he treats in the middle of the night during every possible trauma. He was solid and confident when diagnosing and treating patients and comforting those who had just lost a loved one. The better Matt became as a doctor, the more emotionally freeze-dried he became as a husband and partner. He seldom wanted to discuss work and his experiences during those exhausting twelve-hour shifts. In retrospect, I rarely shared what I did at work with my clients and colleagues, so we lived in a pretend vacuum, a world separate from each other's lives.

The conversation over scrambled eggs and toast was brief and uneventful, as he didn't ask many questions while I rambled on about how we had missed the ferry. We all gathered at Scottie Weston's parents' estate. He said, "I'd like to hear more, but I must prepare for a presentation on the pediatric ward tomorrow morning at six. I'm so glad you're home; thanks for the eggs, and we'll catch up later this week when I'm off for a few days." And with that, he was on his way. After tidying up, I headed straight upstairs to our bedroom, shutting the blinds against the evening light, stripping down, curling up under the cozy duvet, and reflecting that I would never lie to him again, even though it all felt too easy.

Mariah Carey woke me with my radio alarm at 5:30 a.m., assuming

Matt was working while I was still asleep. He was set to give his presentation, and I was about to face all the guys at work who would tease Scottie and me, needing to keep our cool. Both of us are married, and this had to remain discreet. A mix of guilt and exhilaration over our time together was conflicting and confusing as I prepared for work in my Paul Smith classic suit. I looked in the mirror. "Here we go."

"Good morning, Morgan. How was your weekend at the conference? I heard everyone had a wonderful time, and the weather was lovely." My assistant, who was the same age as me and detail-oriented, assisted me with my schedule and organized my daily life.

"Good morning, Carmen. I had a fantastic weekend. I have some letters I'd like you to review and then mail for me. I hope your weekend was enjoyable, too." As I walked to my desk, I noticed that Scottie hadn't yet arrived, but one of the guys beside me was smiling as if he wanted me to know he was aware of what had transpired.

Scottie and I avoided each other at work while everyone searched for signs of a new office romance. I tried to stop staring at him and visualize our night together, but it wasn't easy. He looked incredibly handsome in his white shirt and tie, with a fit, athletic body beneath that had no hint of fat. Two weeks later, after things had somewhat settled around the office and at home, I came into work one morning to find a plane ticket in an envelope on my desk. As I opened it, my heart began to race when I saw Tyee Airlines and a note that read, "Meet me for cracked crab and champagne on my boat at Princess Louisa Inlet this Friday night." The flight departed at four in the afternoon, and it was a one-way ticket.

Oh my God! How did he know Matt was working this weekend and that I was going golfing with a few girlfriends but otherwise had no plans? A weekend on his boat? What boat? I didn't know he had one. I wrote a note and dropped it on his desk. "I need to think about this. TEMPTING."

My butterflies stirred, my cheeks flushed, and I couldn't focus as adrenaline surged at the thought of flying up on a private floatplane to a boat along the coast to Desolation Sound, which I had heard was one of the most breathtaking parts of British Columbia. Spectacular mountains rise from the ocean, with waterfalls cascading off them, free from towns or civilization—just wildlife, eagles, and the enchantment of untouched nature. Damn. After two days of restless thoughts, I asked Scottie to meet me downstairs at the coffee shop and said, "Are you sure we should be doing this?"

"No, but I can't stop thinking about you and how incredible we are together. If you fly in on Friday, I'll have you back in Vancouver by four the next day. You might want to think about something fun on Friday night."

"Okay. This sounds like too much fun for me to say no to. You promise I'll be back by four the next day?"

"Promise."

I kissed his cheek, inhaling his scent, which brought all those heated moments rushing back into my mind. Feeling the heat rise to my face, I noticed his blue eyes twinkling as he whispered, "Tyyyeeeeee," prompting us both to laugh. He pulled me in and kissed me when no one was in the hallway returning to the office.

Chapter Eleven

Two Men, One Heart

That evening, I casually mentioned to Matt that I was going to Whistler Friday night with a girlfriend to golf and stay at her parents' place, intending to return the next day in the afternoon after our round at Nicklaus North. He seemed pleased that I was staying busy while he worked, which was preferable to my complaining about the number of shifts he took and why they always had to fall on weekends when I was free. He preferred weekends because they paid more, and I could keep myself entertained. He became absorbed in his life, the hospital, and the New England Medical Journals, making it easy to deceive him since he never really followed up with questions about where I was or what I was doing.

Parting ways in our lives created an ideal backdrop for deception and my rationalization of having an affair. I noted my ability to live in the moment without guilt and embrace risks, like flying in a floatplane beside a pilot for ninety minutes north. As we soared over breathtaking, snow-covered mountains and turquoise glacier lakes, my heart raced when the pilot pointed out a boat in an inlet with a guy waving from the back. I was dripping with excitement from the anticipation, immersed in the thrill of taking off on the water from the harbour, surrounded by majestic mountains and the raw wilderness with no sign of civilization, and enveloped by the craziness and unease of the two of us here with no one knowing.

We circled above the boat, descending closer as the pilot skillfully manoeuvred the plane through the rippling ocean waves. We came to a halt near Scottie. For a moment, I wondered how I would transfer from the plane to the boat, but then I noticed Scottie hopping into a tender at the back of his boat. He approached me in a PING golf cap, navy shorts, and a casual white tee. Man, he looked good.

After settling onto his boat, he handed me a Veuve Clicquot, which I needed. He wrapped his arms around me and said, "Fancy a swim off the boat before dinner? The water is ten degrees warmer in Desolation Sound than in the city, and you won't believe how amazing it is."

Well, there goes my hair and mascara if I jump in, but I thought, why not? The magic of this place was a thrill beyond comprehension, looking straight up at mountains on either side of the boat and the sun piercing through the inlet with eagles soaring from peak to peak. I was lost in its splendour, and the quiet was only broken by the cascading falls crashing over the steep pitch of the mountain wall. After changing into my bathing suit, we stood at the boat's bow, grabbing each other's hands and yelling, "Tyyyeeeeeee!"

The water was wonderfully warm and buoyant as we floated on our backs, taking it all in, mesmerized by the natural beauty and remoteness. My mind was adjusting to everything, and the champagne helped ease my flurry of emotions, yet we couldn't stop giggling. The crab he had bought from a local fisherman was served with warm butter, lemon, and a salad that he quickly tossed together in the galley. As we cracked the crab and sipped champagne, the darkness of night began enveloping the boat, and we found ourselves in the middle of nowhere with no light pollution, only massive constellations revealed one star at a time.

Orion, with his belt and sword, the big dipper and little dipper, the planets bolder than ever, evident in their brilliance in the sky above this reclusive, private, uncontrolled budding romance. We talked and laughed and shared stories of our lives that we had never explored with someone before. The safety of being so far from the judgment of eyes on our clandestine and surreptitious relationship was liberating. The reality of our marriages not being the most fulfilling romantically or feeling truly loved was the discussion under the Milky Way. Does romantic love and lust last in a marriage, and if not, then at what stage of marriage can we live with it? We were curled under a duvet on a mattress on the back of the boat open to the stars above, giddy from the champagne and naked in each other's arms, where I felt completely loved and adored. It was intoxicating. As I drifted off to sleep with Scottie's body around mine, at some point in the night, hearing the odd rock fall off the cliff nearby, I thought I had never been happier than at this exact moment of magic he created for me. This must be what it's like to have a man appreciate and spoil you, thinking Matt would never do this.

The four-hour boat ride home felt like an adventure as we explored the islands and stopped for lunch at a cool spot called Smitty's in a fishing port, where we savoured steamed mussels and a beer. Many boaters gathered at this place, and while we hoped not to run into anyone Scottie or I might know, it didn't matter much to us at that moment. We felt reckless, coming off a night of blissful infatuation and feeling smitten. All I knew was that I wanted more and more of him. How could I live without this chemistry, this passion, and that feeling of being alive with every sense afire? The music intensified when Lionel Richie's "Hello" played, becoming our song. The lyrics spoke of seeing love in your eyes, your smile, knowing just what to do and say, and wanting to express how much I love you.

The power of music evokes deep emotions without allowing time for the mind to intervene and take control. Unfettered feelings escape from the heart and surface on our skin, liberated from the complexities of thought that might otherwise restrain them. Music resonates profoundly with our primal biology, as it touches our raw nerves and flows through us; we respond with the most genuine expression. This song reached us similarly overwhelmingly, forging a heartfelt connection that lies at the core of our attraction.

I was now living two lives. One was with my physician husband, while the other was with my passionate boyfriend, who continued to surprise me with trips to Carmel for golfing, outings on the boat exploring private coves, and loving me in ways that Matt did not. I struggled with questions swirling in my mind, such as: Is this infatuation likely to develop into a normal relationship? How can this level of excitement and adrenaline continue? How can I focus on my career when I can't stop thinking about Scottie? We must plan to leave our spouses and be together. Are we ready for that? How can I hurt Matt? He's been a wonderful husband but is deeply immersed in his medicine, friends, and life, and he never truly expresses his love for me. I don't hate him; I'm bored with him. How can I justify leaving?

After nearly a year, I decided it was time for Scottie and me to come clean and stop lying about our relationship. It was unfair to Matt and to Scottie's wife and it needed to end.

We met and had a long conversation about it, during which Scottie mentioned that his father wouldn't be pleased. I responded, "Well, he should meet me and see how happy and well we are together." That didn't go over well, and by the end of the evening, I realized that Scottie would never leave his marriage because his father had told him he would be disinherited if he divorced. I felt helpless and angry about the influence of wealthy men. Why didn't Scottie have the strength to stand up to his father for me? Was the amount of money he would eventually inherit so significant that it would devastate him if he didn't receive it? The answer was yes; the money was substantial enough. I needed to figure out what to do next while I sat in the bath that night, crying my eyes out. This wasn't what I expected. Reality hit me like unpleasant, nauseating withdrawals from the drug of lust, infatuation, and delusion.

After a restless night, I concluded that I could no longer see Scottie. I had to stay with Matt and continue building my life with him. This was the right decision, and Scottie and I ended up in tears, but I had to remain resolute. I asked him to transfer to another branch of our office so we wouldn't be tempted to see each other every day, which he agreed to do.

My heart was shattered, my life felt jolted and chaotic, and I felt morally conflicted as I looked into Matt's eyes. He sensed something was wrong. I had been withdrawing from him since the night Scottie and I spent at his parents' estate. Matt knew I was in love with someone else but hoped I would overcome it and move on. I admitted I wanted to move on, but it ultimately destroyed us, and I moved out, accepting the blame and responsibility for the end of our marriage. I was devastated, and the first night in my new apartment nearly broke me as I lay in the bath, contemplating putting my head underwater. Maybe then my heart would stop hurting, and the pain of loss and the guilt of my moral weakness would fade away. At one point, I had two men in my life who loved me, but now I am alone in my downfall, questioning how I ended up here.

I wanted to meet Matt three weeks after moving out to reconsider and apologize. We met at our favourite sushi restaurant, and he made it very clear that we were finished and that he wanted to get a divorce as quickly and painlessly as possible. I walked back to my apartment, shattered and broken. From ultimate highs to crushing lows, I created this situation myself.

As we parted and I hugged him, he said, "I'll be sure to leave your ski gear on the front veranda tomorrow for you to pick up." That was not what I had hoped to hear. The next day after work, I steeled myself to return to our home, which I still partly owned, to collect my skis and anything else he planned to give me. I was trembling as I approached our street. When I rounded the corner, I saw a woman with blonde hair opening the front door, carrying my skis. She returned for the boots, poles, and a bag, placing them on the front deck. I paused to take a good look at her, realizing that I had seen her before. She had been in my home, so I parked and walked up to the front door, knocking harder than usual as I felt my anger rise.

When she opened the door, she said, "Hi, Morgan. Your things are there, and I don't think there's anything else Matt wanted me to leave for you."

"Wait, who are you? I believe I met you at a hospital event, and you work as an X-ray technician, right?"

"Yes, my name is Meg, and I did meet you there."

"What are you doing here?" I asked bluntly.

She turned red, and I figured she was five years younger than me and ten years younger than Matt.

"How long have you been seeing Matt?"

She slowly closed the door, watching my growing rage as my mind pieced together the truth. He's been with her for a long time. He's been having an affair as well and allowed me to endure the humiliation of the guilt, the shame, the moving out, and accepting responsibility for the collapse of our marriage. FUCK!!!

"Are you living here now, in my home?"

I could hear, "You don't live here anymore; Matt and I do," as the door slammed shut and the deadbolt clicked into place.

I wanted to take my skis and ram the front door yelling at the top of my lungs, "Are you fucking kidding me?" My mind was trying to digest this apparent betrayal, and we both were living separate lives. No wonder he didn't seem very emotional when I told him about Scottie. It was his opportunity to have sweet little girlfriend Meg move in and have me move out, accepting all the blame.

If I had felt low before, this was a new level of turmoil I couldn't comprehend. After throwing my skis and boots into the backseat, I had to return to my small apartment and call my mother, which didn't go as I had anticipated.

I was so angry that I had ruined the perfect marriage to my gorgeous doctor husband, about whom she proudly boasted to her friends, and she couldn't let them know I had cheated on him. The elite group in my hometown was made up of the doctors who ruled the city with their sports cars and sprawling homes. I explained to her that our working lives created separate existences, allowing us to engage in relationships we hid from each other—no wonder we drifted apart. The difference is that I came clean to him, while he concealed his love affair from me.

My mother blamed me for not being there for my man and for not having a job that allowed me to put my husband first and always be there for him. Why was I going away on weekends when he was working? Why was I competing with him? She thought that my building a career that earned more money than his ultimately emasculated him so that the X-ray technician wouldn't threaten his ego, income, or masculinity.

My mother said, "Doctors are worshipped in hospitals and expect to be revered when they return home. You needed to do that. This divorce is entirely your fault, and now you must find another man to marry, have children, and provide me with a grandchild soon. It won't be easy since you are now thirty-one years old."

Without the support of my dear mother, whom I humiliated in front of her friends after boasting for so many years about her fantastic daughter married to a gorgeous, athletic ER doctor, she was furious and unsympathetic. It was time to turn to my girlfriends, who would hopefully offer the support and love I desperately needed so I wouldn't drown myself in the bathtub. I wouldn't give Matt that gift.

With my marriage behind me, I needed to concentrate on my job and earn a considerable income to purchase a new home. I also hosted numerous dinner parties with my girlfriends to seek their support and share my perspective. It was a chaotic period, and I was utterly devoted to work. I realized that TIME is the only healer. Well, that and an excellent therapist. My days were spent building my business and rebuilding my sense of self, running for an hour after work or attending aerobics classes to sweat it out and focus on the future. I was on my own for the first time, and it was daunting, but somehow, I embraced the challenge and knew I would make it through. I needed to move past my anger towards Scottie for not jumping at the chance to be with me and be even more furious with his father for wielding his money as a weapon against his son. I needed to forgive Matt, as he was trying to fill the void of love that we both were missing. We never discussed it; instead, we chose to avoid the topic.

This marks the conclusion of my first marriage, which highlighted my innocence and naivety about love, my carelessness about the love we shared, and my tendency to trust a new infatuation—a stepping stone to my subsequent marriage.

Weddings are a magical, romantic occasion, yet they ultimately function as a business arrangement. This becomes clear when common interests wane, the romance fades, and your heart feels devoid of the love you once knew. You endeavoured to sustain the passion, the commitment, and the energy flowing between you. No single event caused this; one of us is a doctor working shifts, while the other is a stockbroker immersed in a different culture daily. Our cultures collided and ensnared us, pulling us into separate worlds and leading us to see ourselves as opposing teams instead of allies. I forgive us and our youth for the forces of two worlds clashing: two hearts separated by an overwhelming desire for love and recognition, alongside a failure to appreciate it.

We drifted apart.

We did our best.

Chapter Twelve

Cultures Colliding

Adjusting from juggling two men for a year to having none was a tumultuous emotional experience. It forced me to question my moral code, my willingness to give it all up, and my reckless behaviour. Was I fully conscious of the repercussions of losing Matt, Scottie, my friends, my dignity, my pride, and, ultimately, myself?

Did I understand the walk of shame one feels when the world learns of your indiscretions, your readiness to cheat and commit adultery? Why didn't I consider that more thoroughly, and why wasn't I able to walk away from the allure of attraction, the adrenaline rush of breaking the rules?

Would I have had an affair if I had remained a schoolteacher surrounded by dominant women and only a few ambitious men who didn't aspire to own a Porsche or lead a lavish lifestyle? Did my culture shape my personality and character, or did I adapt to the role of a risk-oriented stockbroker? It felt natural to be in that environment, and I excelled at the work aspect of the job; the competition was fierce and familiar. When I reflected on the most successful men I worked with, I noticed that every partner in my firm was having an affair with their secretary or assistant. This became evident when a notice was circulated to all stockbrokers. The top of the notice read: Stockbrokers Golf Tournament. Please sign up your foursome along with your handicaps. The date is September 15th, and the first tee-off will be at 2:00, so plan accordingly. You will receive your tee time this week FORE!

I was thrilled to ask my cubicle partners, Halsey, Chris, and Johnny, to play together, and I submitted our entry form with our handicaps. Mine was an eight handicap, the lowest in the group, which made the boys excited, hoping I would help them win the tournament and secure the big prize of $5,000 each. They initially wanted me to put down a fifteen handicap and act as a sandbagger to assist them in winning. Still, I insisted we couldn't do that since one of the partners knew about my previous amateur golf experience.

Halsey and I decided to visit the golf club where the tournament took place to hit some balls and see if we could play nine holes, even though it was a private club. We had a fantastic time chipping and playing little games to improve our short game until the sun went down, signalling that it was time to head home. While driving back, I felt rejuvenated, knowing I was part of this boys' club and truly belonged. The next day, as I sat at my desk, opened the newspaper, and turned on my small lamp, I received a message on my phone that read, "Morgan, please call me when you can. Stephanie."

I knew Stephanie was the President's assistant and looked after all the office details and Mr. Ryan's schedule. Maybe he wants to congratulate me on the latest new client I brought into the firm, a large lumber tycoon I had spent over a year prospecting for.

Rather than call her, I grabbed my coffee and went to her desk. "Good morning, Stephanie; how are you?"

"Oh, Morgan, Mr. Ryan just wants a few words with you. Do you have time now?"

"Sure, love to."

After she checked with him, she came back and said, "You can go in now."

Walking confidently into the office, I felt grateful for wearing my favourite new Burberry suit from my last commission cheque. I settled into the wine-coloured leather chair and greeted Mr. Ryan. He always dressed impeccably, with perfectly styled sandy brown hair, shiny gold cufflinks, Hermès ties, and classy Italian shoes that exuded success.

After I had sat down, he picked up the form I filled out for the golf tournament and asked me if I had an eight handicap.

At first, I thought he was accusing me of lying about my handicap, so I responded,

"Yes, I have an eight handicap, which has increased from a six after working through the summer and not having as much time to focus on my game."

He nodded quietly. "Well, we've never had women participate in our tournament before, which could present a challenge."

My mind was racing, wondering what kind of problem my participation in the tournament could cause. "What kind of problem? I'm a stockbroker, and if you notice, at the top of that sheet, it says Stockbrokers Golf Tournament, so I don't see the issue. You just haven't had women stockbrokers before who play golf, but times are changing, and I'm very much looking forward to playing."

He started to look uncomfortable and said bluntly, "This tournament is for men only."

My face flushed with confusion and anger. I desperately tried to respond to avoid getting fired, so I asked, "Am I a stockbroker, Mr. Ryan?"

"Yes, you are, but the women in the firm would be unhappy if you play and they don't."

"Really? Are they stockbrokers or assistants? It's called a Stockbroker Golf Tournament, and since I am a stockbroker, I want to play and could beat half the men participating." I was so furious that I stood up. As I walked to the door to leave, I turned quickly around and, without thinking, impulsively said, "I'll play you at Shaughnessy, and if I beat you in Matchplay, I get to play in the tournament. If I lose, I will back out peacefully." He stood up, shocked and uncertain how to respond.

I looked him straight in the eye and added, "The Human Rights Board would not be happy with this conversation. Are you in or not?"

Looking down at his desk, he removes his jacket and grapples with the confrontation before raising his head to gaze at me with a subtle smirk of defiance. "OK, we'll play this Saturday at eight a.m. with two of my golfing buddies."

"Game on." I flicked my ponytail and strode out of his office.

Sitting back at my desk, trembling and stunned by what had transpired, I reached out to Halsey to inform him.

He said, "This is absolute sexism, and there's more to this than just their egos being hurt by a woman. Something is happening. Let me find out why they don't want you there." I couldn't understand it.

My focus was shattered for the day. I mulled over every scenario regarding why he didn't want me playing in the tournament, then hit balls on the driving range for two hours. I practised every night after work, determined to beat the President of my firm and show him that I was hired to be equal to all the men and was performing better than most of the men employed at the same time. I just didn't understand.

Arriving at the club earlier than our tee time, I took my clubs to the range and began hitting balls with my pitching iron. When I looked over, I noticed familiar faces gathering at the putting green. Halsey, Chris, and some other brokers were there, holding their coffee-to-go mugs but without any golf clubs in hand. What were they doing here? Then, a few senior partners I recognized started laughing and exchanging bits of paper with Halsey and Chris, who then pointed at me. I waved back, unsure of what these eight or nine guys were up to until I saw Mr. Ryan pull into the lot in his black convertible Porsche 911. Were these guys coming to watch us play? Did I have a gallery following us? No, it couldn't be.

After saying good morning, Chris walked over to me and asked, "How do you feel about today's game with the big boss?"

"I feel great, but why are you guys here?"

"There are considerable bets within the firm regarding whether you'll beat Luke Ryan. It's up to $2000 if he triumphs over you, and Halsey and I are wagering that you will win."

"Holy Shit, are you serious?" Taking a deep breath, I grabbed my driver, launched a ball two hundred yards, and shouted at Chris, "I love a competition!"

He winked at me, "Good luck, Morgan, and crush it!" Luke Ryan and I had a following of ten men in the end, cheering, clapping, or oohing and ahhing whenever putts were missed or made. I relished the competition as familiar, sharpening my focus to pick a target and trust myself. The guys were supportive and surprised that I could play as well as I did, and I was relieved my game was consistent on every hole.

I was two holes up at the eighteenth tee box and had won the match. Halsey and Chris were thrilled but remained quiet and subdued out of respect for their boss until he finally congratulated me, a gesture he had hesitated to make until the final putt.

The gallery cheered and clapped when I sank my long fifteen-foot putt on the eighteenth green for a birdie. Taking the ball out of the hole, I walked over to Mr. Ryan with my hand extended and said, "Good game, Mr. Ryan."

"Impressive game, Morgan. I had no idea you could play that well. Congratulations! Let me buy everyone a round of beer."

We sat outside with the breeze coming off the ocean. I slowly relaxed from the four hours of intense pressure and competition, being watched by this gallery of men, checking me out from every angle and knowing they were quietly commenting on my body. Luckily, I was fit and in great shape but fully aware of the sexualization of their thoughts, which permeated through my mind when I wiggled my butt in the practice swing before each shot. Let it go, Morgan. Your power is your body and its strength and beauty. Something they want but can't have. That's your power over them.

After we exchanged the money at the table and my friends each received $6,000, we said our goodbyes and walked to our cars. Halsey and Chris were thrilled and excited that I'd be playing in the tournament, and I was overjoyed to have triumphed over that bastard president who had challenged me to secure equal rights for my male partners.

Monday morning arrived, and I went to work excitedly, knowing there would be a buzz around the office about what had transpired over the weekend and that I had beaten the boss. There was a gallery of men to witness the humiliation of it all. Walking through the office, I heard clapping and a few cheers of, "Congrats, Morgan! Nice play. Good for you." It was a high that I cherished and felt I had earned, even if it wasn't entirely fair.

As we settled into our desks, the noise and chaos of the business's natural order started. Phones rang, people spoke about buying or selling, shorting their positions, and economic numbers just got released. The energy of the morning was electric. I was getting hungry and realized I had forgotten my blueberry muffin, so I offered to get something to eat for my assistant, Carmen.

Looking up, she was somewhat worried and responded, "The president would like to see you in his office."

The president's door was open, so I knocked and glanced in, thinking he would congratulate me and confirm that I was now welcome at the golf tournament, when he uttered without much hesitation, "The Board has decided you can't play in the tournament after all. I'm sorry, Morgan, but that is how it will be."

Looking down at the floor, clenching my jaw and rapidly digesting this slap overt betrayal, I lifted my eyes and gazed directly into his. "I quit then. I want nothing to do with a firm that doesn't treat women equally and fairly. I will transfer all my clients to another firm that believes in equality. Goodbye, Mr. Ryan. I took you for an honourable man."

Storming out of his office while fighting back tears, I approached Carmen and said, "I just quit because they went back on their commitment to let me play in the tournament. I'm heading across the street to inquire about a position at Scotia McLeod, and I'll let you know where to send my things. I'll call you and the others once I find another job. Please inform Amy in Human Resources that I've resigned and the reasons for my decision. Also, let her know that I'll reach out to the Human Rights Board after securing my next position, which I hope will be in a few hours."

Carmen was shocked but knew she also had to hold it together. "Can I do anything for you right now?"

"You will be transferring my book of business to my new office, and hopefully, I can get you to come with me. I will need you. Carmen, men are all bastards!"

I grabbed my briefcase, tossed my items inside, and avoided speaking to anyone as I headed to the elevator, biting my lip. Afterwards, I left the office. Knowing the location of the Scotia McLeod office, I took deep breaths, walked over to their building, made my way to the fifteenth floor, and entered the reception area.

"Hello. My name is Morgan Cooper, and I want to speak to your manager, Jeremy Sutcliffe."

"Do you have an appointment?"

"No, but he will be interested in meeting with me. I was a stockbroker with Pemberton Securities and quit today to come here."

After waiting for ten minutes, a friendly man with reddish-blonde hair and a smile appeared in the reception area. He extended his hand to shake mine. "Well, Miss Cooper, how can I assist you?"

"Nice meeting you, Mr. Sutcliffe. Could I have a few minutes of your time somewhere private?"

I followed him into his corner office, which overlooked the snow-capped mountains. As I glanced around, I noticed three women in suits chatting. After sharing my story about the golf tournament, my education, my passion for the business, and my desire to build a substantial book of business, he smiled and said, "Pemberton's is notorious for its old boys' club ways, and I'm sure you threatened their plans at the tournament. From what I gather, their assistants or girlfriends all show up after golfing for the big party sans spouses, and I'm sure they were concerned you might inform their wives."

The truth was revealed, and I looked at Mr. Sutcliffe and exhaled. "Thank you for explaining why I could not play with them. How could I possibly work for a company that is so sexist? What is your company like in terms of women and their opportunities?"

"We have five women brokers who are exceptional, and I have asked each of them to report to me any sexist or unfair treatment immediately, and they would be respected and protected. Miss Cooper, we would be honoured to have you join our team. You could set up your desk today, report to HR to set up your security code, sign our contract, and complete any other paperwork. You will have a draw and full commission to establish yourself, and hopefully, your clients will join you here."

I stood up, smiling and relieved, and gushed, "Oh my God, thank you so much for believing in me and giving me this amazing opportunity. I won't disappoint you, and I look forward to meeting the other brokers."

"We have a daily sales meeting at 8 a.m., and I will introduce you to everyone tomorrow morning. If your assistant wants to join us, we can make room for her."

"Carmen is amazing, and hopefully, I can convince her to come and meet with you, as I will need her to handle the transition for me." I turned to walk out of his office, feeling jubilant and excited but full of trepidation about the promise I had just made and hoped I could honour.

Mr. Sutcliffe stood up and shook my hand. "Welcome to Scotia McLeod.

We will need an organizer for our next golf tournament. If you are willing to take on that role, please do."

Smiling as I shook his hand, I responded, "I would be thrilled to take on that role. You have made my day, Mr. Sutcliffe."

"Call me Jeremy, Morgan. We're team members now, and I know you'll be a fantastic addition. Good luck with getting organized. I'll see you tomorrow morning. My assistant, Betty, will help you settle into your desk and complete all the paperwork."

Falling onto my couch that evening, curling up under a cozy blanket with a cup of peppermint tea in hand after a long, candlelit bubble bath, I digested the day, relieved that I no longer worked where Scottie worked or belonged to an organization that treated women like toys in their little game. Shaken by the betrayal of the president, shocked by the news that the guys were having their girlfriends from the office join them after the golf tournament, stunned that this goes on in this industry, and ashamed that I also participated in an affair. Was I any better than them, or had the culture of deception, game playing, lying, and worship of money and power seeped into my belief system, making me think my behaviour was normal? That disturbed me. Was I flawed like them? Can I blame this on their culture, my father dying, Matt for his shift work at the hospital, or my reckless spirit that acted out impulsively?

Reflecting on the power of money. Would Scottie have attracted me if I hadn't seen that magnificent fifteen-million-dollar estate? Would I have gotten excited if he drove a Subaru or a Volvo instead of a black Porsche 911? Was I not receiving the love I needed or the validation I craved in my marriage? The thoughts swirled around so intensely that I concluded I needed to see a therapist.

Growing up, I struggled with my femininity; I took pride in being somewhat of a tomboy. I even remember thinking to myself, "I wish I were a boy," "Boys have it so much easier," and "I get along better with boys."

Unfamiliar with what it meant to be a woman, I began to view life through a more masculine lens, where achievements took priority over pleasure and applying eyeliner. Men's lives seemed more fulfilling, goal-oriented, and rewarding, and, most importantly, they had the power to shape their destinies. Strangely, I wanted to join the boys' club because I resonated more with their belief system than with the women I knew, and I envied their supportive companionship.

They controlled the money and, therefore, the power—the power to love or destroy, to give or take, to uplift or diminish someone's spirit, and to determine their destiny.

I now realized that to be free, independent, and fulfilled, I needed money—plenty of it. I didn't want a man determining my fate and lifestyle. My money mantra became: "I love money and am grateful each day for its presence and wonderful goodness." I was determined to avoid slipping into the vortex of mediocrity.

Fear often stems from the narratives we create for ourselves, so I decided to share a different story than those typically told to women. I affirmed that I was safe, strong, and courageous. Nothing could hold me back... Fear begets fear, and power begets power. I committed to nurturing my power; soon enough, I was no longer afraid.

This became my focus and passion: establishing daily accomplishment targets to achieve my yearly wealth creation goals. These goals did not align with my mother's aspirations for me, which were to remarry and have children, particularly her first grandchild.

It became a recurring theme of conversation, and she showed little interest in my growing success in the business or my career aspirations. At this point, I am a disappointment to her for leaving teaching, which aligns with family values, and for leaving my doctor husband, who represents security and status.

That night, I taped a quote on my fridge door:

If you cannot risk, you cannot grow,
If you cannot grow, you cannot become your best,
If you cannot become your best, you cannot be happy,
If you cannot be happy, what else matters?

Chapter Thirteen

HARVEY ROSS

Determined to build my business with my new company required considerable time and energy but allowed me the necessary time to regain my emotional foundation, which was bruised and beaten up. Luckily, my confidence in selling my firm's benefits and skill set was not impacted by the emotional hurdles I barely navigated through. It was a refreshingly fair and encouraging environment, with the other women brokers being incredibly competitive and hard-working. One woman broker won a silver medal in the Pan Am Games for swimming; another had her MBA from Harvard, so my new mentors were accomplished and disciplined.

One morning, one of the male partners approached my desk, leaning over the cubicle wall, and said, "There's a friend of mine who would like to ask you out, and I just wondered if you would be interested in meeting him."

"What's his name?"

"Harvey Ross, a founder of Ross Capital Corp."

"I've heard of him, and he's a bit of a player."

"He's a good guy and single, and I think you would enjoy meeting him."

"Okay, Gord, but I recently divorced, and I'm not sure I'm ready for another man in my life."

"Great, I'll have him call you."

I had heard about Harvey Ross, who supposedly dated gorgeous models. He owned a house in Whistler, so he must have been a skier, and he strongly resembled Kevin Costner with his sandy blonde hair slicked back. I didn't know much about him, but it made me uneasy to think about the wild life he must lead.

Two days later, while tidying my desk before heading to my aerobics class, my assistant called and informed me that Harvey Ross was on the phone. When I answered, a deep male voice said, "Hi, Morgan. It's Harvey. Are you available for lunch tomorrow after the market closes?"

"Hi, Harvey. Gord mentioned you might be calling, and I'd be more than happy to meet you. Where would you like to go for lunch?"

"Let's meet at Joe Fortes at one fifteen if that works for you?"

"Great, I look forward to meeting you there."

All night, I debated whether I was equipped and ready for a new relationship and how that would impact my work and my emotional journey to recovering my sense of self. As I drifted to sleep, "Don't overthink, don't overthink" was my send-off to la la land.

Needing to portray the successful broker, I wore my cherry-red suit and black overcoat since it was now getting cooler with the fall weather descending on us and the leaves offering that last burst of vivid colours before falling to the ground. I noticed the fiery reds, hues of orange, and brilliant yellows reflecting the afternoon sun as I walked to the restaurant, feeling a nervous trepidation.

As I was about to open the front door, I heard a car pulling up behind me. Quickly glancing around, I noticed a cherry-red Porsche arriving and parking in the valet spot. A man wearing aviator sunglasses and a stunning tan suit brushed his sandy blonde hair back as he tossed his keys to the young valet, saying, "Look after it for me, Henry."

"As always, Mr. Ross. Enjoy your lunch."

I was still holding the door, somewhat captivated by this man's arrival; his energy and overall appearance made me feel a touch starstruck as if I were meeting Kevin Costner, who I had a huge crush. He grabbed the door above me and, almost brushing my face, said, "You must be Morgan. I'm Harvey."

Harvey took my coat and handed it to the doorman. His blue eyes caught me off guard with their brilliance as he shook my hand. His gaze unsettled me, and as we reached our table, he said, "I just want you to know this isn't a date but a job interview for a position at Ross Capital."

"Which position am I applying for again?" I was trying to understand why he mentioned a date. Did I want to go out with him after all? His commanding presence made me feel uneasy.

"You would be an institutional trader stationed at the trading desk, earning three times your current salary. You would interact with large corporations instead of private clients, focusing on major corporations."

"Why would you offer me that position when I've never been a trader, only a retail broker? I'm not even certain I want to leave this company now."

"Let's order lunch and discuss the job and the opportunity it would present for you."

After digesting the surprise that this was not a date but a job interview, I felt a little blindsided but appreciative that he thought I could do this high-powered job. I barely ate my corn fritters, somewhat disappointed by the turn of events.

He asked me a bit about my life as a golfer and skier, where I attended university, and how I felt about being at work every morning at 5:30 am, which meant getting up at 4:30 am. I inquired about the exact role of a trader and what his day involved.

After he described his routine each morning, the clients the company worked with, and the expectations for a trader, I finally replied, "Thank you very much, Harvey, but I need to think about this over and get back to you."

As we left the restaurant, his car idled, waiting for him. He extended his hand to shake mine, saying, "Let me know tomorrow, and you can start next week."

Before I could respond, he had hopped in the front seat, accelerated into traffic, and was gone. However, as I walked away, I could hear the distinct purring sound of a Porsche engine in the distance.

What the fuck was that all about? I need to talk to Gord and figure out how he got this all wrong. I don't want to be a trader, do I? Did he really say I would make what I make three times now? Okay, Jesus. Getting up at 4:30 a.m. instead of 5:45 am sounds brutal, and why me? Why does he want to hire me, someone with no experience in trading?

I stormed into Gord's office since he was one of the senior partners and top producers, which meant he had a beautiful corner office with its own sitting area and coffee bar. As I knocked on his door and let myself in, still wearing my coat, I raised my arms and blurted out, "What the hell, Gord?

He offered me a job as a trader, but there was no interest in dating me at all."

Gord started laughing, stood up, and came around his desk, saying, "Congratulations, that's a job any broker in the city would die for. You know you'll make around one million a year, right? Harvey is very particular about who works with him and won't allow just anyone to sit across from him at the trading desk. He has fired a few guys for not keeping up with him, and he expects people to perform. Harvey is one of the best institutional traders in Canada. He's sharp and aggressive, and he performs well under pressure. There's no one like him on the street. I guess he thinks you have what it takes."

"Do you think he is hiring me because he needs a female to balance out all the men in the firm?"

Gord, laughing again, says, "Harvey would never risk his company to a woman trader that potentially could lose money. He doesn't care about equal rights. He cares about making money and hopes you will make a lot of money for his company. It's about the bottom line with Harvey, and money is Harvey's God. He's one of the best salesmen, and you will learn a ton because a trader must sell their positions, so it's a combination of selling and trading the stocks. We're talking fifty million to one hundred million dollar trades he does over there, many times daily. It would be a phenomenal opportunity, Morgan."

Another night, after a long bubble bath, I curled up under my comforter with my pad of paper titled Pros and Cons.

PROS......

1. Money
2. New Challenge.
3. Potential Partner
4. Only woman trader in Canada

CONS......

1. Disappointing Harvey

2. 4:30 am alarm
3. Staying safe in my space

Drifting off to sleep, a blurred vision appeared of a little red Porsche on a country road, top-down, a blonde ponytail blowing under a golf cap beside Harvey, shifting gears into the sunset.

Chapter Fourteen

Higher Ground

"I know, Mom, I'm turning thirty-three this year, but I don't have a boyfriend to have children with, so just leave it to me. I trust it will all happen in good time." Every phone call, I must explain myself. The pressure from my mother is always there. My need for her approval remains strong; I want her to say she's proud of me.

"You do know that your biological clock is ticking and that your eggs aren't getting any younger," my mother reminded me, unaware of how painful that reminder was. She had me at 23, and it was likely an accident, but our biological clocks aren't changing with the liberation of women. I understood that we were given all our eggs at birth and released one at a time during each menstrual cycle, alternating between ovaries every month. Therefore, I recognized that the healthiest eggs were released first, while the less healthy ones were released as we aged.

"Remember that your career ambitions might deter a suitor who doesn't enjoy competing with his partner for attention. You may achieve greater success by remaining in his shadow." Unfortunately, this message often conveyed a sense of judgment rather than the supportive encouragement I needed to make my business thrive.

Fuck, that was my first thought, but then anything my mother said tended to bang around in my mind, especially in the dark recesses of the night. Bang, bang, bang! With that in mind, I accepted the position at Ross Capital and informed my company that my last day would be this Friday, jumping into a chaotic frenzy of an uncertain world. Still, somehow, I knew I needed to jump. Underlying these risks was a subconscious understanding that I could cope, survive, and hopefully thrive in my new environment. It was only me to look after, so if it didn't work out, I wasn't letting anyone down and could return to the retail world if needed.

I never got accustomed to waking up at 4:30 a.m., even with coffee at the trading desk. The 5:30 a.m. meeting was intense; you had to be wide awake and concentrate on that day's trades, the overnight economic news, the market's anticipation, and what clients might buy or sell. It was a whirlwind of activity, and you had to stay alert to avoid costly mistakes. Harvey was like a maestro, juggling different phones from various corporate accounts while listening to the squawk box blasting trades from the trading desk in Toronto simultaneously. He would sell a new stock issue at $23 ¼ to one client while purchasing stock from another, then yell to the squawk, "Sold Inco at $23 ¼ to HSBC, and buying Teck at $42 ½." After that, he would swivel his chair to take in the breathtaking view of the pink sunrise reflecting on the snowcapped mountains, shouting, "Morgan, get Bill Cranston on the phone and see if he wants a piece of the new Inco issue."

I had stepped into an intense firestorm. I needed to get the numbers right and sell them quickly to these clients, who were still adjusting to a female voice at the end of the Ross Capital line. The more urgent I sounded, the more likely I was to receive a response. These clients were well-informed about Canadian companies and knew precisely what they required in their portfolios and what they needed to sell.

We were instruments for those trades, but every client wanted the best price for entering and exiting. Then they would negotiate the commission, and I would hear Harvey say, "A half point is our lowest, Wayne, and we'll make it up to you on the sale. You know that. Thanks, Wayne; we'll chat tomorrow." It was fast-paced and intense, and the clients didn't want lengthy conversations like I was used to as a retail broker.

There were days when I had to step away, sit in the stairwell, and cry. It felt like a pressure cooker, and one mistake could cost the firm millions. Harvey reminded me of that every single day. My life revolved around work because I could not stay awake past eight o'clock, and there was no time for a man, much to my mother's chagrin.

Harvey was impressive. He would leave work every day at 1:00 p.m., often going for a run, golfing with clients, or meeting his model girlfriend, who was on the cover of Vogue Europe last month. Portia was tall, glamorous, short dark hair, and stunning. I wouldn't say I liked it when she came into the office to meet Harvey. He put on an air of sophistication and charm that seemed contrived compared to the guy who sat across the desk from me. He arrived before me every morning, having the papers all read and wired on his coffee, sometimes even sharing cheese scones that Portia made for him. She seemed crazy about him, and they made a gorgeous couple. So, when I asked how things were with Portia one day, he gave me a quick stare and responded, "I don't talk about my personal life."

Harvey was hilarious with his clients on the phone and quite entertaining with the partners in Toronto, but he kept his distance from me. During market hours, there was no time to discuss anything else. Someone was always shouting positions to buy or sell from the squawk box, so there was never a moment of silence until the market closed.

One day, Harvey's assistant walked in and placed a cheque in front of him for our monthly commission, then set my cheque before me. Harvey, deeply engaged in conversation with a client about a merger between two companies and how they could benefit from it, allowed me a glance at his cheque before mine. I had to do a double-take. It was $180,000.00! I kept counting the zeros before realizing that was his earnings from the previous trading month. My cheque was $25,000.00, which kind of blew me away, but Harvey's was astonishing. I quickly grabbed my calculator and multiplied his commission by 12 to get $2,160,000.00. Knowing he was also a part-owner of his firm; he would receive additional dividends. Holy crap, I thought, as I got up to grab my lunch in the staff room, grasping the reality of this segment of the industry.

One of my clients, who founded the institutional firm Caldwell Partners, invited me to lunch one day, which is rare in this business. We had developed a strong working relationship during my first year at Ross, and I respected him for his accomplishments. Thus, chatting with someone without the pressure to close a deal would be refreshing.

Sam Caldwell was a very handsome, fit-looking man with blonde hair who was self-assured and humble when you meet him. Gentle and intelligent, he built his business from the ground up with hard work, determination, and an incredible team around him. Most men offer a hint of flirtatiousness when I meet them due to a lack of familiarity with an attractive woman in the business. Their go-to was to get a response from me, but Sam was not interested and only showed ultimate respect and curiosity about my position at Ross Capital.

"You know you are the only woman trader in Canada and getting recognized for your ability to sell and keep up with the notorious group of aggressive males. It can't be easy."

"Thank you, Sam, but I had no idea about the pressure to sell blocks of stock every day, and Harvey is relentless as a mentor. He's brilliant at what he does. It's been quite overwhelming, even though it's been a phenomenal learning experience. Harvey can speak and listen at the same time. It's completely wild to observe, and he never misses a beat."

"Most people burn out with institutional sales. I will get right to it, Morgan Cooper. I want to set up a retail arm of my company with 8-10 brokers and would like to find someone to establish this for me. I need them to find office space, hopefully, in the same building we are currently in, and hire the brokers and assistants; since we chat almost every day on the phone, I thought you would be great at doing this for us. I know Harvey will kill me, but I wanted to run this opportunity by you. Then, you would be the office manager and bring in a retail business book with help from our corporate client base. I understand you had a healthy book of business when you left to go with Ross. Do you think they would be interested in coming back with you? Our model portfolio has been annualizing around 20% with a US-based focus unique to many retail clients today."

As Sam spoke, I thought, Oh my goodness, another work change in less than three years. Harvey won't be pleased after training me, but it seems like an excellent long-term opportunity to live a more normal existence and hopefully not be under pressure every day like I am now.

"Thank you very much for considering me, Sam. This is an incredible opportunity, and I appreciate your trust in me with something vital for your firm's next stage and development. I truly value your kind words. If it's all right, I would like to take some time to reflect on this this evening and possibly over the weekend. I may initially respond with a few questions we haven't discussed here, but I am genuinely interested and excited about this."

This was a night for a long, hot bubble bath, followed by one glass of my favourite Super Tuscan wine as I curled up on the couch under a cozy blanket, listening to Luciano Pavarotti belting out Nessun Dorma, which inevitably brings tears to my eyes; even with the Italian lyrics, he elevates me to higher ground. I close my eyes and soar with angels. This was followed by Van Morrison's Whenever God Shines His Light. Both songs permeate my soul and cut to the core of my being, touching me like angel wings wrapping around my inner spirit. I curl up in it. Music transforms us all, allowing us a moment to sit and reflect on our human spirits, taking us to higher ground.

By Monday morning, my mind was made up after spending time at my Tall Tree Therapy in Lighthouse Park, surrounded by ancient cedars and the sound of ocean waves crashing against the cliffs of Juniper Point. I enter the forest to lose my mind and find my soul. That is my church, my saving grace. I inhale the fresh air from the lush cedars and Douglas firs, along with the moist sensation of the ocean against my face. There's wisdom I absorb from trees that are 250 years old, having withstood the abuses of weather and humanity, along with the knowledge that nature has existed here for centuries before me and will be here for centuries after. Nature will endure even if humanity doesn't. That is a power I respect and feel humbled by. I look up at their branches reaching into the sky, close my eyes, and listen, breathe, and be. It's my meditation, providing answers when I need them most.

After 18 months of working in this most stressful, frenetic, and not overly satisfying environment, I let Sam Caldwell know that I would be honoured and thrilled to open a new office for him and get underway as soon as possible. I want to take two weeks to decompress and will be ready to go on the first of June.

Then, the anxiety of letting Harvey know was building over the morning due to his anger over a trade that went sideways. His energy level was high, and his temper was a bit erratic. How do I let him know that I am moving on and that one of his clients I covered offered me a job? The anticipation nauseated me, so I thought I would tell him when things calmed down. He just dropped the phone, so now may not be the best time.

After one more night of tumultuous sleep, I knew I needed to tell him, no matter his mood. Since I could not speak to him during trading hours, I waited for the final bell at 1:00. He grabbed his jacket from the back of his chair when I stood up and said,

"Harvey, I need to speak to you about something. Do you have a minute?"

"Yeah, just a minute, though, as I'm teeing off at 2."

"I will be brief and get to the point. I met with Sam Caldwell last Friday, and he has offered me this fantastic opportunity to open a retail operation to complement his institutional business. He wants me to find the office space and hire a team of retail brokers to handle discretionary money management."

Harvey was restless and anxious to leave but responded, "What did you tell Sam?"

I sheepishly blurted out, "I said I would love to do it because I feel I'm burning out here, Harvey."

He put the jacket on that he had been holding onto and looked directly at me as he turned to the door, saying, "Good because it was my idea. You will excel in that world, and this is a dog-eat-dog side of the business. Congratulations."

He was gone while my mouth was still open, trying to process that information. What? Was it his suggestion? Did he propose it to Sam? I decided to call Sam, and he confirmed that he and Harvey had skied together last month. Harvey outlined what Sam needed to do and noted that I would be the best person to launch this subsidiary of Caldwell Partners. Sam clarified that this initiative was Harvey's brainchild and remarked, "He's a brilliant visionary, and he thinks very highly of you."

Heading down the elevator, my mind swirling with the thought that it was Harvey's idea and that he thought the world of me, I was stumped. Harvey has never given me a compliment or a hint of recognition for what I had accomplished in a short time there. He tolerated me and often felt I was not meeting his expectations.

Stepping out of the building into the fresh air, I smiled at the sight of cherry blossoms on the trees, heard robins announcing their arrival for spring, and felt euphoric that Harvey thought highly of me. I envisioned Mary Poppins dancing down Cherry Tree Lane, with the robins singing and animals dancing along with her, and I had an overwhelming urge to kick up my heels and dance.

Chapter Fifteen

Thirty-Three and Me

Not many people arrived at the underground garage at 5:30 a.m. each morning, except for one guy I got to know for his excitable energy. We would take the elevator together, and his loud sports car with plates that said it all, "SUN TOY," would pull into the garage and park a few spots away from me. I used to ask him if he was wired on caffeine at that hour or just excited about his job. He smiled cheerfully and said, "No, I can't drink coffee and hate my job. This is just me." He stepped out on the tenth floor before I continued to the fifteenth for Ross Capital.

He asked how things were going on this rainy, dark morning, which might be my last at Ross Capital. I replied that I had just quit the day before and needed two weeks off to decompress before starting a new position with Caldwell Partners. After eighteen months of encountering each other and riding the elevator together, we had exchanged names and the companies we worked for. I knew he was a very handsome, dynamic lawyer at Davidson and Co. named Hans Becker, but I didn't know much about him aside from the fact that he made me laugh and was the happiest person I had ever encountered. His vibrant love of life made you feel good; it was contagious. After I mentioned needing two weeks to decompress, the elevator doors opened, and he stepped out, looking back and saying, "You should go to London and stay with my friend Ellen." The doors shut, and I contemplated London. I hadn't thought about where to go for two weeks in May, but London sounded lovely.

While processing my last day and coming to terms with leaving Ross Capital, I received a phone call from Ellen, who spoke with a British accent. "Hello, Morgan. My name is Ellen, and I'm Hans's good friend and ex-girlfriend. I would love for you to stay with me for two weeks. My husband travels frequently, and you'd have your own bedroom and a separate floor in our home in Sloane Square. I'll pick you up at Heathrow once you inform me of your travel schedule. Come next week for the Chelsea Flower Show, and we can take the Chunnel to Paris on the weekend to visit my brother and his wife."

"Hi, Ellen. Besides being my morning elevator buddy, Hans works efficiently, and I don't know him well. This is incredibly generous and kind of you. I haven't thought about going anywhere since I quit my job yesterday. Can I take some time to reflect on it and get back to you?"

"Don't overthink it. London is magical in the spring, and Hans says we'd get along famously. I won't overbook you; you can stroll through the parks, explore the museums, and do whatever you fancy. Just let me know your flight details, darling, and I'll come to pick you up."

Everything was happening so quickly, out of my control, and I just needed to say yes to what life had planned for me. How amazing it was to spend two weeks in London with someone I had never met, but I trusted Hans, my elevator friend, not to lead me to the arms of some crazy English woman.

Exactly one week later, I was strolling through Kensington Park with Ellen, listening to her share about her relationship with Hans Becker. I loved that they remained friends. She still adored him and stated that his enthusiastic personality was authentic, genuine, and infectious. She confessed it was hard to keep up with him, and I could easily see why with his magnetic yet exhausting energy.

Ellen showed me London like a long-time friend would, with theatre tickets to Les Misérables and The Phantom, both mesmerizing productions, although a bit depressing. We hopped on the Chunnel for a weekend in Paris, staying with her brother and experiencing the local perspective of the city in bistros, gathered around large family-style tables, enjoying course after course of delicious French cuisine, sipping delightful Burgundy wines, and trying to join in the conversations after my year in Aix-en-Provence a decade ago. There's a reason they call it a romantic language; when Parisians become passionate about their food, wine, art, or love affairs, it's enthralling and captivating to sit back and soak it all in. It transports you to another world.

Ellen encouraged me to stay for a month instead of my original two-week plan since her husband was rarely home. Sam Caldwell was okay with it as he would also be on holiday while I was away. We agreed that we could begin once we both returned.

Landing back in Vancouver, well-rested and refreshed from a month of cultural extravagance and leaving Harvey and the stress of the trading desk behind was the best mental health reboot I could have asked for. Ellen was a gift from Hans, and I will be forever grateful to him for initiating that connection with someone so generous, funny, and kind. I arrived in London a rattled, jumbled mess of exposed nerves with a frayed heart after my divorce from Matt, the end of my whirlwind love affair with Scottie, and a year and a half of trying to survive in a hotbed of institutional trading, where my nerves were frayed from the pressure to impress and achieve, desperately attempting not to let Harvey down. Flying across the water allowed me to let go of all I had in Vancouver: what I created, what I destroyed, the loves, the losses, and the understanding that it was time to heal.

After living with Ellen for a month, my apartment felt quiet and lonely, filled with a packed schedule of daily events that never required my consideration. It was a true gift to experience long walks through all the parks of London, stroll down the mall to Buckingham Palace, cruise past Big Ben in black London taxis, pop into lively pubs for a Guinness, enjoy exquisite Indian food, and indulge in plenty of shopping on Oxford Street and Sloane Street. At Ross Capital, I earned more money than I ever thought possible, allowing me to treat Ellen and myself to incredible restaurants while discovering British designers like Paul Smith, Burberry, and Alexander McQueen. Naturally, I needed a new wardrobe for my exciting career move ahead. I finally felt joy, laughing and soaking in the sounds of life and love. I was awakening, blooming toward the sun and its energy. After the jet lag had faded with caffeine, I decided to run on a sunny, gorgeous day to recalibrate my return to reality. I hadn't run in over a month, and as I stepped outside, I took a deep breath of ocean air; that salty breeze was rejuvenating. My jogging shorts felt a bit tighter, snugger than I remembered, and it must have been all the croissants, Indian food, halloumi sandwiches, and oat biscuits with old cheddar cheese that Ellen laid out every afternoon. Food fueled my soul, and I would burn off the added calories by running and returning to my routine.

As I ran along the water, passing some of Vancouver's most stunning and expensive real estate, I had to stop at the intersection to check both ways. I heard the roar of a sports car engine as it pulled up to the crosswalk, and glancing back, I saw it was a red convertible Porsche. It halted to let me cross, and I realized Harvey was in the driver's seat. He pulled over to the side of the street and looked up at me. "Hey, Morgan, when did you get back?" "Hi, Harvey. I returned yesterday and am trying to cope with my jet lag." I wanted to tell him how great he looked and how thrilled I was to see him again, which surprised me.

"Hey, I'm having some friends over for a BBQ tomorrow evening and was wondering if you'd like to join us. It's very casual. Come around six."

"Sounds great, Harvey, but where do you live?"

"Right there," he said as he pointed down the street. "Two houses down to the right. 3080 Pt. Grey Road. See you tomorrow night."

Off he went, turning into his driveway, garage up, car nestled in, garage door closed, and he's gone. Starting to jog again, I take note of his stunning home on the ocean and remember the monthly cheques he was getting, so I'm calculating that it didn't take long for him to buy this Nantucket-looking beach house. I wonder what Harvey Ross likes to socialize with because he's an intense ball of dynamic energy and even walks assertively. I couldn't imagine him relaxed and cajoling with friends, but maybe a glass of wine lightens him up. I had heard he loves to party, but I just had never experienced that with him, and it would seem strange not having a trading desk between us. I wonder if his tall, elegant model girlfriend will be there. Hopefully, she's walking the catwalk somewhere in Europe and not at the BBQ tomorrow night, making me feel shorter and chubbier than usual.

My breathing is not great after taking so much time away from running, and my thoughts race to what I will wear tomorrow night, hoping my white pants will fit ok, even though white pants are not flattering when tight. Harvey looked so good in that sports car driving into that magnificent beach home, and that whole look was super sexy. He has it all going for him, with the looks, the brains, the athletic body, the blonde hair, the blue eyes, the sports car, the house, the charm, the money, the career, except forget it, he would never be interested in me and my five foot five, now slightly chubby body, and boyish personality. Don't even go there. You are not in his league.

The white pants were too tight, but thankfully, I found a navy-blue polka dot mini skirt and a cute red silk top in my closet that worked. I had been single for almost two years, and it was time to start thinking about returning to the dating scene to tell my mother I was finally seeing someone. Maybe I'll meet one of Harvey's cool, wealthy friends who enjoy golf and skiing.

The music was loud, and voices could be heard on the street as I walked into Harvey's open front door. I had brought a bottle of wine and walked in, looking for a familiar face. One guy I recognized had been in to visit Harvey a few times at the office, and he came up to me and said, "Hi, Morgan, I'm Tim, and we met at Harvey's office. Let me get you a drink, and I'll tell Harvey you are here."

Harvey approached me with a margarita and said, "Come in and meet some of my good friends, Morgan." They were a friendly and outgoing group, joking about a golf game and someone who had cheated. A few women rolled their eyes while sharing golf stories. I enjoyed it, and it was clear that they had known each other for many years. Tim remarked, "We all went through high school and university together, so no one has any secrets here."

As I sipped the delicious margarita, I glanced around to see if the tall model was in sight. I leaned over to Tim's girlfriend, whom I had just met, and whispered, "Is Portia here?"

"Harvey broke up with Portia a few weeks ago, thank goodness. None of us could tolerate her. She didn't fit in with our group and was far too young. Harvey is Vancouver's most eligible bachelor now, but I'm sure he won't hold that title for long."

With that information, I glanced at Harvey, wearing aviator sunglasses, pale pink gingham shorts, a white shirt, and boat shoes, and thought he was the most attractive single guy in the city. Someone would be lucky to end up with him.

After admiring Harvey's art collection and casual, chic decorating style, I was on the covered deck overlooking the North Shore mountains, listening to the waves crashing rhythmically against the shore. I was drawn to a fascinating couple who had started their own sporting goods business and were incredibly passionate about sports and their importance for children growing up. Harvey joined us, generously offering more of the fish tacos he had prepared, and he was a gracious host, complementing his many other qualities. I knew he had been married once while living in Tokyo for four years before returning to establish his own company, and I also learned about a young daughter with whom I would overhear him chatting on the phone at work. It was refreshing and appealing to see him joking around with friends, revealing a lighter side, I must say.

As people began to leave, I felt an arm around my waist. "You don't have to leave with everyone. Why don't you stick around for a nightcap?" I looked up into those sea-blue eyes that captivated me and melted my resolve to go. There was no reason for me to depart, and by the end of the evening, I was smitten with Harvey Ross and his irresistible charm.

We sat on a comfy couch on his deck surrounded by pillows, under a cashmere blanket with the soft light of candles, watching the full moon light up the mountains and creating a line of light across the ocean towards us. He left and returned with two glasses of port and a cigar, asking me if I minded. At that moment, I thought the smell of a cigar would only enhance this scene and my growing infatuation. Bette Davis Eyes by Kim Carnes played softly in the background, offering a space of safe reclusion, swallowing me up in a tranquil romantic ambience.

We chatted about my new business opportunity with Sam Caldwell and the people he thought I should contact to become clients. "I have a substantial list of contacts who would love to have their money managed by such a respected team at Caldwell. Once you get the office established, the art purchased, and the brokers hired, I will give you the list of high-profile people to connect with. Sam knows that I will be helping you as it was my idea."

We discussed our upbringing, our marriages that ended, his daughter Jenny, and how difficult it was to live and work in Tokyo. The Japanese liked having business dinners without their wives, making it difficult to maintain relationships as he was never home.

Harvey opened up and was vulnerable like I had never seen before. When I asked about the model Portia, he said they had nothing in common. He couldn't talk to her about his business, and she didn't golf or ski. He looked straight at me, inhaling his cigar deeply. Both of us were now a little drunk from the margaritas and port, and on the exhale, he quietly said, "I have been waiting for you to be ready to start a new relationship."

"So, do you think I am ready now?"

"Let's hope so. I don't know how much longer I can wait."

I smiled, aware that my cheeks were flushed. He leaned over and kissed me like I hadn't been kissed before, and the taste of cigar mixed with port was erotic and sensual. The barn door opened, and the horses left the stable. We were free to express all the pent-up emotions and mutual attraction we felt for each other for so long, and neither knew what the other was feeling. We never revealed our growing desirability, and I had learnt from that one office romance that had almost destroyed me, so that was never happening again. Plus, I believed he liked tall, sophisticated models on his arm and someone subservient to him.

It didn't take long before the mini skirt and red silk top were on the floor, and his gingham shorts were on top of my skirt. A flurry of heated activity led to his bedroom and living room, and then he collapsed back on his king bed. He leaned over, whispering, "There's a new toothbrush on the counter I left out for you and a white T-shirt to sleep in if you want."

As we curled up in each other's arms, he whispered, "Nice getting to know you, Morgan. Sleep well. Night, night."

"Night, Harvey."

Chapter Sixteen

Hello Darkness

After spending the weekend with Harvey, I finally returned to my apartment to reflect on what had transpired and what this all meant going forward. He was even more interesting a character than what I knew while working together. Harvey grew up in a home where he witnessed his father going bankrupt from the recession and having to close the sawmills he owned, making his mother work night shifts at the hospital as a nurse. His father took the stress and humiliation out on his eldest son, Harvey, which became unbearable for him, so Harvey moved out and in with wealthy friends who looked after him while he finished high school. That friend Tim Katz was at his party, and they went to university together, with the family inspiring Harvey to create his wealth and vigilantly protect it so he never goes bankrupt. I now understood where his intense motivation to succeed and create wealth came from, so he would never have his wife need to work and never be humiliated in the community by losing everything he had. That childhood trauma impacted him most profoundly.

During the summers, Harvey decided to caddy at the local private golf course to meet some members and get to play at the end of the day. One of the members he caddied for was a successful stockbroker who drove a Bentley, so he asked numerous questions walking down the fairways with this man he respected and wanted to emulate. That summer of caddying set him on a path of focus and determination to be a distinguished and affluent stockbroker, with nothing getting in the way of this ambition. He determined early on that dealing with private clients was not his thing and wanted to be more emotionally removed, so dealing with people representing corporate, banking or family offices allowed the relationship to be strictly business. There were no tears or blame if money was lost, as there was an intellectual understanding of the market's natural volatility.

Starting a new job and relationship simultaneously would take some energy, but both inspired me, and I knew Harvey and Sam would assist in getting this company off the ground.

My weeks were spent ordering office equipment and meeting with various brokers to interview and determine their integrity and capacity to bring in clients or their existing book of business. Rumours were getting around town about this discretionary money management company with tremendous credibility and a respectful track record in the community. It was fun overseeing these decisions, building a team that would work well together, and hiring assistants who did not want the pressure to be a mistress to their boss, but it was a respected career choice. They liked that they would not be discriminated against and that I was heading up the team and would continue to create a safe and protected environment for them.

In the meantime, I spent most nights with Harvey, preparing his favourite chicken dinner and updating him on the progress of Caldwell Partners. We found time to golf on the weekends and thoroughly enjoyed playing together. A true character is fully revealed on the golf course, and Harvey was honest and respectful of golf etiquette. We loved playing the game side by side. We often shot similar scores, around 81-84, and encouraged each other on the course. It was a fun and flirtatious time outdoors doing what we loved. I cherished those four hours on the course, as we both shared a passion for the game and enjoyed even the ritual of practising hitting balls on the range and doing putting drills. Harvey was a natural athlete, nine years older than me, competitive, and handsome, so watching him play was a pleasure.

Harvey wanted to join me in picking out the art for the office as he loved going through galleries and getting familiar with new artists. His knowledge and eye for art were superior to mine, so I welcomed his input and advice. My mandate from Sam was to purchase only Canadian artists, and I found predominantly women artists I loved. I needed to get final approval from Sam, but he agreed to all the pieces I chose. The budget for the art was unlimited, so it was a fun exercise and an enjoyable project to share with Harvey.

One day, Harvey called me from one of the art galleries we often visit, saying, "Hey, Morgan, can you come to Buschlen Mowat to check out this new artist the gallery just started representing? You must see his new pieces; they're just hanging now."

"Yes, love to; I will be twenty minutes."

Harvey and the owner of Buschlen stood in front of a large piece of art resembling the Stanley Park seawall. As I approached, I overheard Harvey say, "I'm going to buy this one. I run around the park once a week, and the depth of colour used here is fantastic."

"Oh, hey, Morgan. Do you remember meeting Don Buschlen last week? He just introduced this new artist, Ross Penhall, a firefighter from West Vancouver."

"Hello, Don," I said as I shook his hand, unable to take my eyes off the bold colours in the artwork. The trees resembled those I walk among, presenting a more playful vision of Emily Carr's renowned forests populated by ancient red cedars. Ross showcases a distinctive style defined by rounded trees and vibrant greens, with the grit of the earth beckoning one along a winding path into the enchanting interplay of light and shadow in the forest. He captures the essence of losing oneself in the power of nature, creating a space to listen—to listen to its life force truly. I am amazed by his dynamic blend of green tones and the light and shade he skillfully manipulates, drawing us into the painting to the extent that we can almost smell the cedars and feel the salty air.

Harvey and I were captivated by this young landscape artist whose talent had yet to be recognized. After an hour at the gallery, Harvey bought two paintings, and I acquired two for the office. We were excited about our purchases and knew they would soon increase in value once this painter received the recognition he deserved.

Two days later, the artwork was delivered to the office, and two other brokers assisted me in hanging it: one in the reception area and the other in my office. The piece in my office depicted giant ancient-growth cedars and Douglas firs, sheltering a sun-drenched pathway below, meandering through the woods and enticing you to step into its enchanting forest, breathing it in.

After two months of the summer spent almost every night with Harvey, he leaned over while I poured a glass of wine for us and said, "Let's go on a little trip tomorrow for the weekend. I have something to show you."

"I love surprises. Should I bring my clubs?"

"No, we're taking the weekend off from hitting balls, but bring your hiking gear."

Driving north to Whistler always offered the most scenic, breathtaking views I had ever encountered. It was even more spectacular with the top down, gazing up at the mountain peaks piercing the blue sky. One couldn't help but feel free and alive, invigorated by the fresh mountain air and swept up in the overwhelming sensation of falling in love. Harvey was thrilled to be driving his Porsche on Highway 99: "See how it hugs the corners and rides like a plane around each one?"

We drove into Whistler, and I still didn't know the surprise. I soon found out when we pulled into the driveway of a house on a golf course with a SOLD sign on the front lawn. Once the car was turned off and it was quiet enough to talk, I looked at him and asked, "Whose place is this?"

"Sam bought the one next door, and I bought this one this week. We will be neighbours, and I wanted you to check it out. I have a few renovations to complete before the ski season, but I hoped you could help me with some ideas."

When we walked through the place, it was a gorgeous townhouse looking out over the ninth hole of the golf course. It had three bedrooms, a massive fireplace, an open kitchen, and a living area. As he showed me around, he pointed out what he wanted to do or upgrade. My only input was suggesting a large centre island for cooking and six chairs for entertaining.

"What do you think, Morgan? I thought you might like living on the golf course like you did growing up. Plus, we need to get some skiing in this winter."

"It's phenomenal, Harvey. I'm so happy you bought this, and to have Sam next door will be amazing. I can't wait to tell my mother."

We drove to the city and picked up some sushi to enjoy on his lovely deck. It was a wonderful day, and we nestled into that couch just in time for the setting sun, casting pink and orange hues as we sipped on a glass of Pinot Noir. Harvey had lit his favourite cigar, inhaling deeply when I impulsively asked, "Are you considering having more kids? If not, I understand, but I want children, and we can't keep seeing each other if you don't want another child."

I think I shocked him just as I shocked myself. A subconscious thought made a unilateral decision to be voiced. There was no filter.

He took a few puffs on his cigar, uncertain of his response. Harvey was 42, and life appeared nice, simple, and under control, so I held my breath as one does when hoping for the correct answer. "Stick around; I'm in."

When I jumped onto his lap, I think I knocked the cigar to the ground, but I couldn't stop showering him with kisses on his face, neck, and lips to thank him for wanting to have a child with me. At that moment, I felt like the luckiest person alive. We celebrated our commitment to this idea even though we hadn't discussed a plan. Men!

A week later, my apartment rent was due, and I felt I was wasting money storing my furniture since we never spent time at my place; his place was far more beautiful.

Since we had agreed to have a child together, I should move into his place. I called the landlord and gave my notice, thinking that Harvey would be okay with it all. That night, I said, "Harvey, I think I should move in with you since I'm always here anyway, and it would be much easier. I notified my landlord today, giving two weeks' notice."

An uncomfortable silence hung in the air before he asked, "You're not moving your furniture or anything else, are you? Just clothes since this place is fully furnished."

I hadn't collected anything of value besides my country pine furniture, which I suggested could go into his new place at Whistler; he thought it was a good idea. It surprised him, especially since we had only been together for three months, but things were progressing quickly.

I spent the next two weeks figuring out where everything was headed. I was excited about living with Harvey; the company was about to get started in a month, and I had stopped taking the pill. At 33, I realized life wouldn't wait for me to get pregnant at the perfect moment. My mother was finally informed that I was dating the guy I worked with, who founded

Ross Capital. She was delighted and relieved, knowing I would be well taken care of financially and would try to get pregnant this coming year. She wanted to come out in the fall to meet Harvey and stay with us, but we were both working hard during the day and had our nice little routine established in the evenings. After we ran along the beach or I attended my aerobics class, we would cook dinner together. Then, after my bubble bath, we'd curl up in bed, catching each other up on our days while watching a hockey game, a taped PGA Golf tournament, or NFL football and usually making out when I arrived warm and naked from the bath.

In early September, Caldwell Partners opened its doors with nine partners and eight assistants who all got along exceptionally well. There was no overbearing ego among us, and everyone arrived with enthusiasm and high expectations of professionalism that were invigorating. Sam Caldwell was our fearless leader in establishing the culture and creating presentation materials to ensure consistency in our sales pitch. We offered clients the same track record that Sam and his team established over the previous fifteen years.

There wasn't a day that I didn't look forward to going to work and connecting with the eight male partners, aged 35 to 55, along with the female assistants, ensuring that everyone thrived and achieved their individual goals. I loved the compatibility and collaboration that developed as the days and months passed. With each new client introduced, much like in a golf game, I felt thrilled when my opponent sank that birdie putt; yet beneath my happiness for them lingered a desire to do the same and receive equal recognition. The competition for the highest revenue flowing into the firm was fierce but friendly. Teasing and joking with each other while dropping in and out of one another's offices added much-needed levity to an otherwise monotonous day spent on the phone or at the computer. Being on my home golf course with my young male buddies felt like our office environment: Friendly yet competitive, supportive yet demanding. We constantly strove to be our best and win the game. Finding my tribe, my nexus, ultimately nurtured and sustained me, allowing me to flourish.

Moving in with Harvey was a breeze. He needed to clear some space in his massive closet for my clothes, and my dishes, pots, and pans fit neatly into the kitchen. The move took place while he was at work, allowing me to organize everything without him feeling too anxious. His home was so beautiful and tastefully decorated that there was no need to rearrange anything, and his artwork added depth and colour to each room.

During the Thanksgiving weekend, we were invited by a long-time client of Harvey, who had become a close friend, to a fishing lodge on Quadra Island in the Gulf Islands. Wally Chambers was exceptional; after starting his own business, he raised millions for cancer research and became one of Canada's leading philanthropists. Having grown up in poverty, Harvey held Wally in high esteem, seeing him as a role model and a mentor. We took the ferry to the island, where fishing guides were arranged to take us out the next day after Wally prepared a scrumptious dinner of Congolese mussels, homemade French fries, smoked salmon, and Caesar salad. Thankfully, I brought an apple crisp and pumpkin pie to complement the generous meal. Wally's wife, Kate, was actively involved with their two daughters and volunteered at the Children's Hospital. We enjoyed a delightful evening around their harvest table in the charming log fishing lodge.

We had our cozy little cabin by the ocean, featuring a fireplace and a deck, with a substantial four-poster bed adorned with quilts and blankets draped over the end. It was a snug retreat. During dinner, I noticed a slight pain in my left side but thought it might just be cramping since my period was due any day now. I had only come off the pill a month ago and figured it would take a few months to clear from my system. With the wine and all the delicious food, we nestled in and fell asleep in our charming cabin in the woods. However, I could still feel those cramps morphing into an unfamiliar pain on my lower left side. When I turned to that side, it became a sharp, stabbing pain that I could pinpoint. I tried to ignore it, knowing there wasn't much I could do.

Harvey's alarm rang at five o'clock, which was late compared to his usual 4:30 a.m. wake-up call. However, as I looked around groggily, I noticed he was already dressed and ready to go fishing.

"Good morning. You were tossing and turning quite a bit last night; I even heard some groaning. Are you okay?

"Good morning. I have this pain in my left side, and I don't think I should go fishing. Bouncing around on the waves in a boat seems far too painful. Why don't you and Wally catch some salmon? I'm fine, curling up, reading, and strolling around the property until you return. Is that all right? I think it's just cramps from my period. It's my first time off the pill, so maybe that's what's going on."

Harvey kissed me goodbye and said, "I hope you feel better."

I grabbed the white flannel housecoat from the back of the door and looked out the window as he and Wally walked down the dock, carrying their fishing poles over their shoulders like two little boys heading off to catch some fish.

Putting on my grey sweats, red plaid flannel shirt and down vest, I wandered up to the lodge to get some coffee, but then, as I was opening the door to the lodge, I doubled over in pain and felt the blood rush from my face. Falling to the ground, my last vision was Kate running towards me.

I fell in and out of consciousness as various faces asked me questions, and there was a panic of activity about what should happen. I can't speak; I drifted away into darkness. Then I heard a loud voice: "The helicopter is coming from Campbell River Hospital. The doctor is on the phone." Then nothing.

I have a slight memory of being lifted onto a stretcher and the loud sounds of propellers above, wind and dirt in my face, and a flurry of anxious people racing, but I was in darkness and only peeked out now and then, aware of a crisis. At one point, I heard Kate's voice through the noise of the propellers. "Frankie, go out and get Harvey and Wally right now. They went to Heriot Bay and get them to the hospital as soon as possible. She may not make it."

When I emerged from the darkness again, a man in a white lab coat appeared. His face was blurry beneath a bright white light, and he leaned in closer while placing a mask over my nose. Hello, Darkness!

A nurse stood over me when I woke up in the recovery room. I tried to focus despite the excruciating pain, unsure of what had happened. My throat was sore from the tubes that had been down it, but I attempted to speak, "Hello, what happened to me?" Then I started shaking uncontrollably, my teeth chattering and my hands trembling. "I am soooo cold!" She left and returned with a warm flannelette blanket, which helped to stop my teeth from chattering together. "Please tell me what happened. I have no idea."

"I'll get the doctor, and he will explain everything. You are okay now, but it was a close call. Your husband is coming by chopper and should be here shortly."

My mind was still groggy from the anesthetic, and I had no idea what had happened, but I remember the pain and collapsing, then nothing.

"Hello, Morgan Cooper. My name is Dr. Baker, and I performed the surgery on you. You had an ectopic pregnancy in your left fallopian tube, which we had to remove. It burst, which caused you to go into shock with extensive internal bleeding, and it was touch and go with your vitals when you arrived here. You were lucky the team at the lodge called a helicopter for you. You will need to remain in the hospital for at least five days as you have lost a lot of blood, and your hemoglobin is seven, and it needs to be at least fifteen.

"Will I be able to get pregnant again?"

"You still have one fallopian tube, but there may be scarring in that tube as well, so I have referred you to an infertility specialist in Vancouver when you can travel home."

"I have to stay in the hospital for a week?"

"Yes, at least five days."

Relieved to be alive, I placed one hand on my bandaged stomach, not fully conscious, and drifted off to sleep. Under the warmth of the flannel blanket, I faintly heard, "Hello, darkness, my old friend. I've come to talk with you again."

Chapter Seventeen

The Pressure of Life

When I slowly entered back into my life, I looked around, forgetting where I was and what had happened to me. A nurse beside my bed, checking sacks of fluids being directed into my arm by tubes, gently said, "How are you doing?"

"I am in a lot of pain. Can I have more pain medication?"

She glanced at the clipboard and replied, "Yes, you're due for some morphine. You have a catheter, which we will need to remove at some point. To access the fallopian tube, they cut through your abdominal wall, so it will be difficult to sit up for a few days. I will set up a pulley system to assist you. We'll aim to get you walking down the hall tomorrow with your waltzing Matilda pole."

Yikes. None of that sounded good.

Harvey walked into the room with the fishing clothes he had on the last time I saw him and came up to the side of the bed, "Thank God you're okay and didn't come fishing with us. The doctor said you probably wouldn't have survived. Your tube burst, and you went into shock from the internal bleeding. I can't believe it. I guess we got pregnant but in the wrong place." He leaned over, kissed me on the cheek, and said, "I've let your mother know and work since we are both staying here until they say it's ok to go home. How are you feeling right now?"

"It feels like a bus ran over me, and I can't sit up because they cut through my abdominal wall, but I'm grateful to be alive. I don't remember much. Thank God Kate was at the lodge where I collapsed."

"No kidding! Thank God she called 911 and insisted on a chopper coming to get you. She was scared and hoped to visit you once you were ready for visitors. From what I gather, you've lost quite a bit of blood, Morgan, so you must take it easy."

Harvey sat on my bed, holding my hand, but I was drifting off to sleep again. When I woke up, he was still there chatting with the doctor who went through the details of the surgery and said that they needed to fly in AB- blood from Victoria for me since only 3% of Canadians have that blood type. Dr. Baker told Harvey and me that there was a chance of another ectopic due to potential scarring in the other fallopian tube. He explained that when the egg is released from the ovary, it goes into the fallopian tube en route to the uterus; then, if the sperm meets the egg in the tube and becomes an embryo, it stays in the fallopian tube for seven days to absorb as much protein as possible before descending to the uterus and embedding in the uterine wall. If the embryo gets stuck in the fallopian tube and continues to grow, the tube will burst, causing shock and internal bleeding. He said more women should be aware of the risks of an ectopic pregnancy and get to a hospital as quickly as possible with the symptoms.

"You are lucky, Morgan."

"Thank you, Dr. Baker, but I don't feel so lucky. I just lost our potential baby, and that makes me very sad."

"We had no choice but to operate; we had to save your life." I will check in on you tomorrow, but the nurses will be monitoring you all night long and managing your pain. Try to rest now; I'll see you tomorrow."

Harvey biked over to visit me every day, taking the ferry and bringing treats made by the staff at the lodge, even though I had little appetite. He got me a TV so he could watch the baseball games, as I didn't have the energy to socialize. I hated the sponge baths the nurses gave me, so one day, I used the pulley to lift myself, found a shower down the hall, and went in, leaving my arm still attached to the pole with the fluids. With one arm, I washed my hair and rinsed off the yellow dye from my tummy. The problem was that hospitals didn't have blow-dryers, so I got caught, but it felt so good to finally shower after three days of lying in bed and taking fifteen-minute walks every few hours.

Seven days later, I could finally leave the hospital. Harvey picked me up, and the nurse said I had to sit in the wheelchair to be taken to the front door. I had all my vitals checked that morning, and it turned out I had lost eight pounds, weighing in at 123, with hemoglobin only at 10, and I felt as if I had no muscle strength whatsoever. How am I going to get back to work? Sam had called to say I needed to take another week at home before returning; the partners were looking after all my clients, and Carmen oversaw any meetings I had scheduled.

When Harvey and I arrived home, I curled up on the couch under that cashmere blanket. We ordered pizza, and while it was on its way, we watched Dirty Dancing, which was just right.

This marked the beginning of the infertility challenge and its impact on a woman's psyche and confidence. The pressure to conceive became overwhelming, with every call from my mother about my latest period, what I was doing to address it, and the most recent article she had read about getting pregnant. We took my temperature daily for a month, and then I would call Harvey at work to get home right after the market closed. HAVING TO HAVE SEX is not romantic for either of us. Let's figure out the quickest and most efficient way possible; then, I would lie there with my butt propped up on pillows to help send the swimmers toward the one fallopian tube I had left. Harvey and I had only been together for five months when I had the ectopic pregnancy; we had not discussed marriage or a future game plan.

After one year of dating, Harvey called me at work and said, "Can you meet me today after the market closes at Toni Cavelti's?" This caught me off guard since Toni Cavelti's is a prestigious jewellery store in town, where everyone buys diamonds.

"Sure, I would love to."

Walking to Toni's, I wondered if Harvey was buying me a watch or a bracelet. Upon arrival, I saw Harvey and Toni sitting at the counter, surrounded by numerous rings on the glass top. The store felt like it was all ours. Toni welcomed me in, and as Harvey hugged me, he said, "Time to pick out your perfect ring so I can propose one day."

As I tried on the rings, I was astonished. We had never discussed a wedding or marriage, but I couldn't have been more excited. As I gazed at these magnificent, sparkling diamonds, I said, "It must fit under my golf glove, so I can't have a large rock on my left hand. I think the eternity rings are the best, and I love the diamonds all around for their significance."

Toni put away the trays of massive diamonds and brought out only the eternity rings. I asked, "What do you think, Harvey?"

"You will wear the ring, so choose whichever you prefer. I want the highest quality diamonds that Toni has available." I tried on several, but I kept gravitating back to the $80,000 Asscher Cut platinum eternity ring adorned with ten diamonds. It was breathtaking and felt wonderful on my finger.

Harvey looked at me and the ring. "Is that the one?"

"Absolutely, I love it, Harvey. Thank you!"

"I'll polish and size it for you, and then you can pick it up tomorrow, Harvey," Toni said as he began polishing it.

He shook both of our hands and said, "Congratulations. You make a very handsome couple."

As I walked back to the office, I wondered when Harvey would propose and what kind of wedding we would have. Harvey didn't care for grand events; we had both been married before. I was content with something intimate and private.

We both got busy with work, weekend skiing, and dinners out with friends, but I wanted to see the ring, so I searched Harvey's closet to find where he hid it. The little, unique places I thought it might be turned up empty. He must have stored it in a locked drawer at his office or his safety deposit box, so maybe he's waiting for a special occasion like Christmas, my birthday, Valentine's Day, or perhaps when we go to Maui in January.

The next three years were spent trying to get pregnant, seeing an infertility doctor regularly, and building the company. Thank goodness I had my work to occupy me as the focus on getting pregnant dominated my thoughts, especially with the numerous friends getting pregnant now with their second and third kids. I escaped to work, and sadly, so did Harvey. Every month when I got my period was a sad day, a day reminding me that my body was not fulfilling what it was meant to do, to reproduce and combine our genetics. The biological imperative to perpetuate our genes and to see ourselves in our children has propelled human evolution. To pass on characteristics through inheritance seems as much a Darwinian mandate as it is an emotional desire. It is the nature of living things to reproduce.

"If there are living beings on Earth today, it is because other beings have reproduced with fervent eagerness for two billion years," wrote Nobel laureate François Jacob in "The Logic of Life." "Let us envision an uninhabited world."

Children represent our projection into the future. They serve as our bridge to adulthood. Parenthood is the ultimate rite of passage, an experience that, for many, fulfills life's journey. In a broader sense, it's our contribution to society. Children are the building blocks of the nation. The desire to have children is so fundamental, essential, and natural that, for most people, the journey to parenthood begins with a single kiss.

In the prime of our lives, at the peak of our personal, physical, intellectual, and financial capabilities, we need assistance. Our trust in our bodies, love for one another, and faith in a higher power appear shaken and fractured.

Infertility is not a classic disease, but it affects women the same way a disease does, emotionally and physically. It brings our usual healthy existence into a precipice of grief and loss. Our next stage on this infertility track was to go through in vitro fertilization, which involved retrieving my eggs, fertilizing them outside my body in a petri dish with Harvey's sperm, and transferring the growing embryo back into my uterus.

Three years later, I still don't have that beautiful ring, and I am about to go through my first round of IVF. Harvey has been going out on Thursday nights with the boys and not getting home until two in the morning. The pattern began shortly after I moved in, but I didn't think it was a problem until he rolled into the driveway at four in the morning. Then, I knew he had to be unfaithful. All the bars and restaurants close at two in the morning, and he wasn't in a car accident, so you go from worrying that he's in a hospital or dead to him betraying you just in the time it takes to hear him stumble up the stairs and into the bedroom. You go from praying he's not hurt to wanting to hurt him. Thursday night was the brokers' night out to drink and release some steam from the stress of their week. Harvey could barely walk when he stumbled home, and I was always awake, waiting for the sound of his Porsche coming into the driveway, the keys dropping into the bowl, him entering the bedroom reeking of booze, and passing out until his alarm went off two hours later. He would always get up, still drunk, shower, and make it to the office by 5:30 am. I don't know how he did it. Was it because of me not getting pregnant that our sex life was impacted by the demands of making a baby and the letdowns of it not working? Sex for fun was something we no longer wanted. There was too much emotional weight attached to the outcome of sex now. It disappointed us when we needed it most to work, create a life, and have a baby. The emotional demands were complicated for both of us. Still, the increase in drinking was a significant concern for me, as I had stopped drinking any alcohol to do everything I could to keep my body healthy. Was one bottle of wine every night too much? After two glasses, he was slurring his words and becoming verbally abusive, putting me down in every way he could. I grappled with the definition of an alcoholic, intent on determining whether Harvey had an alcohol use disorder and what steps I should take regarding it.

I decided to see a therapist about my concerns and to define an alcoholic for me, as I was in denial for these past four years. She said, "If a person's drinking is impacting the relationships around him, then he has a drinking problem. If he must control when he drinks, then the drinking has control over him." She also said, "Alcoholism is contagious. It impacts the people around the alcoholic with being equally obsessed about the alcohol, and how much they are having."

My skin crawled as the cork popped out of the bottle, signalling that the wine was about to be poured and that Dr. Jekyll was ready to kill Mr. Hyde.

I asked Harvey if he thought he needed help and if he would consider AA or seeing a therapist. I would help him in any way I could, but he consistently responded the same way: "I don't have a problem."

There was nothing I could do, and I needed to continue with our IVF cycle, so I chose to cope with it. Living with an alcoholic creates a delicate dance around the drinker's mood that evening and which topics to avoid, maintaining calm to prevent stirring Dr. Jekyll. We enjoyed activities during the day, like golfing and skiing, where drinking was prohibited. At five o'clock, when the beer is poured, followed by a bottle of wine, the door of my anxiety creaks open, and I walk on tenterhooks until he has gone to bed. That is when I exhale deeply and release the tension in my body, stemming from the fear of his verbal attacks, the threat of a physical altercation, and the growing awareness of my resentment toward him. I was learning to compartmentalize my life and become skilled at it, pretending to the world that the Power Couple we were recognized as living the most glorious life. Little did they know the truth, the private hell I endured, but I found ways to survive, and I needed to devise an exit strategy.

My focus and obsession were on my work and having a baby, and I needed to believe Harvey would be there for me, his Thursday nights would stop, and his drinking would become curtailed.

After a week on Clomid, which prompted my body to release hormones that increased the likelihood of my ovaries releasing a mature, ready-to-be-fertilized egg, I found myself drenched in night sweats and suffering from headaches as I began the IVF cycle. Each morning, I needed to arrive at the clinic by eight for an injection in my butt, then return for another injection at two in the afternoon. This routine continued for seven days, and now both hips throbbed with every step. Then, Harvey was called to do his part in the morning, and I was scheduled to arrive at noon for the egg retrieval, where they puncture the vaginal wall to suction out as many mature eggs as possible. The eggs and sperm are combined in a petri dish in hopes that they will find each other agreeable enough to form a healthy embryo or two. This is when one begins to pray to a higher power.

That night, I had another dream of my baby in my arms. Dream babies appear when I call them. They've been waiting, waiting for the right moment, the cue, for you to say, "It's time, Baby. We're ready. It's time." Then they slide into the frame, into the present, wrapped in baby blankets and pink lotion, small and whole, and you hold them until your empty arms no longer ache.

Then, in the quiet of my bedroom, I awaken.

After a restless night, I wear my housecoat and head downstairs to make a cappuccino. My hips ache from the injections, my insides hurt from the poking to retrieve the eggs, my body feels out of sorts from all the medications, and my emotional state is on the brink of collapse—knowing we must wait three days to determine the viability of the embryos. The waiting game is torture, and we've been playing it every month for three years, hoping and praying that my period never arrives. When it does, the mourning and grief begin anew for that dream baby. As I sit in the kitchen watching the Today Show with Katie Couric and Matt Lauer, nursing my coffee, I'm captivated by the baby photos on the fridge door, which I've adorned from top to bottom with magazine cutouts. One in particular catches my eye; she gazes back at me with her angelic blue eyes, chubby cheeks, and curly blonde hair. I say, "I'm waiting for you, and we will have a magical life, you and me."

The house is quiet, and my mind drifts to envision raising this baby alone and surviving without Harvey. Is that too selfish, or must I safeguard my baby and myself?

Chapter Eighteen

Miracle Baby

Three long days finally ended with a phone call from my gorgeous Greek-South African doctor, who, thankfully, I believe, helps with the hormones. He said, “Morgan, we have good news. You have four healthy embryos we can implant tomorrow morning. Sleep well tonight, and I’ll see you tomorrow at eight. You will be here for four hours after they are implanted in your uterus, where you must remain still so Harvey can pick you up around two in the afternoon.”

I was so excited and immediately called Harvey to share the good news. He was relieved and happy that we could proceed to the next step in our infertility journey. I realized how easy this whole process has been for him. No poking and prodding, no hormone injections in his backside, no periods, no pain—just masturbating in a room with Playboy magazines. It’s not his fault, I suppose, as it’s my scarred fallopian tubes that caused infertility, so I must be grateful for his patience and support as we go through this together as a team. This isn’t a time to question the creation of a man and a woman or why the woman carries the child, but God must give us the strength and nurturing qualities to create life. I deeply long for a life from the depths of my being, the biological imperative to reproduce.

Harvey dropped me off in front of the clinic, wished me good luck, got out of the car to hug me, and said, “You’ve got this, Morgan. Our baby is waiting for you.”

I hugged him back and whispered, “Who knows, maybe we’ll have more than one.”

He instantly held his head back and said, “That’s possible?”

“I really hope we have twins, Harvey. How magical would that be?”

We hugged again, and he waved as I walked into the clinic, knowing this was now up to me and my body to receive these little embryos that had full life potential.

The nurses got me ready in a surgical room, and up in the stirrups I went. I looked down to see those beautiful Italian Ferragamo shoes walk into the room, knowing Dr. Christo had arrived. We chatted briefly, and then he put the four embryos in my uterus, which caused some cramping and discomfort. Still, I closed my eyes and started visualizing them attaching to my uterine wall.

He held my hand and calmly squeezed it, saying, "Relax now; the four embryos are in your uterus, and hopefully, the healthiest will attach and begin to grow. You need to lie still in the recovery room for four hours, without getting up to go to the bathroom or lifting your head to eat. You can drink water while lying down with a straw. A bedpan will be provided if you need to use one. I have faith in a successful pregnancy, Morgan. I will call Harvey to let him know when he can pick you up. After that, you must return in ten days for blood work to check if your HCG levels have increased. Take it easy until then. No jogging, exercise classes, or jumping; take it easy. You can go to work if you are mostly sitting and not on your feet all day."

"Thank you so much, Dr. Christo. I look forward to seeing you in ten days to hear the good news."

"I believe we will," were his last words as he turned with his lab coat and Italian shoes, leaving the room. Two orderlies wheeled me down the hall to a recovery room and told me I must lie flat without even a pillow under my head for four hours, praying I didn't need to pee. They brought me a food tray, but eating with my head down was impossible. I sipped water through a straw, then closed my eyes, dreaming of a beautiful, healthy baby.

Ten days felt like ten years as I panicked each time I sat on the toilet, praying not to see any blood, hoping not to feel cramps, and walking as slowly as I could wherever I went. I went to bed early, avoided coffee and wine, and abstained from sex. I arrived at the clinic early and calm, convinced it must be working and tried to remain positive. The nurse greeted me and asked how I felt as I followed her into the room for a blood and urine sample. She asked me to wait in Dr. Christo's office while he reviewed the results and said he would be with me shortly. When he walked in, I tried to gauge his expression, which was neutral, and that worried me. "Everything okay, Dr. Christo?"

"The numbers look promising, Morgan. Your HCG levels are somewhat elevated, which is excellent, but I must caution you not to be overly optimistic, as I'd have preferred to see them rise a bit more. Please return for a final test in four days and continue to take it easy."

As I stood up to leave, I looked back at him sitting at his desk, about to pick up the phone to make a call, and said firmly, "I know how to handle bad news, Doctor. That's all I have been doing every month for over three years. I'm preparing to handle the good news, and I don't need anyone telling me not to be too optimistic."

How can you envision the outcome while remaining cautious or "not too optimistic?" I was upset and resolute in focusing on that little angelic face I hoped to see in nine months.

After giving blood and urine four days later, they told me the doctor would call me the next day with the results. "The next day? What time? I must wait another day?"

I was sitting at my desk at work, trying to stay busy and distracted, unable to eat, and feeling a combination of worry and excitement. The only person at the office who knew I was going through this IVF cycle was my assistant, Carmen, so she would understand my new routine of leaving the office every morning and afternoon. I needed to share it with someone at work; she was a great confidant and supporter.

I was on a call with a client late in the afternoon when Carmen came to my door and said, "Dr. Christo is on hold for you."

I immediately started shaking and could barely pick up the phone to say, "Hello, Dr. Christo. It's Morgan."

"Hi, Morgan. I have good news for you. You are pregnant, and your due date is December 16th. You will be referred to Dr. Hudson, an OB-GYN specializing in high-risk pregnancies. Congratulations, Morgan."

Collapsing into my chair, I looked out my office window and gave Carmen a thumbs-up. She began to tear up, covering her face with her hands. Then, she hugged me and brought me a glass of water.

After calling Harvey, who was so relieved and excited, and my mother, screaming on the phone, I called Pippa Walker, my good friend and doctor, "Pippa, I'm pregnant and have a due date!"

Her first reaction was of caution. "How far along are you?"

"Three weeks, I think."

"You shouldn't tell people until three months, just in case."

"But, Pippa, I am pregnant today and have never been pregnant before except in my fallopian tube, so today and every day until my baby is born, I celebrate that."

"Congratulations, Morgan! You're going to be an incredible mom. I pray you have a healthy pregnancy, and I can't wait to see you this summer at the cottage. Your mother must be absolutely thrilled."

The next day, a case of fine Italian wine and a bouquet of vibrant flowers were delivered to the clinic, accompanied by a note that said, "Thank you for all your expertise and kindness in helping me become pregnant. I will treasure every moment of creating this miracle. Love, Morgan."

I was floating with joy in a way I had never thought possible. We drove to Whistler to relax by a fire and absorb the reality of our news and the plans we needed to make. Harvey had been keenly interested in a log home being built across the golf course from us and mentioned after dinner that he would like to see it the next day, even though it still needed to be finished. Harvey's passions included real estate, new homes, modern architecture, and dealing with stocks and property.

We met the builders of this stunning log home, who allowed us to walk around and take in the expansive view over the golf course to the Whistler and Blackcomb Mountains. The house featured a totem pole in the centre as a support, an exquisite piece of art; the floors were made of knotty pine, and the massive red cedar logs provided a warmth and glow that I had never experienced before, bringing nature into the home. Harvey chatted with the builder, inquiring when he thought it would be finished and whether the owner had any input on the final touches. It was one of the most beautiful houses I had ever been in, with an astonishing view of the mountains, the lush golf course, and ample privacy from other neighbours. I loved the open concept with the stunning kitchen, dining, and living area nestled among the trees on either side, offering a feeling of living in a treehouse. The centrepiece was the fireplace, crafted from local river rock, displaying various shades of rust, grey, and brown, rising to the twenty-foot ceiling. It was a work of art, with those rocks fitting together so perfectly, along with the artistry of the totem pole depicting a bear holding a salmon, the cedar logs so perfectly fitting seamlessly, and the floating staircase, all forming an extraordinary compilation of nature in its purest and most authentic art form.

As we said thank you and goodbye, Harvey asked the builder for his number and said he would like to follow up with him over the weekend. That night, we chatted about the house, and I sensed that Harvey loved it, although he stated he needed to think it over.

The following day, Harvey wanted to walk over to the log house to see what the morning light was like and chat with the builders. It was a beautiful spring day, with patches of snow still on the ground, yellow daffodils poking through the greenery, and the distinct chirps, whistles, trills, and croaks of birds filling the air. The magic of the fresh mountain air and my feeling of nausea confirming my pregnancy made for a sensational morning of pure joy.

We met with the builders, and I wandered around the property alone, leaving Harvey and John to discuss constructing a log home and the natural insulation provided by logs. Other visitors arrived to inquire about the house, prompting Harvey and me to stroll into the village. We talked about the incredible location of this house, with its stunning views, and I noted that this property would only appreciate. I sensed that Harvey would likely act on it when he contemplated this, but I couldn't let my hopes soar, as it was the most beautiful home I had ever visited.

That night, over prawn linguine, Harvey raised his wine glass to my water glass, saying, "We will need a place to get married. How about it be at our new log home?"

I sat there, stunned, my mind racing. We finally discussed marrying five years after picking out that ring at Toni Cavelti's. "You bought the log house? Today? How much did you pay for it? Married? Do you want to get married there? Just us? Any friends or family?"

"I imagined we could get married there, with Hans and Shelby standing up for us, and then host a gathering with family and friends at the house in town. Maybe a band and catered food could be outdoors around the pool for about sixty people."

"Ok, someone has been thinking this through, and it all sounds incredible."

"Let's not tell anyone until after we get married and then let them know, like our mothers."

I didn't know how to keep it a secret from my mother, but she was so happy and excited about my pregnancy that she wouldn't expect a wedding anytime soon. Harvey closed on the log home a month later. We moved all our furniture in from the other place, but it needed to be more significant to match the size of the logs and required more substantial-sized couches, chairs, and coffee tables. We needed a large harvest table for the dining room, so Harvey and I visited a shop in the city that imported the most beautiful French country antiques from the south of France: stunning character pieces made from oak and walnut. We purchased an oak armoire, a walnut dough box with beautifully carved inlay, two overstuffed cream-coloured couches, a coffee table, and stools for the counter. We got everything we needed from this one shop, and they agreed to deliver it to our Whistler place that week.

During my lunch hour the next day, I went to Holt Renfrew and bought an off-white Armani jacket, a chiffon mini skirt, and off-white Prada shoes. I felt they hid my growing tummy, and I did not want to wear a wedding dress if it was just us getting married with our two dear friends. It was Whistler chic, I thought, and we had a white limo pick us up after to take us to a French Bistro called Les Deux Gros. Our friends were so excited about standing up for us. They arrived with a massive bouquet of gorgeous white lilies and a playlist for us to listen to while we got married. What a Wonderful World by Louis Armstrong had me in tears while we stood at the window exchanging our vows, with the snowcapped mountains in the distance and the rumblings of our little miracle in this spectacular log home to start the beginning of our married life together.

"With this ring, I thee wed." The ring! There you are, finally on my finger. Stunning.

"Till death do us part."

The champagne cork was popped, the phone calls were made to our mothers, and in the happiest moment of my life, I toasted Harvey, thanking him for all his support during our infertility journey and for providing the most stunning log home for us to raise our baby girl. I was about to burst with joy, grabbing crackers for the limo ride, and I took a deep breath, bathing in the magic of the universe. As we drove off to celebrate our marriage, becoming Morgan Ross, I stared at my ring, which reflected rainbows around it like a prism in the evening light.

Chapter Nineteen

Miracles Do Happen

After nine months of relentless nausea, only eased by Stoned Wheat Thins or thick banana milkshakes, along with cravings for brunch featuring Indian cuisine or grilled cheese and tomato sandwiches at bedtime, I finally began experiencing contractions. With just ten days until my due date, and as luck would have it, Harvey happened to be in Toronto for a Christmas party. The contractions were so intense that I decided to head to the Women's Hospital, my little suitcase packed months in advance, and I called Harvey to let him know I was in labour and that he needed to return home.

I pulled into the parking lot, and when I checked in at the front reception, I announced that I was in labour and would need pain relief as soon as possible. The nurse looked at me, clearly skeptical, and asked me to go into the room and lie on the bed to be assessed by the doctor, who would inform my physician if I was indeed in labour. As I walked, now forty-five pounds heavier than I was nine months ago, I couldn't help but hear my mother's voice saying she never gained more than twenty-five pounds during her pregnancies. All I wanted was to have this healthy baby girl out without any pain and to put an end to the persistent nausea.

"Should I start the drugs now because I heard you don't want to be too late?" I asked the doctor when she came in to examine me. After a quick check, I learned that I was, in fact, not in labour but experiencing Braxton Hicks, which are contractions that generally do not last long, do not occur very frequently, and do not build up.

The doctor said, "Your contractions will become more regular as the muscles tighten and the pain intensifies. You can go home now and wait for the contractions to be about one minute apart before returning to the hospital."

I rolled off the bed, grabbed my little suitcase, and trudged away, feeling somewhat humiliated. I tried to grasp that this was nothing compared to labour and that I would know when the real contractions occurred. It's difficult to walk. Yikes!

These painful sensations drove me home, and I felt a twinge of panic about the impending birthing experience, determined to get drugs to ease the pain. Whoops. Harvey was on a flight home and likely missed the company Christmas party. I hoped he wouldn't be upset when he got home and found me there. Perhaps I'll go into labour tomorrow and he'll be relieved to be with me.

Four days later, I knew it was time, and this time, I got the drugs, but not until I suffered for hours and threw up too many times to count, nurses begging Harvey not to give me more orange juice, as they had to keep changing my gown, but I was so thirsty and so nauseous. I thought every woman, including my mother, lied to me about the pain of childbirth, and imagining a bus hitting me and then rolling back over me was the only parallel I could think of. During one of those dreaded contractions, I heard a newspaper rustling and opened my eyes to see Harvey reading it and sipping coffee while I was writhing in pain. "Harvey, put that fucking newspaper away and do something to help me!" The nurse handed him a cold facecloth for my forehead as I squeezed her hand until it was blue, swearing so the whole ward could hear me—my only strategy for coping with such agony. Why do people have more than one baby after experiencing this? I wondered.

After fifteen hours, I was now exhausted and worried about my baby being delivered safely.

I heard from Dr. Hudson, after a session of pushing, "Morgan, the umbilical cord is around her neck, so she is under stress. You need to stop pushing the moment I say STOP. Alright, let's push and give it everything you've got. STOP!!"

My thoughts turned to a friend who lost her baby a month ago due to an umbilical cord wrapped around her healthy baby boy's neck. I stopped and prayed for the sound of a cry.

Harvey was holding my hand when we heard a gurgling cry and a massive sigh of relief from my doctor and the nurses. "Congratulations, you have a healthy baby girl."

They handed this little bundle to me, all wrapped snugly, and I saw these beautiful blue eyes looking back at me from the blanket wrapped around her sweet little body. It was instant love for the most precious miracle, our miracle.

I looked up at Harvey, who had tears streaming down his cheeks, as he whispered, "She's perfect."

"I love you, Harper Ellison Ross. I finally get to meet you."

The nurses were excellent; I hated being home alone with Harper, not having them help me with everything from proper breastfeeding to changing her diaper to knowing when she needed to be fed. Every mother must have this sense of panic at the overwhelming responsibility of not only raising this little newborn child but keeping her alive and protected from the world.

My mother wanted to come out and help me, but it was two weeks before Christmas, and we decided to escape to our Whistler home, so cozy in the snow, with that big, brilliant fireplace, and cater to Harper and her needs. I loved my walks in the snow, all bundled up with her little face sticking out of the snuggly, those intense blue eyes peeking out under her soft pink hat, such a sweet, gentle soul, so trusting, so loving, so mine.

We cherished bonding with our little miracle, calm, happy, and at peace in this winter wonderland. It was a great excuse to do what we wanted and sleep when needed. We decided to attend a Christmas Eve chocolate and champagne party just down the street at our neighbour's log home, which our builder had just completed.

We took Harper in the baby bucket, and I was so pleased these days. After nine long months, I was no longer suffering from nausea. Not eating crackers, Indian food, banana milkshakes, and burgers felt like a huge relief.

The Taylors' log home was decorated for Christmas, featuring an enormous tree they had cut down, reaching right up to the twenty-foot ceiling. It was breathtaking. I placed Harper under the tree so she could gaze up at all the twinkling lights above her as she nestled among the presents, and I caught her smile for the first time. We enjoyed a glass of champagne, and Carole prepared over ten chocolate desserts, each creatively presented on her harvest table, tempting me to indulge in a bite of each one. Many neighbours and friends arrived, dusting off the snow, hanging their heavy winter coats and hats, switching from boots to shoes, and chatting about the expected snowfall. Oh, how I love winter. The sharpness of the cold nips at your cheeks, and the fresh, crisp air causes the warm moisture in our breath to condense into tiny droplets of water, forming a small, misty cloud.

The feeling of stepping away from the cold outdoors and warming up by a fireplace with hot chocolate is a luxury and a tradition that only those living in places with seasons can savour. Harper was born on December 10th, and I was born on December 20th. Our winter blizzards will always enchant us, the magic of snowflakes and their hexagonal shapes reflecting the light like tiny fairies gliding down from the sky. The joy of Christmas makes it seem like the world celebrates our births alongside Jesus and his transcendent arrival—another miracle.

We didn't stay long, but we got to show off our new baby girl, only two weeks old, and bundled up to walk home to our cabin in the woods. Snow was gently falling, flakes landing on Harper's tiny cheeks, and as we crunched through the snow under our boots, I looked up at the full moon filtered through the haze of snowflakes, thinking my life was a dream. I love being a mom, and I'm overwhelmed with love for this little human being who just had a snowflake drop on her tongue, experiencing that first sensation of nature's magic.

Harvey and I curled under the duvet, sinking into down pillows as we kissed each other goodnight. I knew I would wake in a few hours to feed Harper, but I drifted off while the soft light of the full moon touched my hand. Smiling, I quietly whispered, "Goodnight, moon."

Chapter Twenty

The Juggling Act

My male partners expected me to return early in the New Year and believed that a month's "holiday" was sufficient when having a child. I was the only female partner among twenty-one partners, and there was no established policy on maternity leave, so this situation was entirely new for them. When I informed the CEO and CFO that I would be back in May but would stay in touch with everyone for crucial decisions regarding corporate strategy or client communication, they were perplexed about managing this. My CEO, also my partner, was the most understanding as he has children and suggested I return in May for our conference in Palm Springs at La Quinta. In the meantime, my CFO suggested I consider taking Unemployment Insurance, which would pay me $800/month instead of my monthly commission of at least $30,000/month.

The response went something like this: "Thank you, John, for that suggestion, but do you think I lost my fucking brain during childbirth? My clients are well taken care of; therefore, those commissions and fees are mine, from which the firm takes more than half. Please don't treat me like an idiot, John. I look forward to seeing you at the conference in May and giving you a run for your money on the golf course. Return to your job, and I'll return to mine."

After that call, I felt mad but chuckled, grateful it wasn't a video call. By noon, I was still in my housecoat, my hair piled up on top of my head with an elastic, my face unwashed, and I was still nursing my cold coffee, thinking it was time for toast with crunchy almond butter.

It was time to hire a nanny who would arrive every morning and leave at four o'clock each day. I needed to feel at ease with someone caring for the most important person in my life, ensuring they were part bodyguard, mother, nurse, and respectable cook.

Life took off in unknown directions when Harvey and I flew down for the conference in May, leaving Harper behind. It felt like I was abandoning her, pulling her off breastfeeding the week before and leaving her with a Filipino nanny whom I prayed was kind and loving when I wasn't around to witness her with my baby. I left a complete mess, but I had to put on my work hat and get my act together quickly.

The partners and their wives were very complimentary about how I looked now that I had lost all the "baby fat," which was close to forty pounds, but it was a constant in the conversation. It did feel good being back to my 126 pounds and feeling fit and strong, even if I was having withdrawals, and my boobs were hurting like hell, not knowing what to do with the milk.

On the golf course that afternoon, after our meetings, I was putting on the fifth green when Harvey looked at me with a shocked look. He pointed at my top, my boobs which were leaking like crazy and leaving two big circles of wetness around each boob. I was only golfing with men, so I was somewhat horrified. I missed the putt and then got in the cart.

Harvey said, "Hold on." He drove the cart quickly through a large puddle, which splashed over the cart's hood and drenched me.

"What the hell?" Then I looked down at my top; it was wet and soaked.

"Wow, Harvey, this might work. Thank you."

My golf top was dry at the end of the next hole, and the milk circles were gone. Brilliant.

Leaving my five-month-old baby, who had been attached to me around the clock, filled me with gut-wrenching guilt that nature never intended. Mothers shouldn't leave their babies at such an early age. I counted the minutes until we left for the airport, knowing I would return to work full-time the following Monday and dreading how that juggling act would affect us all.

I felt torn every day. Each morning was tormenting as I left at six a.m. before my baby woke up. If Harper was awake, I had to hand her over to Elly, the nanny. I would drive over the Lions Gate Bridge in tears, leaving her behind. Then, guilt would set in at four o'clock as I left work and my partners behind. Was I contributing the same way I did before, when I often stayed at work until after dinner many nights, or was I simply more efficient now? The guilt of not being the best mother and not being the best partner was a constant dilemma swirling in my mind and heart. I needed to figure this out. Men were lucky.

They suffered no guilt.

The first alarm on my desk went off at 3:30 to signal that it was time to wrap up and hand over any outstanding matters to my assistant, Carmen, while the second alarm rang at four o'clock, announcing that it was time to grab my jacket and coat, get out, and head home. I would become immersed entirely with my clients and the work, only coming up for air when the first alarm rang, never going out for lunch or wasting time. As I drove home, I could feel myself leaving the workwoman behind and transitioning into the mother. The craving to see Harper intensified, praying she had been cared for and loved that day by someone I trusted with my baby's life. Guilt was a constant ache.

I focused on Harper and my work, so Harvey must have felt somewhat left out during those first few years. Balancing energy and time was challenging with a new baby and a growing career. He maintained his routine, which remained unchanged after Harper was born. He would get up at 4:45 in the morning, arrive at work by 5:30 for the eastern conference call with coffee, leave the office at 3:00 for a run or a round of golf in the summer months, and return home for dinner, prepared by our nanny or me, accompanied by a few glasses of red wine, before heading to bed by 8:30. Over time, I became engrossed in my child and my work. Harvey, too, immersed himself in his job and a bottle of red wine. The gradual erosion of our relationship stemmed from both of us hiding from our vulnerabilities, childhood traumas, our inability to trust in love, and the need to control everything. Having chaotic childhoods, we, as the eldest children, developed skills to manage our outcomes. You can't let others in while continually maintaining control of your surroundings. Harvey was a heavy drinker, particularly on Thursday nights. I felt scared when he came home, unable to communicate, mumbling obscenities, angry at the world; if I happened to be in his way, I didn't know what he might do to me physically, so I hid. I also needed to protect our little girl from witnessing her father when he drank.

His attempts to control me were manifesting themselves more often and more vocally when he drank at night, attempting to turn me away from family and friends.

"Why do you need to go back East every summer to see your mother?"

"We don't need to invite those people over for dinner again. The only people I agree to have for dinner are the six friends, but nobody else."

"Your mother is having too much influence over Harper. Tell her to mind her own business."

My work didn't threaten him; he liked me making money but also gave me power. I started a "Safety Net Fund" just in case I needed to run. It's a wild way to live with someone who is supposed to protect you and make you feel safe. I was starting to pull away physically and emotionally, protecting myself from his verbal attacks. Harvey hated me visiting my mother and family back at our family cottage on the St. Lawrence River, where my daughter could spend time with her Nan and extended family. It was a magical place that my mother built after my father passed away. It was a classic cottage with cedar shakes and white wood trim around a Nantucket-style frame, with a screened-in porch with pink geraniums in white wicker baskets, looking out over the river to one side and the tennis court and gardens over the five acres of manicured lawns and maple trees to the other. The long, winding gravel road meandered through massive oak trees on guard, like soldiers greeting you, protecting you, as you slowly drove into the compound towards the cottage, little guest house and tree house. The dock had a laser sailboat, canoes, and a beautiful Hinkley mahogany boat for trips down the river or into town for groceries or lunch at Chez Piggy. Harvey never wanted to come as he could not handle being somewhere he was not in control. The only time he returned to our cottage in sixteen years was for my brother's wedding, when I told him I would initiate divorce proceedings if he did not show up.

"Harvey, this could be an expensive decision if you don't join us at the wedding where Harper is a flower girl. I want you there as a member of our family. Please, Harvey. You have never seen how wonderful our cottage is, and you can play tennis with everyone, but your daughter would especially love to have you there."

He arrived the day before the wedding and left before the out-of-towners' brunch, and the gifts were opened the next day. It was a glorious wedding, with the Tragically Hip arriving by barge down the river to our dock while singing, "Ahead by a Century." After the ceremony, we could hear the whop, whop, whop of a helicopter approaching, getting louder as we left the tent to see what the noise was; I looked over at this crowd of 120 people sounding like the Munchkins in the Wizard of Oz.

"What is it?" and "It's coming towards us!" "The helicopter is landing in the farmer's field."

A few minutes later, walking towards us, a man in a tux I recognized as my mother's wealthy friend Michael yelled, "I'm looking for Mr. and Mrs. Cooper."

Everyone giggled with excitement, searching for Ben and Carly as they were now running towards Michael, Carly having kicked off her white heels and was carrying them in one hand, with one hundred people running behind, women kicking off their shoes to watch the newlyweds get in the helicopter and take off. Ben lifted Carly and carried his new wife to the chopper, blonde hair blowing, white veil and dress being frantically held as the wind from the rotors was gaining speed, they climbed into the door of the cherry-red chopper, and slowly, effortlessly lifted from the field into the air above us, turning on its side so Ben and Carly could wave to all the guests, delighted by this magical moment.

The Munchkins were waving and yelling, "Bye Bye Bye!" Watching them fly over us, waving as they began their new life together, was an exhilarating scene and a thrill. The guests gradually returned to the tent for a much-needed glass of Rosé, savouring the fresh shrimp and oysters being passed around. It wasn't long before we heard the distinct sounds of the helicopter returning to the field to drop off the married couple, allowing them to continue celebrating with their family and friends. It was time for dinner, toasts, roasts, and special friends expressing beautiful love notes to Ben and Carly. I gave a toast to my baby brother, highlighting his life of adversities offset by numerous blessings, and wishing him a lifetime of joy and good fortune. It took me back to the moment when Dad handed him, all wrapped up in a little blue blanket in the hospital, and said as he placed Ben on my lap, "You will learn to love him and look out for him."

Tears slowly crept down my cheeks and onto my pale pink silk dress, knowing how happy my father would have been to see the man his baby son had become. I glanced at my mother, searching for the strength to finish my speech, but she understood my thoughts beyond the words and was holding a tissue over her eyes. My father, her husband, has missed so much of life, and we all needed him dearly. We miss him every moment, especially on days like this. I shook my head, noticed the empathy from the guests, saw tears welling in Carly's eyes, and thought I should change direction.

"My father would have given anything to be here to wish his youngest son the healthiest and happiest life with his new bride, and I know he would want this song to celebrate the two of you. From Dad to you with love."

The air slowly filled the tent with the high, sultry baritone voice of Elvis Presley singing "Can't Help Falling in Love."

Ben took Carly's hand and led her to the dance floor, encircling her waist and pulling her closer as they swayed to Elvis. He felt as if it was Dad singing those words to him, recalling the sweet, innocent baby he once was. Soft sniffles from women who knew my father filled the air, echoing the profound impact of that voice, those lyrics, and the heartache of losing him at such a young age. As Ben twirled gracefully around the dance floor, he looked at me, a tearful smile breaking across his face, and silently mouthed, Thank you.

The DJ recognized it was time to shatter the lingering pain of our father's loss and reignite that giddy, joyous spirit of celebration, so the music intensified. Everyone hit the dance floor, even Harvey, who danced with Harper. It was a moment to cherish and savour, knowing these instances are fleeting.

We danced until the early hours under this massive white tent, until the bridal party decided to jump off the dock. Black jackets were tossed in the air, pink floral dresses billowed above the water, and one stunning white taffeta dress soared through the air like a cloud shimmering in the moonlight, disappearing into the dark waters below. The giggles and joy as they popped up meant everyone survived and was relieved to see the bride getting helped by her groom up the ladder from the weight of that spectacular gown, now soaking wet, makeup running down her face, perfectly straight hair dripping wet. No longer curly, the bridesmaids all looked like raccoons with mascara below their eyes, which made the men laugh even more. They were all soaking wet, so the towels came out; the reality that the clothes would have to come off at some point made me run into the cottage to grab whatever sweats, sweaters, pants, and bathrobes I could find. Since I was still dry, I started making hot chocolate. I saw homemade ranger cookies for the bridal group of twelve as they sat around the screened-in porch lit by numerous candles, now bundled up in an array of cottage clothes under the light of the full moon, reminiscing about the phenomenal night and their special friendships.

Looking at my handsome baby brother glowing with joy at this moment alongside his bride and best friends made me think that Dad would have cherished every minute of this. Ben was only twelve when he lost his father, and there's so much of his life Dad has already missed. Quietly leaving and shutting the screen door behind me, I made my way barefoot along the path through the garden, past the treehouse with the red door named "Bunky," guided by the moonlight reflecting on the water, feeling the presence of a loving spirit, to the guest cabin where Harvey and Harper were sound asleep.

Glancing up, my hand on my chest, I deeply breathed and whispered, "Good night, Dad. Good night, Moon."

Chapter Twenty-One

Do I Stay

The gradual awareness of emotional abuse became increasingly apparent as I achieved more tremendous success at work. With that success and money came power—independent power—fuck you, money—which provided me with the enhanced exit strategy I needed if Harvey's drinking did not stop. He attempted to dictate what I could and couldn't do, who I could spend time with, and which social events we could attend, isolating me from others whenever possible. He desperately tried to demean my mother, stepfather, and brothers, a behaviour I didn't comprehend, as they posed no threat to him. Did my love for them threaten him? It made no sense. The more he tried to control me, the more I distanced myself, until one night in the kitchen when he grabbed my arm so tightly that I thought he would break it. The bruise lingered for weeks, serving as a painful reminder of the direction of our relationship.

I did everything I could to protect Harper from the growing tension between us in the evenings when we both became obsessed with the wine bottle. The squeaky sound of the corkscrew twisting into the cork was followed by the friction of the tightly sealed cork rubbing against the glass as it was removed from the bottle, with a pop announcing that it was time to hide. I could feel the nerves along my back coming to life, accelerating into flight or fight mode, knowing this was not a healthy way to live.

We had experienced him passing out in his dinner at Hans and Shelby's Whistler home, disappearing on New Year's Eve to find him in a neighbour's hot tub with four naked women, driving so drunk he could not get out of the car without falling over, mumbling his words now after two glasses of wine, and never kind words.

A doctor informed me that if he's having one beer and a bottle of wine every single day, then he is supplementing the alcohol in his system, and it doesn't take much to become inebriated.

I could do nothing right, and I learned to dance with the danger that he imposed on my safety and my daughter's well-being. I learned to create the façade of a beautiful life, a privileged life with a private school, a stunning beach house, a log home at Whistler looking over the mountains, golf club memberships, and travel to Maui, Europe, and all parts of the world whenever we wished to go. It was idyllic, the life of envy by many, but I lived behind the façade in fear that when his eyes blackened, the demons were now in charge, and Harvey was gone. He would never remember the next day after the demons took over and never believed me, even when I showed him the bruises.

I finally confronted him, urging him to seek help at AA or through therapy, and I would support him in any way I could. "I love you very much, Harvey. I appreciate the wonderful life you have provided for Harper and me, but you are destroying yourself with alcohol and dragging us down with you. Please seek help and save your life from this addiction or disease. Can't you see what it's doing to you and your family? I walk on eggshells the moment you open that bottle of wine because your mood shifts, and you become defensive, aggressive, judgmental, angry, and bitter. I feel scared and unsafe when I'm with you at night, worried that I might say or do something to upset or offend you. Please get help and save us all. I love you, Harvey, but I detest the alcoholic.

"I can't quit drinking," Harvey quietly uttered.

That's the moment I knew our marriage was over. Harper was only ten years old, but I needed to protect her and show her that I was not going to tolerate abuse and set this as her example of what marriage is.

After a year of therapy, he never joined me once, and a year of attending Al-Anon at the local church, St. Francis-the-Wood, where Harper was christened, helped me understand the power of addiction, the power of emotional abuse, and the power I needed to leave.

Harvey knew I was thinking of leaving. We hadn't had sex for a long time, yet we continued the dance, pretending our relationship and family life were perfect. Friends had a glimpse into my life now and again when they witnessed his verbal abuse at a party or if they popped over while he was ordering me around.

We attended Tegan and Tim O'Reilly's party on the water to celebrate Tim's fortieth birthday, and they certainly knew how to throw a fantastic party. The theme was Pucci, and as guests arrived, we took photos with the hosts. Our cars were valet parked. An Aperol spritz was handed to us as we made our way down to the pool, which was adorned with orange slices, massive coloured balloons, and a fantastic band playing on their deck for the one hundred guests, all dressed in stunning colours with top designers fully represented. I adored my long, form-fitting Prada dress with high-cut sides and a low front in a sea-blue shade, paired with bright pink high-heeled shoes, which I knew would be kicked off once the dancing started.

I loved socializing at these parties, as the atmosphere was fun and lively, allowing me to escape the reality of my secret life with Harvey. When I noticed Harvey mumbling or stumbling, it was my cue to escort him home from the party, no matter how early it was. I usually do this out of embarrassment and fear that he would say or do something that might reveal my world. To explain his stumbling, I would make up excuses, such as that he got up at 4:30 a.m. and was tired by 8:30.

On that night, I didn't want to leave. The band played such incredible music that it was impossible to resist dancing. Although Harvey never danced, all the women loved to gather on the dance floor, so I didn't feel out of place dancing without my husband. I noticed the expression on Harvey's face as he watched us dance. He looked quite drunk, and I felt safer there than going home.

Garth began dancing at the edge of the swimming pool, tempting fate as he called out, "Let's do the corner dance." With wine and spirits flowing freely, many people thought it would be fun, without considering the consequences of missing the mark. Janie, dressed entirely in white, jumped excitedly into the corner and danced around the pool; within seconds, she slipped in, prompting hysterical laughter.

However, I knew it wouldn't be a pleasant sight when she climbed out of the pool. Fully attired in white, her outfit was completely see-through, revealing her Hankie Pankie thong and lace bra. I quickly grabbed some towels and started drying her off. While kneeling and trying to balance on my high heels, I was suddenly pushed forward from behind, landing on my knees.

Not just me, but the entire group of dancers around the pool overheard the loud, mumbled words: "You just have to be the centre of attention all the time, don't you?"

The music stopped. I glanced over my shoulder and saw Harvey stumbling up the stairs while friends gathered around me, one of them saying, "Maybe it's time, Morgan."

I looked at her and replied, "I'm done. I can't do this anymore."

Someone handed me a Rosé, someone with an Aussie accent, someone I had not met before, and he said, "I don't know who you are, but you should not be treated that way."

With tears in my eyes, knowing the truth had been revealed and glowingly exposed, I looked up into his mischievous blue eyes and felt completely free. This Aussie accent validated my feelings and summarized what I needed to do. It was time. As he turned to walk away, he said quietly with a flirtatious smile, "You're stunning."

I kicked off my high heels, held tightly to the Rosé, and walked up the stairs to the distinct sound of Santana and Rob Thomas playing Smooth. Santana's crystalline tone and clean arcing sustain make him the rare instrumentalist who can be identified in just one note, resonating through my body. When I got to the top of the property, I glanced back at the sight of the full moon, now bright orange, which must have reflected from the orange slices in the pool. Now, that's the power of a good party planner, orchestrating the moon to match the night's theme. I smiled and felt giddy from the magic and energy of that party. I glanced down at the people dancing to Santana and caught the Aussie in the crowd smiling at me. As I slowly headed home barefoot, I heard the lyrics resonating through the trees loudly and clearly.

As I approached the front door, I opened the gate and prayed Harvey was asleep. I held my breath, glanced at the sky filled with flickering stars, placed my hand on my anxious heart, and whispered, “Good night, seductive Aussie. Good night, orange moon.”

Chapter Twenty-Two

Risking

The home phone rang at 6:00 a.m., which was unusual, even though I was awake, and Harvey had left an hour earlier. "Turn on CNN and look for your brother." Then, Harvey hung up.

I quickly grabbed the remote and put on the TV in time to see Matt Lauer asking Tom Brokaw what had caused this pilot to lose control of his plane and fly into the World Trade Tower. The footage was shocking to see a large commercial airline go straight into the top of the Twin Towers and realize the people in that plane would have died along with all the people on those floors that it careened into. Katie Couric was shocked as she and Matt tried desperately to get information about what has happened when the live camera on the first tower filmed the second plane go straight into the other tower. The screaming was real and visceral on that set. The instant reality that this was not an accident; this was done by men who could kill themselves and everyone else for a cause was beyond comprehension. While glued to the screen, I tried to call my brother on his cell, and it went straight to voicemail; I called my sister-in-law, and it did the same thing. They lived and worked in the financial district and regularly go to Windows of the World for breakfast meetings; the restaurant on top was now billowing smoke from all its windows. I called my mother, who was frantically trying to locate Ben and Carly, and the world was now being informed with footage of the first terrorist attack on American soil.

It took several hours to locate my brother, who had been in Dallas on business with his phone turned off, and his wife, Carly, who walked home in slippers from a pedicure place because her heels were ruined. It became evident that no one would be flying in US airspace anytime soon. As the Twin Towers collapsed and New York was plunged into chaos, people fled from the windows, aware of their imminent death; terrified individuals covered in soot ran from the towers to save their lives. Firefighters rushed into the two buildings, knowing they might not survive. The heroism, bravery, and determination to help those trapped in those burning buildings were witnessed by those of us in the safety of our homes miles away.

The new world order of America was under siege, and I couldn't help but shake as I witnessed such trauma and horror live in the incredible city of New York. I called my girlfriend Katie, who had just moved from London to New York with her young family five months earlier. Her voice was unrecognizable as she, haltingly, through tears and gasps, said, "I can't find John, and his company is in the North Tower."

I knew John had merged his company Tullett and Tokyo with Cantor Fitzgerald, whose headquarters are located between the 101st and 105th floors of the North Tower of the World Trade Center, just above the impact site of American Airlines Flight 11. Eight hours later, I got a call from Katie, exhausted and traumatized, her voice broken. "John just walked in the door. He's been walking for seven hours, covered in ashes after witnessing people jump while he stood at the bottom of the Twin Towers, late for a breakfast meeting at Windows on the World, missing death by eight minutes. Still, his thirty employees weren't so lucky. I must go, Mugs. He's alive but shattered beyond belief."

This horror paralyzed the nation, stunned every New Yorker and the world, and changed our lives forever as we knew it. Evil exists on American soil, and now the new weapon is suicide terrorism. It is unfathomable, incomprehensible, and a reminder of life's fragility.

My mind turned to the Aussie, and I wondered if he was in New York for business. Shortly after the party, I learned that he and his family had recently arrived from Australia so he could become president of Canada's largest diversified mining company.

Five days after the worst terrorist attack in the US, I got a phone call from the Aussie, Joey Dutton. "I've been thinking about you and wonder if you would consider meeting me in London for a few days next week.

I'm there on business but have my nights free."

The silence was deafening as I tried to catch my breath. His accent created slower speech with a deep nasal tone, and he exuded confidence and charm as I attempted to process the suggestion he was making.

"Thank you for calling, Joey. I'm glad to hear you weren't in New York. You know I'm married, and I believe you are, too. It would be nice to get to know you, but going to London for that feels a bit premature."

"I'll contact you when I return from London. Take care, and I look forward to getting to know you better."

My cheeks flushed, my heart raced, and my mind spun. Along with a strong espresso, I felt jittery, fearful, excited, and alive with that first brush of infatuation. It had been years of Harvey diminishing my spirit through persistent emotional abuse when he drank, and as I pulled away to protect myself, his nastiness intensified. I knew I was vulnerable and found ways to escape by travelling with girlfriends, shopping sprees, and immersing myself in Harper's life and work. For a while, I thought I had everyone fooled with my acting, presenting our perfect life of privilege in the right circles, doing the right things, and behaving the right way. Yet, I was crying myself to sleep many nights, hugging my pillow when Harvey lay beside me, sound asleep. The truth was that I had been madly in love with Harvey for years when he was sober, but the drinker eventually consumed the sober Harvey. Dr. Jekyll slowly and methodically killed Mr. Hyde. I no longer trusted Mr. Hyde to be as humorous, generous, and kind as he once was. He now poked at me with comments he knew would hurt; he recognized it would punish me, and he chose this path rather than pursuing sobriety, love, or redemption to save his life and his family. I wanted nothing more than to have sober, healthy Harvey by my side for life until death do us part. Death now held a new meaning when one believed that the husband who made that vow could also be the one to cause your death, killing not only your spirit but also ending your existence.

First, I am defined by my feelings. If I am unhappy with how I live, I need to take action to improve my situation. The first risk I must embrace is admitting that I am not where I want to be, that I am not feeling as I believe I should, and that I am not content. Each person fears three general types of loss in life: the loss of love, the loss of control, and the loss of self-esteem. We all confront the threat of these losses throughout our lives.

The following two months were spent figuring out what I needed to do, whom I could confide in, and how I would manage my emotional state amid the intense fear of leaving Harvey, ending our family life, and the heart palpitations caused by the Aussie. Was he giving me hope or serving as the catalyst, saying, "You don't need to be treated this way?" Was he shaking me from my make-believe trance, suggesting that perhaps faking this life wasn't working and nudging me towards being with a new man? Joey Dutton contacted me frequently throughout the day to chat and plan when we could get together. It all felt wrong, yet, like a drug, it was overwhelming, intoxicating, and addictive, making me crave the next hit. His voice was irresistibly sexy and captivating, and each call left me flushed, perspiring, and shaken. I needed to sit down, regroup, and collect my bearings before moving on to my next client, my next errand, my reality, and the pickup at Harper's private school, where his children also attended.

It felt like a volcano brewing, with no control over the timing of its eruption or the outcome of the destructive lava flow. In what direction will this lava flow travel, and how many people will be affected by its stream of molten rock? I had made up excuses to avoid meeting Joey, but when he suggested meeting for a drink in his company's boardroom, I immediately replied, "Yes, but I need to be home by seven."

I lied to Harvey. I told him I was going to a meeting at the school for the upcoming fundraiser and would only be there for a short time. Since he had little interest in school activities, it was easy to head off after giving them a quick dinner.

The entrance to the mining company's main door was locked, and no one was around until Joey arrived in a beautiful suit and paisley tie, looking every bit like the president of Canada's largest mining company. That day, after my analyst issued a solid buy signal for Joey's company, I purchased thousands of shares for clients eager to continue adding to their positions; it felt impressive.

When he opened the door, my first instinct was to hug him to calm my racing heart and sweaty hands. Instead, he took one of my damp hands and led me through the enormous office with a breathtaking view of the snowcapped mountains, now tinged with pink from the setting sun, and into the boardroom. I have been in many boardrooms, attending client meetings and conferences. However, this one was grand, featuring a mahogany table that could seat thirty, a lounge area with couches, a massive screen above a fireplace, and a spacious gourmet kitchen off to the side.

He took me into his arms, saying, "What have you done to me?"

"I could say the same thing, and I'm unsure about what we should do, but my cravings for you are intense, and I'm not certain I can resist the power of infatuation I feel for you."

His blue eyes were a stunning shade of aquamarine, glistening in the light. I was mesmerized by them and have always been drawn to blue eyes. My father had blue eyes, while my mother had brown, so my immediate thought was likely influenced by that.

Then the kiss—gentle yet firm, kind yet lustful—sought a response. Two bodies, two souls yearning for passion, thirsted for new love; the adrenaline rush of desire and longing enveloped us. Being led to the couch in the lounge felt both wrong and right, adulterous yet electrifying, and neither of us nor our bodies wished to stop until more than an hour later. He was the lover I had never known or experienced before; the intensity of two bodies craving each other for months—perhaps even years—was pent-up energy unleashed, like two starved athletes restrained from reaching their full potential. Every muscle and every part of my being vibrated with his scent, the taste of his neck, and the freedom of unrestrained expression. Fear had no place here; worries about what to think, what to say, or who might judge us were absent, leaving only the raw essence of desire and connection between us.

As I put my dishevelled clothes back on, sorting through the pile on the floor, my mind instinctively vowed to be free. "It's time to be free, Joey. Thank you for showing me that there is hope."

We joked about our wobbly legs, rumpled clothes, and flushed faces as he walked me out. Our hands trembled when he hugged me goodbye, but both relieved and exhausted, we finally honoured our intense passion for each other.

After sixteen years with Harvey, the guilt crept into my conscience while driving home, the guilt of lying to him and Harper, so I needed to figure this out, and soon, before the volcano blew and hurt too many people.

Harvey made a snide comment about my tardiness as I walked in the door fifteen minutes after seven. Judging by the bottle in front of him, he was on his fourth glass of wine, and I headed straight upstairs to see Harper and soak in a hot bubble bath before the scent of Joey could be detected.

It was both conflicting and enticing, all-consuming yet liberating, sad but exhilarating, and filled with emotional turbulence, making it difficult to think clearly or focus on anything else.

Going through the detached motions of marriage feels numbing. Pulling away out of fear from his verbal abuse was isolating, but I learned to bury myself to protect my heart and my child. I kept saying I could handle this, but was it strength or fear of stepping into the unknown? Is it genuinely teaching your child the best lesson to remain in an unhappy relationship and sacrifice your joy and mental health for the sake of society's repercussions and judgment? I desperately wanted Harvey to articulate how much he loved me and to stop drinking to save us and our family. My life was devoted to showing him how much fulfillment and adventure we could have toward ultimate peace and contentment. I wanted nothing more than to remain in my marriage and not disturb my daughter's stability, dismantle the fabric of our lives, pull apart the pieces of our home and our friendships. I tried to not shatter the dream until one day, Harper made it crystal clear that enough was enough. She held my hand after witnessing Harvey call me a big shot for using my money to build the treehouse at the cottage. Harper held my hand and guided me outside to the quiet and privacy of our garden.

My little girl's sweet, freckled face looked into my eyes and quietly yet firmly said, "It's time, Mom. It's time for us to leave Dad and find our place to live."

I realized then that my daughter had also been walking on thin ice; she no longer wanted to play the game or pretend we were a happy, functioning family. Here I was, believing she wasn't aware of the abuse, that I had protected her from it with my acting, keeping her separate from the slow disintegration of our marriage and the unhappiness I was hiding. She was the mature one among us all.

Chapter Twenty-Three

The Catalyst

Harper and I were now a team, but despite being a parent, I still had to approach this as methodically and objectively as possible. Who was I kidding? This was all emotion, all heart, with very little logic to guide what happened next. I spoke to no one about the conflict I was experiencing, as I couldn't trust anyone with this information—this bomb that was about to explode. My therapist needed to help me devise a game plan that best protected Harper and me from any violent responses. If Harvey was going to continue drinking, which he claimed he would and couldn't give up, then I had no choice but to leave to save myself from going under and losing myself entirely. My nerves were frayed from the obsession I now felt for this Aussie man who offered a lifeline from the sixteen years of marriage to a man I once loved and wanted so much to stay with—if only. The power of alcohol to destroy relationships and families felt like being in a slowly sinking boat; you either surrendered to going down with it or struggled fiercely to get into the lifeboat and row to shore, saving yourself and your child's life. I needed to do everything I could to understand this addiction and help Harvey seek rehab, attend one AA meeting, or even admit he had a problem. I attended weekly meetings at Al-Anon; I knew the Serenity Prayer and recited it every night when I closed my eyes:

God, grant me the Serenity to accept the things I cannot change,
Courage to change the things I can,
And the Wisdom to know the difference.

I researched every source, but the Al-Anon leader once asked me, "Is your husband across the hall at the AA meeting, Morgan? Since you've been attending these meetings regularly, I assume he's doing everything possible to combat this disease."

"No, he is not. He has not come yet, and I can't convince him to come. He is at home, enjoying a bottle of red wine."

"At some point, you will need to inform your husband that you have a zero-tolerance policy regarding his drinking and that you must give him an ultimatum. He either needs to quit drinking and seek professional help, or you will have to prioritize your well-being and leave. If you need our support, we can assist you with an intervention. That's why we are here: to help family members implement a plan to save their loved ones."

I broke down in tears, my head in my hands, knowing an intervention would never work with Harvey, knowing I had no choice now but to implement my plan of zero tolerance and had no choice but to leave him. My therapy and attending Al-Anon were not moving him in the direction of getting help or quitting.

That night, I lay in bed staring up at the stars, my eyes stinging from a flood of tears, hearing the crashing waves of the ocean and feeling the salty sea breeze on my face, dreaming of a life free from this perpetual anxiety, this obsession with Harvey's mood when he drank, and wondering what I had done wrong this time. Alcoholism wreaks havoc on intimacy and trust, and his paranoia also heightened as I pulled away. I caught him searching my office, rummaging through my desk, and when he found a Valentine's card, he believed I hadn't bought it for him, and he lost his mind.

Since his mother was visiting, I went to bed earlier than he did that evening. They could chat and keep each other company while I put Harper to bed. I wanted to curl up and enjoy quiet time after my Al-Anon meeting. Harvey's mother was sweet and kind, yet somewhat intimidated by him when he drank. I heard her coming up the stairs and stepping into the guest bedroom, which I had prepared with towels, fresh pink tulips, and lit bedside lamps. I loved that bedroom with its white wainscoting halfway up the walls, the soft yellows and pinks in the fabrics creating a warm, happy atmosphere, and a big comfy chair in the corner under the window providing an ocean view.

I tensed up, knowing Harvey was going to bed later than usual. He was angry with me over the card he had seen and was not convinced I had bought it for him long ago. I had hoped his mood would improve by spending time with his mother, but I realized I was in trouble when he slammed the bedroom door. He was tossing things around in the bathroom, and I feigned sleep. Before I realized it, he was on the bed, yanking the covers off and shouting at me that he knew I had someone else; his hands were around my neck, choking me as I tried to scream and get away. His eyes were dark with horror and unrecognizable evil in them. He squeezed harder, then let go to hit my head and face as hard as he could.

When he let go of my neck, I struggled to get air but jumped off the bed, ran out of the bedroom, slammed the door, and heard him screaming, "I'm going to kill you!" Without thinking, I opened his mother's door and slid under the covers beside her, hoping she would save me from her son.

Harvey opened the door and yelled, "Is she in here?"

Pulling the covers over my head, his mother responded, "No, go back to bed."

I heard the door slam, then Harper's bedroom door opened and closed as I prayed to God that he wouldn't hurt our little girl. I shook uncontrollably, my teeth chattered, and Mumbo's flannelette nightie against my bare skin felt comforting. I realized my nightie had been torn off as I lay there, trembling and terrified for my life, my neck and head pounding, my heart thrashing against my ribs, hearing Harvey run around the house, opening and closing doors, then silence.

"He's returned to bed, and hopefully, he passes out. I'm so sorry, Morgan. Is this what you've been living with?" Mumbo quietly whispered, placing her hand on my lower back.

"Yes," was all I could say, shivering out of control.

Terrified that he would find me in his mother's bed, I stayed awake until I finally heard the shower turn on in the master bedroom. His footsteps passed our bedroom, the garage door squeaking as it opened, followed by the revving of the Porsche engine as it backed out of the garage, shifting into first gear, then second as it gained speed down our street. I knew it was five o'clock in the morning, and I needed to call a lawyer to plan my escape. The physical attack made it clear that I had to jump into the lifeboat before he returned home from work.

I got out of bed, leaving Mumbo snoring peacefully, and checked on Harper, who was thankfully safe and sound asleep. I hesitated to look in the mirror, fearing the reflection that would stare back at me. My neck was bruised, a mix of blue and red, swollen near my ears, making it difficult to turn my head in one direction. My face was alarming, all puffy from a lack of sleep, with my cheeks swollen from the impact of his fist and one eye half-closed, changing shades of blue, evidence of abuse. It was the most dreadful sight, and I wanted to break down and weep, but I had to hide it from Harper, uncertain if she had heard anything.

I called my good friend, knowing she was an early riser, and thankfully, she picked up right away. "Are you okay, Morgan?"

"No, Paige, I need to consult a lawyer and meet with you after I drop Harper off at school. Harvey assaulted me last night, and I'm not sure if I should call the police and file charges."

"Oh my God, Morgan. I'll reach out to Meryl, and she'll find the best lawyer and get back to you immediately. Come and see me as soon as you're able. It's time, Morgan."

After showering and attempting to cover my face and neck with a scarf and makeup, I welcomed Harper for breakfast, pretending everything was normal. I chatted with her while gazing out the window, trying to discuss her day and the field hockey game she had after school. I was still trembling, and I felt reassured when she didn't say anything at all. I wasn't sure if she had heard my screams from the night before—the frantic rush to the guest room, Harvey slamming doors, searching for me in the house. I prayed she had slept through it, but how could she have? I couldn't bring up last night at that moment for fear of completely breaking down in front of her, and I didn't want an eleven-year-old to see her mother frightened and unstable. She had always viewed me as strong, and I needed her to know I could manage this.

I hugged her as I dropped her off at school, wearing my sunglasses even though it was only eight a.m. and overcast. She sensed that her life would change that day, and I didn't realize how much.

Paige had a steaming cup of coffee waiting for me, and her lawyer friend Meryl arrived shortly after. This is assault causing bodily harm. My advice is to meet with Jeffrey Keith, the best lawyer in town. He will take photos of your neck and face, gather details of what happened, and provide you with the best advice possible. He has rearranged things to meet you this morning at eleven.

Paige wrapped a Hudson Bay blanket around me to help curb my shaking from exhaustion—shock, fear, my new reality, my painful face, and my neck. I needed to gather the strength to drive downtown and face the lawyer, aiming to strategize in a way that would de-escalate the trauma and enable me to see a path forward without fear of retaliation.

I arrived early for Jeffrey Keith and, for the first time, felt safe in this austere, regal law office. Its Brazilian red cherry wood-panelled walls felt solid and protective of me and my rights as a wife and a human being. I took a deep breath and visualized myself climbing onto the life raft, raising my arms to lift Harper onto the front of the raft, and then putting on our life jackets, saying, "Let's go and row ourselves into a new life of freedom and safety."

Jeffrey Keith came out to greet me, shaking my hand and looking at me and my face with empathy and kindness. "Hello, Morgan Ross, nice to meet you. Let's go and figure out a game plan you are happy with."

As I settled into his office, he offered me a glass of water. I suddenly realized that I hadn't had any and was quite parched. He asked me to share everything, which I did hesitantly. At times, I needed to pause to catch my breath.

There was a knock on the door, and he said, "I hope you don't mind, but I've asked my partner to come in and take photos of your injuries and the apparent physical abuse. Are you okay with that? We haven't discussed pressing charges or involving the police, but I wanted to have photos and evidence of the attack before we decide how you wish to proceed."

I rolled down my turtleneck sweater so they could take photos. The worst part was behind my ears; one eye was nearly swollen shut now. As I was leaving, the man with the camera said sorrowfully, "I'm so sorry this has happened to you." Then he went out the door. I wasn't accustomed to people feeling sorry for me and pitying me, but I had put myself in this position and needed to get myself out of it and into a place of joy and peace for both Harper and me.

With that thought, I looked at Jeffrey Keith and said, "I don't want to file charges against my husband; I want to file for divorce. I want him out of the house today, and he can go to Whistler. I want to give him an ultimatum: if he quits drinking today and agrees to go to rehab right away, then I will support him in the best way I can. If he does not agree to go, then he will have to divide his assets in half and lose his family. It's the wine or us!"

I asked my lawyer if I could borrow his phone to make a call.

"Hello, Harvey Ross here."

"Hi, Harvey, it's Morgan. I'm at my lawyer's office, but I need to meet you at home today at 1:30 so you can hear about your options. I have decided not to involve the police or press charges of assault. We have taken photos to determine whether we need to reconsider that decision. I will see you at the house at 1:30. You and your mother will spend the night at the Whistler house. See you at home."

"But, Morgan, I don't remember anything."

"My face and neck should remind you when you see me."

Jeffrey Keith smirked as he leaned back in his chair. He remarked, "I believe Morgan Ross will be fine. When necessary, you are a resilient woman and representing you would be an honour. Are you comfortable with your husband at home, or would you like me to be there?"

"I am furious about what he has done; he should be the one feeling nervous about being alone with me. He worships his money and knows I now have the power to halve it. Thank you, Mr. Keith. I will contact you tomorrow to discuss our plan of action. I need to stay in that house until I purchase a home for Harper and me, which I have the funds to do. I have a healthy reserve set aside, Mr. Keith, in my 'Fuck You' account for this very purpose."

"If you can get him to leave the matrimonial home while you find a new one, that will work in your best interests."

"Trust me. If he does not agree to get help with his drinking, the path forward for us is crystal clear. Thank you for meeting me on such short notice in this crazy crisis."

"Good luck today, Morgan. Try to get some ice on your eyes and face. You're going to be okay."

When Harvey walked in through the front door, I stood in the kitchen, pressing a bag of frozen peas to my face. He looked weaker and somewhat hesitant as he approached me. My resolve was clear, but I needed to remain firm, even as tears threatened to spill down my cheeks. I didn't want to reveal that emotion right now, but it bubbled up with the harsh reality that our magical life together was over. The sad truth was that I did love Harvey deeply, but I loved sober Harvey, not cruel, drunk Harvey, and I could no longer live with both. How could I love a man who had tried to strangle me to death? Yes, I was torn by the guilt of another man's affection. Yet, the slippery slope of abuse had me treading water, searching for that life raft, and being buoyed by the kindness of another man was proof of my unhappiness and fragile vulnerability.

"Harvey, we need to talk. You almost killed me last night. You would have succeeded if it weren't for your mother protecting me and hiding me in her bed. Do you remember what you did?"

He slowly sat down, taking off his jacket, looking pale, as I handed him a glass of water. His hand shook as he took hold of it. Confused, he looked at me and asked timidly, "I did that to you?"

"Harvey, your eyes were black with evil in them, and I know you don't remember because you blacked out, but your vicious intent was to kill me, and I will never trust you again. Look at my neck, where you tried to strangle me to death, yelling how much you wanted to kill me. You have been getting more and more abusive when you drink, and don't blame me again, like you always have. I went to a lawyer, and not the police, for our daughter's sake and your sake, but we do have photos of the assault if you don't want to go along with my proposal."

Looking up at me, his hands now visibly shaking, and for a moment, I felt sorry for him and the power and destruction of this wretched disease, of how such an intelligent, beautiful man whom I fell madly in love with did not have the strength to fight its insidious control.

His eyes were no longer black demons but soft blue eyes full of shame, and he was tired and sad and did not want to hear my proposal.

"Harvey, I want our family to stay together more than anything. I have dedicated sixteen years to you, yet you have gradually eroded my respect and love through persistent abuse and reduced my spirit in every possible way. It's time for you to confront this disease, and I will support you in every way I can. We have the funds for you to enter rehab, such as the Betty Ford Centre in Palm Springs, where your friend Ted went and got clean. I can't live with you if you continue to drink. I'm going for a walk around the neighbourhood to give you time to reflect on this. This is your intervention. Quit drinking today, whether it's through AA or rehab, or continue drinking and move to Whistler to give me time to find a new house. If you choose the latter, I will file for divorce next week and want fifty percent of our assets while ensuring that you and I remain equal parents in raising Harper. You will not have Harper overnight if you keep drinking, though. When I return, I expect your answer: your family or your addiction. That's your choice. It's that simple. Is that clear?"

My heart pounded so fiercely that it hurt; indeed, everything hurt as I slowly walked down our street, hoping no one would see me. I welcomed the hidden dirt path to the ocean, sat on a log washed up on the beach, listened to the rhythmic crashing of waves as flickers of sunlight caught the tips of each rolling wave, and became enchanted by the noisy, white-tipped seagulls with their mewing. Their wings beat against the salty air as they approached the fishing boat with numerous lines dragging on either side, rippling in the calm water. They cried and made their inverted arcs, hungry and tenacious, as the fishermen waved them away, but they are part of the ocean world where all is connected.

Taking a deep breath, I placed both hands on my strung-out heart and prayed that Harvey would choose his family and do everything possible to battle this demon and take the first step. I had Ted's phone number ready to dial if he opted for rehab, as Ted had spent months at the Betty Ford Centre, returning home with a fresh start and turning his life around after achieving sobriety and gaining control over his addiction. I noticed he spent less time with his old friends who drank too much because he needed to protect himself from relapsing. I prayed that Harvey would have the conviction to fight for us, for me, and for his health through sobriety.

I struggled to get up, to determine my fate, what I wanted it to be, and what I would do with each option. Stumbling home from the weight of my reality, I opened the door to find Harvey still sitting where I had left him, though his head rested on his hands.

"Have you had enough time to think it over?"

"Yes, and I can't stop drinking. I want to try to make our marriage work, and I don't want to lose you and Harper."

"You can't quit drinking, or you don't want to try?"

"Both."

"Unfortunately, that isn't an option. Drinking and family don't mix. If that's your choice, I need you and your mother, who's waiting upstairs, to drive to Whistler and stay there until I find a new home for Harper and me or until you secure one for yourself. We're done, Harvey. I can't do this anymore, and I have zero tolerance for your alcohol abuse. I need to pick up Harper from school now, and when I return, I don't want you here."

"I'm sorry, Morgan."

"Me too."

The Disease Won
When do you give in
When do you give up?
Is it always a sin
To let the disease win?
Every bottle of wine and beer
Turns a life into chronic fear.
How does one acknowledge
When one is on the edge?
The bottle is opened…
Walking on eggshells begins.
The personality changes,
Dissociation sets in.

It must be Thursday, and anxiety appears.
The barriers go up, along with the fears.
Can I be free tonight?
Or be careful; he is in sight.
When do you give in
When do you give up?
Alcoholism is contagious
I must survive and be courageous.
It will drive one to self-destruction
As it begins to numb all the senses.
It will damage any feelings one had,
The focus on drinking, or not, is bad.
Will you ever stop drinking, please?
Or can you not take control of the disease?
It is so sad to see
In the end,
You have chosen the wine over me.

Was the Aussie the catalyst that Harvey noticed after seeing a Valentine's card I knew I wouldn't give him (too sexy), or did the Aussie give me the strength to leave and not spend another day in this turmoil of alcoholic hazing? Yes, he did bring everything to a wild, dramatic, run-for-my-life ending, but I was grateful that there was an end to this façade of life, living on thin ice, never knowing when I might fall through. Your central nervous system remains on high alert, anticipating five o'clock beer time, followed by a cork popping from the wine bottle, stepping up to the front lines, wondering where the next attack will come from while trying not to provoke the enemy. I never trusted anyone with these fears for the worry they might spread around our circle of friends. I had to manage this and its outcome; consequently, I was never vulnerable or honest with my friends about my home life, even when they saw Harvey mumbling and stumbling at parties. Our sweet little girl, with her innocent eyes, witnessed the truth of our reality, walking on thin ice for years, learning from me how to handle her father. That was the role model I never wanted to be. I needed her to see me achieve the outcome of demonstrating that one should never accept abuse under any circumstances.

For once, I had clarity as I looked at my reflection in the mirror. Staring back was a bruised, beaten face with swollen eyes and bluish-green skin that ached to the touch, distinctly marked by puffy finger impressions on my neck. I thought, enough; this is my life, and I must save it.

The next day, I made two phone calls: one to my mother and the other to the Aussie. Both advised me to stay with Harvey, suggesting that leaving was too impulsive, ultimately wanting what was best for themselves. They did not consider my safety or mental health, only the ripple effect it would have on them.

"Don't worry, Mom, I have enough money to buy a new house. You convinced me to stay years ago when I tried to leave Harvey at four in the morning after he had come home drunk and been with another woman. You're not going to do that to me again. You'll have to tell your friends the truth for once."

"Don't worry, Joey. This isn't about me leaving Harvey to be with you. I'm grateful you were my catalyst, helping me break free from a relationship where I was slowly slipping into oblivion. Thank you for giving me hope; I will always be thankful. I'm just relieved that he didn't kill me. You need to sort out your marriage, just as I need to sort out ending mine."

Ultimately, I realized that men, money, and my mother have influenced every decision I've made. The power to persuade, the power to manipulate, the power to love, and the power to destroy.

Discovering this new Nantucket-style home, nestled among magnificent oak and maple trees, allowed Harper and me to heal beneath a dome of safety and cultivate the peace we desperately needed. I brought the artwork I had purchased and all my significant possessions, leaving the rest for Harvey. I encouraged him to visit the house because I wanted him to know where we would be living, and he needed to understand that I could buy this home without his assistance. He was shocked to learn I could acquire this beautiful four-bedroom, multimillion-dollar house with a pool and a lovely garden on the quiet crescent where we once lived. The new house had just been completed, so we immediately moved in. Everything felt fresh and spotlessly clean, which I appreciated—free from anyone else's dirt or use, especially in the kitchen. Harvey walked through the house silently, exuding sadness from every pore, and appeared broken. I couldn't help but feel sympathy for him, even though my bruises were not fully healed, and my heart was still shattered. As he left, I hugged him, saying, "Please get help."

Rising early on our first morning and manoeuvring around the boxes, wrapped in my cozy white terrycloth robe, I made my Nespresso. The early morning aroma of coffee jolts my senses to life, starting my day with, "Welcome to a new day, a new beginning." Curling up in my favourite red Adirondack chair, sipping cappuccino from my Emma Bridgewater mug under a large red maple tree, I listened to the robins chirping and the little black-capped chickadees vying for attention with their distinct high-low pitch of feee beee, feeee beee. The birds make me smile, welcoming me back to the neighbourhood and reassuring me that Nature prevails; Nature is like a warm blanket of consistent, unconditional love—predictable, robust, and always there to restore my soul. Nature never lets me down. Nature fuels me as I close my eyes, with the morning light dancing on my face as it peeks through the fluttering leaves, and the gentle breeze joins the chorus of sensations, gently waking me to the first day of the rest of my life. How they come together—the birds singing, the light breeze, the warmth of sunshine, and the foliage—neither taking, yet both giving and receiving just the same, each an intrinsic part of the now.

Our new life was about to begin, with boxes to unpack, artwork to hang, and healing to initiate one day at a time. The conflicting array of emotions was daunting and felt beyond my control. I allowed each emotion to surface as I listened, respected, recognized, and responded. My overall feeling was one of deep sadness, with a flicker of joyous freedom, as though I had escaped a long struggle with a disease I ultimately could not defeat. I was the lucky one. I could walk away from it, but Harvey could not. Furious at the disease that was slowly destroying my husband, I forgive Harvey, yet I will never forgive or forget the disease and the destruction and devastation it has left in its wake.

These quotes provided me with comfort and solace, affirming that my departure from Harvey was a lifesaving decision to escape a severe addiction that could have dragged both Harper and me down with it:

"A man who drinks too much on occasion is still the same as he was sober. An alcoholic, a real alcoholic, is not the same man at all. You can't predict anything about him for sure except that he will be someone you never met before."
—Raymond Chandler, *The Long Goodbye*

"Alcoholism, as a disease that ravages the mind and body, often becomes intertwined with domestic violence, heightening its destructive impact"
—Rove Monteux, *What is Wrong with Society Today*

"Alcoholism can be understood as a spiritual disorder," Ross told me the first time we met in the treatment room at NYU. "Over time, you lose your connection to everything but this compound. Life loses all meaning. Ultimately, nothing is more important than that bottle, not even your wife and kids. Eventually, there is nothing you won't sacrifice for it."
—Michael Pollan, *How to Change Your Mind: What the New Science of Psychedelics Teaches Us About Consciousness, Dying, Addiction, Depression, and Transcendence*

"If you're one of us, the bottle takes your shit, that's all. First a little, then a lot, then everything."
—Stephen King, *Doctor Sleep*

"If I am this capable of loving an alcoholic so much, imagine how awesome I could be at loving myself."
—Grace W. Woldson, *So You Love an… Alcoholic? Lessons for a Codependent*

"The life of the Addict is always the same. There is no excitement, no glamour, no fun. There are no good times, there is no joy, there is no happiness. There is no future and no escape. There is only an obsession. An all-encompassing, fully enveloping, completely overwhelming obsession. To make light of it, brag about it, or revel in the mock glory of it is not in any way, shape or form related to its truth, and that is all that matters, the truth."
—James Frey, *A Million Little Pieces*

"The drinking parent lied to the sober parent; the sober parent deceived the drinking parent. Most children of alcoholics have learned that no one can be trusted."
—Abraham J. Twerski, *Addictive Thinking: Understanding Self-Deception*

"Alcohol is a far greater killer than all opiates. You can buy alcohol on any street corner throughout the world. It gets your brain and your liver. It destroys your morals, destroys your vitality, kills your sexual potential, and you become sluggish. It was a great pity that Prohibition failed. The experiment was too radical. Instead of barring it altogether, the dispensation of alcohol should have been under prescription or some other control. Prohibition was one of the worthiest attempts of a group to impose their will upon the rest of the people. But of course, if you prohibit something, you deprive people of an essential liberty; when you deny the right of choice, you oppose the greatest gift in the world. People will not stand for it. Alcohol makes man mad and leads to such strange behaviourism. Yet, beer and liquor ads maintain newspapers, television, and a huge portion of the national and world economies. Drinker that I am, I think essentially, I am the victim of an addiction that is here in the world, revealed to all, exposed to all. It is there. We who are weak take to it and are destroyed by it, but it is essentially a weakness of governments everywhere to allow this poison to circulate like a river through the bloodstream of humans. As one of the heartiest drinkers in the world, I speak with a voice of authority."
—Errol Flynn, *My Wicked, Wicked Ways*

Chapter Twenty-Four

Man Drug

Harper is an old soul—mature, supportive, and kind. She wanted to return to her old neighbourhood, where her close friends lived nearby. She didn't care about the ocean view, the massive media room, the gym, the infinity pool, or the status associated with our beachfront home's luxuries. Instead, she sought a safe and cozy space, craving joy and freedom. Free from tension, abuse, and walking on eggshells, she desired to invite whomever she wanted for dinner or a sleepover without worrying about what her father might say or do. Free from alcohol and its destructive effects on all of us, she wished to live without criticism and soar like our favourite birds.

Safety and freedom were what we found in our tranquil home across from Hans and Shelby Becker, who had four wonderful children that would visit whenever they pleased. The front door was always open, cookies filled the cookie jar, and popcorn was ready to be popped for movie nights featuring our favourite chick flicks. I couldn't believe the love and kindness that blossomed from those clean white walls, free from fear, without diminishing my spirit, and devoid of harsh judgment, like a suit of armour slowly crumbling to the ground. I felt lighter, laughed often, slept better, loved harder, entertained frequently, made homemade pies and cakes for friends, and thirsted for life without wine or beer.

My senses ignited, and I felt giddy with excitement about music, meeting new people, travelling, dancing in the kitchen while I cooked, and filling our home with friends. The financial security of ten million dollars after the divorce was finalized also brought me peace. The image of a butterfly leaving its cage flashed before me, and I couldn't wipe the smile off my heart and face.

While navigating through this turmoil, my company was sold to the

Royal Bank, and I had no desire to work for a bank. It was an easy decision to sell my shares to the bank and retire from a career I cherished, excelled in, and loved every day. It was an opportunity I would never have again, as it perfectly suited my personality and competitive spirit. However, I also have only one chance to raise a beautiful little girl who has been an innocent victim of our marriage, which was dominated by alcohol's devastating impact. Creating a safe and loving environment for her to grow up in, with a consistent parent offering her all the support and guidance she needs, is all I care about now.

Friends noticed my distinct joy and lightness. My laughter and openness were undeniable. At the next dinner party, Joey Dutton commented on how great I looked, admired my dress, complimented my longer, blonder hair, and expressed a desire to spend time with me alone. My heart raced, and the attraction felt vibrant and alive. I was now free, but he was not. That was the dilemma, yet my reckless exhilaration softly whispered, "Yes, I would love that."

With his sexy Aussie accent and husky voice, he said, "I'll call you tomorrow."

Two weeks later, sitting in 2A and lifting off from the Vancouver runway en route to Maui, I reflected on how impulsive and wild this was. Still, the adrenaline rush felt like a thrilling adventure unlike any other. Harper was spending the weekend with friends, so I didn't need to worry about her; no one needed to know. Joey was taking a scuba diving course and would be busy for a few hours each day, but this left us time to golf, play tennis, walk the beaches, go out for dinner, and experience what it would be like to be on our own for three days.

It was a captivating dream to be with a man full of vibrant energy; his mind ignited by curiosity and brilliance, a thirst for adventure, natural athletic ability in sports, and unbridled passion. His intellect was matched by a determination to achieve and succeed, understanding that patience was vital in uncovering gold and copper. Joey's energy was relentless, and I often found myself unprepared as I tried to keep pace with him physically and mentally. The challenge was both daunting and liberating after years of holding myself back. When you tiptoe around, you stifle your emotions;

your spontaneous behaviour and words become cautious and restrained, resulting in a lack of freedom.

Joey had a wonderful family, including a supportive, kind, loving wife and three beautiful children. I understood why he couldn't leave or chose not to go.

For a year, we played together on the ski slopes, our snowflake-dusted faces sharing slippery wet kisses among the snow-laden trees that left me weak at the knees. Golfing together felt unprecedented as all my senses were ignited; my mind, body, and soul throbbed with electricity. Meeting him at local hotels on Wednesdays or at conferences in Toronto or Boston came the risk of losing my friends' respect as well as and my inner turmoil of being the other woman betraying his faithful wife. Why was I able to do this, and how much longer could I sustain this affair, this hallucinogenic high, this intoxicating danger, without everything collapsing around us? I didn't want to be the reason he left his wife; he needed to leave because he was unhappy in his relationship, and it was unfair to both his wife and me to keep engaging in this deceptive game without a resolution. He assured me we would be together one day, and for a time, I believed him; I didn't know when that day would come. Eventually, it struck me that he relished having both a wife and a mistress, a role I realized I had taken on, and I cringed at the thought of it.

He was like a drug, and even though I have never experienced drugs due to my need to be in control and my respect for my health and brain, it was what I imagined. The extreme highs are addictive, like an intoxicating danger that you crave every minute of every day, and then the lows are unbearable from the withdrawals. The obsession of when you will get the next hit, the next high, the subsequent escape from the monotony of everyday life. I could not get enough of him, but he had the control strings to when I got my next hit, my next dose of danger. There was no seeing each other on holidays or weekends, only when it worked for him.

I wasn't functioning after all my craving for freedom; I had found myself in a new kind of cage that I took full responsibility for creating. I held the door open, fully aware that I was stepping into a world of deception, sleeping with another woman's husband, and lying to anyone who inquired about my relationship with Joey. How long could we maintain this charade, and who would ultimately get hurt? There were many potential victims in this game, with Joey's family being the ultimate casualty, and for that, I would never forgive myself. The guilt of harbouring this longing matched the overwhelming desire to be with him.

Skiing on weekends with friends was essential for my sanity and maintaining my sense of normalcy, except when Joey joined our group. In those moments, I could not focus and acted like a schoolgirl, with my friends aware of our obvious attraction and flirtation. We had been seeing each other for nearly a year when we went spring skiing with six friends in our group, trying to find the best runs without ice or patches of mud peeking through. It was mild and breathtaking, and everyone was excited to ski together in this haze of spring fever. I felt exhilarated skiing with Joey, and he always managed to position himself beside me, placing his hand on the seat beneath me as I settled onto the chairlift, whisking us into the air. The adrenaline made all my nerve endings tingle, heightened by electric currents.

The group took off down a steep, icy slope. I caught an edge to avoid a rock and began sliding uncontrollably towards a cliff, picking up speed. Panicking, I gripped a tree that jutted over the cliff and wrapped my arms around the trunk, hanging there with one ski still on and the other sliding on the ice above the cliff, burying its tip in the snow twenty feet below. Everyone had skied on, including Joey, and no one saw me fall. I needed help. I swung my free leg over a branch to dangle from the tree, hoping it wouldn't snap. The tree was at least forty feet above the base of the cliff as I struggled to retrieve my phone from my chest pocket without losing my balance or ski glove, hoping to call Tim from our group to get the ski patrol. My hand was shaking, and instead, I accidentally called a friend in Vancouver, telling her I was stuck in a tree on Flute Bowl and needed rescuing. All I could see below were ice and rocks, and I desperately tried to remain calm, praying that the branch wouldn't break. Julie told me not to move and that she would get the Patrollers there.

I felt scared and angry that I had crashed, upset that my group would be waiting, and worried about me. Clinging to the tree, I saw Joey's name appear on my phone. I couldn't move for fear of falling, so I let the call ring.

Three patrollers finally arrived. The problem was unclipping my boot from my ski while dangling from the tree. A female patroller climbed up from below, assisted me in taking off my ski, and gave me ropes to wrap around my waist. Two male patrollers above me pulled me up as I slipped on the ice. The two male patrollers had to secure ropes around my waist and help me climb back up, digging into the ice with my ski boots and trying not to slip.

They helped me collect my other buried ski and get to a secure spot to put my skis on again, and then off they went. My legs felt shaky and weak, but I had to find my group. I skied down cautiously and took the chairlift to the top to see their anxious faces, all waiting for me. When I skied over to them, I fell into Joey's arms and started to cry. My girlfriend had called them, so they knew I was stuck in a tree, but still, the emotions of how close I came to falling over the cliff were overwhelming.

We decided to head down, and I felt relieved, aware that I was still shaken; my nerves had already maxed out, so it was time for a break. My legs regained their strength and stability as I cautiously skied down the mountain, choosing my fall line and avoiding skiers and boarders in the centre of the run. I could see the bottom where the group was gathering and taking off their skis when someone suddenly helped me put them back on, handed me my toque and goggles, and asked if I was okay.

"What happened?" I felt dizzy, and my head was pounding. Oh my God, please don't tell me it's another accident! I must have blacked out.

"You got hit by a snowboarder and think you hit your head," a young guy was saying to me when he left me sitting on the snow and took off down the mountain.

I struggled to get up and back onto my skis, thinking I could make it to the bottom of the run. I skied straight down, and when I stopped near my friends, their faces were all agape in shock as they looked at me. I must have put my toque on in a funny way while wiping the snow from my face, which turned out to be blood. I glanced at Joey, Tim, Chloé, and Tegan as they approached, and then I collapsed, blacking out.

I was coming to when I realized I was lying in an ambulance, with two medics asking me questions. As an oxygen mask was placed over my face, I noticed the orange jacket on top of me—Joey's ski jacket.

"What is your name?"

"Where do you live?"

Now, lying on a bed in the Whistler Medical Clinic with my ski boots still on, someone was wiping my face and asking too many questions that I could not answer. The nurse has placed bandages on my nose and cheek. They've wheeled me into a large X-ray room and positioned my head in the loop of a CT scan. All I want to do is sleep, but they won't let me, even though I still have an orange jacket draped over me. Whose jacket is this again?

One of my friends in our ski group, Henry Morris, was sitting next to me. He was a plastic surgeon and was chatting with the doctor about my concussion, wondering if I had a brain bleed. They were discussing sending me to the trauma centre in Vancouver by helicopter. Another helicopter ride, I thought. This isn't good. I started asking Henry questions about Harper, and I now remember my name, but I had no idea what had happened to me. Did I fall from that tree?

Henry told me Harper was picked up from ski school by Tegan and went to the city for the birthday party. Oh yes, I remember something about a birthday party.

The room was bright and blurry, and it started turning when I tried to lift my head. A different doctor said I needed to remember three words before they could let me go home: "We will check in with you every twenty minutes to see if you can tell us the three words: cat, tree, and ball. We don't believe you have a brain bleed, but you have a severe concussion and will need someone to stay with you tonight. Can you sit up without being dizzy or stand yet? How many concussions have you had?"

"This makes five concussions, and no, I can't stand up without falling over."

"You have a concussion called a coup contrecoup injury, which hits the front of your head and then the back. You have a large bump on the back of your head, and you hit your face very hard. It occurs when the brain moves back and forth inside the skull after a blow to the head. You will need to take it easy for a few months, and you can't risk having another concussion, or it could be fatal."

Shit, what, fatal? Now, he had my attention.

As I sat up, I instantly felt nauseous, but I wanted to take my ski boots off my feet. Henry helped me do that and then tried to get me to stand up, but the room started moving from under me, and I fell over.

A nurse would peek her head in for the next four hours and ask, "What are the three words?"

I would glance at her and respond, "Not a clue," or come up with three words like "horse, road, sky."

Henry returned with my red Adidas running shoes, jeans, and a chai tea latte. He looked tired, and it must have been late, yet he was still in his ski clothes. I suggested he go home, but he said he would grab something to eat and be back.

Two hours later, around 10:00 p.m., still unable to remember the three words, the nursing shift had changed when an Asian nurse pushed open the curtain and yelled, "What are da tree words?" Tree? I think that's one of the words. She slammed the curtain closed and walked away. Okay, I have one word now. I need to remember the ball and the cat. The cat plays with the ball. I'll keep saying it until a nurse returns and lets me go home. I need a bath.

Henry pulled back the curtain and said, "We need to get you out of here. When I see the nurse, I'll give you some coaching just before so you can remember the words."

He glanced down the hall and noticed the nurse rushing to my room as he said, "Cat, tree, and ball."

The curtain flew open, and before she could say anything, I said, "Cat, tree and ball!"

"Alright, that sounds great. I'll inform the doctor and check if you can go home now."

I was allowed to leave but not be alone, so when Henry dropped me off at her log home, Tegan was waiting for me. She had my jammies, a bag with my clothes and a cosmetic bag. How did they get into my place, I wondered.

"Morgan, I must wake you up every three hours tonight, and I am so sorry for your crazy day of two accidents. Luckily, you are going to be okay. Do you want anything to eat?"

"I feel dizzy and nauseous from the concussion, and I can't take Advil for my headache, so I'm grateful to go to bed and sleep, Tegan. Thank you for helping me with Harper and letting me stay here. This day was absolutely wild, and I still can't believe it."

Exhausted with mixed emotions about being rescued from the tree and being taken by ambulance to the clinic after a massive hit to my head. It rattled all my senses, and I needed to lie down and get some sleep. The stress of remembering three words every twenty minutes in the clinic was draining. As I put my head down on the pillow, I thought, what were those three words? Damn, maybe I'll remember them in the morning.

After touching my shoulder when the alarm went off every three hours, Tegan went to another bedroom to sleep, knowing I would be okay after waking up most of the night.

The sound of Tegan's voice outside my room woke me up, and I spent a few moments trying to get my bearings and remember why I was in this strange bed. After a restless sleep, my head still hurting, I got up to the morning light and looked in the mirror at a face I did not recognize. My nose and cheek had large brown plasters on them, my one eye was black from smudged mascara and bruised with shades of green, my hair was a knotted mess, and I felt weak, my head still aching. After washing my face and brushing my teeth, I wrapped myself in Tegan's white terrycloth housecoat and got a coffee, which may help keep my head from aching.

"Good morning, Morgan. How are you feeling?"

"Like an idiot, Tegan. Falling into a tree before sliding over a forty-foot cliff and then getting a concussion all in one day is incomprehensible. Thank you again for waking me up. I am so sorry you had to do that, but I appreciate it."

"Joey Dutton called and wondered if he can drive your Range Rover down since he doesn't think you should drive. How do you feel about that?" By the look on her face, she knew.

"I think I can drive my car, Tegan. If you could thank Joey for his offer,

I would be okay with driving to the city." Did Tegan know about us? She was a friend of Joey's wife. I wanted Joey to drive me down to spend time with him, but I couldn't encourage this much longer; plus, I didn't want him to see me looking like this. While I was packing my bag, I could hear Tegan chatting with Harper on the phone, letting her know I had made it through the night and was about to drive to the city.

As I hugged Tegan goodbye, she hesitated to let me drive, but as long as I kept my head still and looked ahead, I was fine to take the wheel. The moment I got behind the wheel, I needed my sunglasses, even though it wasn't particularly bright outside. The light hurt my eyes and head, and I recalled this being one of the symptoms of a concussion.

I drove down the Sea to Sky Highway, taking in the magnificence of the mountains blanketed in snow, I had some quiet time listening to David Gray reflect on these scary accidents, knowing they were caused by my inability to focus and function with this out-of-control infatuation and my failure to be with him, sharing our relationship openly and honestly had to happen or I would spiral.

I need to be alone and sort this out.

The next day, Joey reached out to check on me and suggested getting together next week if possible. I asked him whether he had received his orange ski jacket back and thanked him for the comforting sign that he was with me, while also offering to drive me to the city. I mentioned that everyone knew, and he agreed that we couldn't keep it a secret from our friends any longer.

"Maybe the universe was telling me that I was wrong to love you and that I needed to end this clandestine relationship. Two accidents yesterday, both of which could have ended my life, feel like a massive sign to get my life and love for you in order."

"Let's meet next week to discuss what we need to do. It's no longer an accident waiting to happen. I'm sorry, Morgan. Thank goodness you are okay."

After checking into the hotel and finding our favourite room, Number 305, with its mountain and ocean view, I felt nervous and overwhelmed, knowing he must decide to leave his wife to be with me or to leave me to be with his wife. My cheek was still bruised, and the cut on my nose was healing but still evident. He looked so good when he walked into the room in his beautiful navy suit and checkered pink tie, but the pain in his eyes told me of his conflicted heart.

I voiced my concerns about the guilt that plagued my body and thought he needed to take time to sort out what he wanted. I believed that we should not see each other until he clarified what was best for him and his family. I needed to pull away, which was the hardest thing imaginable, but he felt he needed time as well, so we both ended up in tears. Music was always our thing when we were together. We loved playing new music that we had discovered or that related to our love affair. "This Year's Love at Last" by David Gray, "With or Without You" by U2, and "Hands Clean" by Alanis Morrissette were just a few. After holding each other for a long time, without speaking, Joey got up and played a song he thought was relevant. It was by an Aussie named Alex Lloyd and was titled "Amazing."

We sat quietly, listening to the words. "You were amazing." I realized Joey had chosen to play this song to say goodbye. Perhaps he had deceived me about our future together. I plunged headlong into a dangerous love, fully aware that I could get hurt. Knowing he must have done this before, during his marriage, I felt insecure. Still, I risked my heart and self-respect for the thrill of forbidden love. We were both caught between the fear of being discovered and the devastation it would cause him, his family, and all our friends, not to mention the impact on his career. As I composed myself, my eyes red and puffy, afraid of letting go and feeling painfully sad, I pressed the hotel elevator button, knowing this year's love was sadly over. As I reached into my purse to retrieve my car keys, my hands shaking and heart aching, I touched something I had pulled out upon arriving in the lobby: four one-hundred-dollar bills.

He likely wanted to pay for the day room at the hotel, but it felt strange, wrong, and shameful. I felt relieved that the affair was finally over, convincing myself we could not keep lying, but the withdrawals from this drug were going to be brutal. I was alone in facing the withdrawals and had no one to confide in about a year of wild, unbridled passion, where every sense was aflame, and every moment consumed by thoughts of him, my handsome, athletic drug. My nerves were exposed to the elements of madness, unprotected and vulnerable to whatever came my way. There was no way to live on eggshells with Harvey, nor could I manage my raw, exposed nerves around Joey, feeling out of control with both men. I needed to shield myself, so I withdrew and focused on expelling that man from my central nervous system, trying to understand why I was drawn to dangerous, risky love.

Months went by, poems were drafted at all hours of the night, tears were shed, emails were written to express my love and sadness, and I slowly crumbled, knowing he was sharing his bed with his wife and life was moving on for him. Withdrawals like this were torture, and my freedom was something I needed to regain again in my life: another man, another tortured heart.

Just as I accepted that Joey was remaining faithful in his marriage and coming to terms with his decision not to leave her to be with me, a good friend called. "Hi, Morgan. I must tell you something you may not want to hear, but I thought you should know. Joey is having an affair with the in-house lawyer's wife at his company. Joey's wife found out, kicked him out of the house, and wanted to divorce him. It sounds like he may lose his job, as the Chairman loves this lawyer and partner at the firm and is not happy about Joey's behaviour, so it's caused a real mess. I thought you should know, and I am so sorry to be the one to tell you this."

"Wow, on so many levels, Chloé. Thank you for letting me know. I'm shocked, and I guess our affair was not a secret after all. He must love the game of playing with women's hearts and lives, so he deserves whatever happens to him."

"We all knew Morgan and worried about you but hoped you would figure it out alone. He had a reputation for cheating in Australia, but you were smitten, and none of your friends felt it was our place to intervene. I hope you see who he is and feel lucky you are no longer with him as his mistress. He just blew up three marriages now, hurt you, and his wife finally said it was enough."

Then, she quietly asks, "Did you leave Harvey for Joey, Morgan?"

"He was the catalyst I needed to leave Harvey, and for that, I am grateful."

My hands shook when I said goodbye to Chloé and collapsed on the chair outside for fear of Harper hearing the call. I was stunned and heartbroken from a sense of betrayal. He promised he was sorting things out with his wife, but only two months later, he is cheating on his wife and feels like he's cheating on me as well, which seems so messed up. With space and time, I had prayed he would not be able to live without me. I loved that man with all my heart and lost my mind over him and lost so many months and days obsessing over him, craving his touch, his mind, his laughter, his hook of toxic charm. He stole my attention away from what mattered in life.

Instead of leaving his wife for me, he sought out another woman for an affair. Was he seeing the lawyer's wife at the same time he was with me? Could that be why he ended things with me? I suppose managing three relationships can get complicated. My mind shifted to anger, unresolved grief over losing him from my life, and confusion—so much confusion. I can't trust myself to choose the right man in the end. I walked toward danger and jumped, fully aware of the risk of heartache and the potential pain I could cause another innocent woman, fully mindful of the consequences of being with a married man. What the fuck was I thinking? I should have known better. Like a drug, I had to stop using it, or it would destroy me. After spending the evening oscillating between shock at the fact that he's with another woman and berating myself for being weak and unable to set boundaries against his charm, I took a ZZZ Quill. I climbed into bed far too early, but my brain and heart needed a rest.

As I drifted off, my final thought was of an animated Tasmanian devil whirling around our neighbourhood, stirring up dirt and dust everywhere, indifferent to the destruction left in its wake. Why am I drawn to narcissists? The narcissist often presents as a model citizen—charming, kind, and charismatic. They light up a room, shake hands like politicians, and win over business associates, friends, and acquaintances. They're the town's mayor, kissing babies and making everyone feel special. Yet behind that perfect façade lies a far darker reality. When the doors close and no one is watching, they reveal their true selves—manipulative, abusive, and cruel.

Their charm is merely an act—designed to deceive and extract what they want from others. This duality can leave you feeling confused, clinging to the hope that maybe, just maybe, they will be that kind and loving person to you as well.

Here's the hard truth I've learned from my experiences with narcissists: It's all a performance, and like any act, it can't last forever. They only reveal their true colours to those closest to them—those who know them behind the scenes. If you've witnessed that side of them, trust what you've seen. Don't stick around for the encore. Embrace the truth and walk away. Protect your peace and choose yourself over their endless manipulation. You deserve more than the scraps of affection they offer to keep you hooked. The hook felt like a drug to me—something I believed I needed, no matter how destructive. The addiction was real, even knowing that this power could ruin my life.

After a turbulent night of tossing, I got up early with the birds and morning light, retrieved my favourite Emma Bridgewater mug and filled it with espresso and foamed milk. Curling up in my cozy white housecoat and sitting in my favourite Adirondack chair, I took a deep breath through my nose and let it out through my mouth. All muscles relaxed as I read:

Rise
Don't get angry
Or enraged
Or insulted.
Rise above the bullshit,
Flick your light back on,
And shine it brighter than ever.
And fall so deeply in love
With your own life
That anyone who tried to wrong you
Becomes a laughable, ridiculous,
Distant memory.
By Cara Alwill Leyba

Chapter Twenty-Five

The Iron Man

After a year of emotional turmoil, shifting from anger to resentment to loneliness and finally to a sense of liberation from my emotional ties to men and the drama they bring, I decided to explore the world of online dating. My new home was tastefully decorated, providing a safe, shabby chic comfort. My daughter gradually moved on with her friends, hoping I would become less needy and more independent of her for my social life and sense of purpose.

Many friends have suggested that I go online to find a man to share my life with, but it felt more like searching for my latest outfit, new Prada shoes, or something I had to have. I have genuinely enjoyed a lovely, pain-free, drama-free, man-free year. Is it necessary to have a man in my life? The reality, however, is that I would need to present myself with all my best photos, showcasing my best features, my favourite sporting moments in golf and ski outfits, and conveying my joyful disposition. It seemed like quite a lot! Is that truly what I'd have to represent at a bar, party, or golf club if I met someone? Could I wrap my head around the idea of marketing myself online?

I signed up on Match and uploaded lively, fun-filled photos of myself being active, smiling, and eager to showcase my intelligence, character, athleticism, and sharp wit. However, I didn't include pictures of myself in a bathing suit or posing suggestively in my image collection. When I first posted my profile, I quickly received notifications stating, "Your profile is getting a lot of attention!" Soon after, photos of twenty men appeared, and I cringed.

One long-bearded man in camouflage pants stood beside his Harley-Davidson, holding a large orange cat with the message,"I think we have a lot in common."

Another man, sporting a protruding stomach and standing at the door of his Winnebago, proclaimed, "If this lifestyle excites you, let's ride."

I suddenly felt exposed, as though my privacy was laid bare for anyone on Match who wanted to view my life through photos and witness my vulnerability about being alone now.

One guy winked at me and quickly remarked, "Are these photos current? You don't look your age."

Another, who had taken far too many close-up selfies at unflattering angles and had teeth that could benefit significantly from a good Crest White strip, winked and said, "I'm heading to a barn dance, and you look like a country girl who would two-step with me on the dance floor."

I cringed before promptly deleting it. What part of my profile suggests I would two-step? If he resembled Blake Shelton, I would be thrilled to two-step and take any step on the dance floor, but not with this guy, Carter, who has bad teeth.

After a few weeks of chatting with some nice guys, but not the right ones, I decided to seek precisely what I was dreaming of. I entered these requirements into the search bar. I was curious whether I could find a man who is younger than me, athletic, sports-minded, kind, has children, ambitious, successful, passionate, with a generous spirit, possesses a sense of humour, is six feet tall or taller, has dealt with past emotional issues, and has beautiful blue eyes. Giggling to myself as if sharing my desires with the Universe, specifically with Match.com, felt akin to buying a new dress for a party.

I closed the app and went to pour myself a glass of Rosé. After getting ready for bed and curling up in my comfy chair, I opened my laptop to check if Match had found me my perfect guy. I was shocked and put on my glasses to see the images filling my computer screen. It was a beautiful, handsome man's face, with photos of his athletic body biking, running, skiing, and there he was laughing in one picture. I instantly pressed wink... and got excited about the possibility of this guy winking back. I thought this good-looking, younger guy would look at my age and hit delete as quickly as I pressed wink. Oh well, I tried. I felt this way as I brushed my teeth, then heard the distinct ping on my phone. I grabbed my phone, checked the Match app, and saw that he winked back. Oh God, now what? I decided to do what the app suggested. It's your move now; say something.

Hi, Eddie. Seeing someone normal with a similar lifestyle on this site is great. Plus, you're not holding a cat in front of your Harley.

He replied promptly, "The cat is sleeping next to the Harley in my garage, and I thought sharing that might alarm someone like you."

Humour?? Seriously?

I replied, "I hope it's not orange!"

We chatted for the next two hours, well past my bedtime. He was a delight to get to know and asked many meaningful and intriguing questions. We decided to exchange cell numbers and agreed that a walk with coffee would be an excellent first meeting. If either of us felt the "ick," we would turn around and head back.

That Sunday morning, we met at 10:00, and my friends said, "Whatever you do, don't take your golden retriever." So, naturally, I brought Phoebe, my wonderful but wild dog, because I figured that if he didn't like dogs, I wouldn't like him. I walked into the coffee shop he chose, careful not to reveal my upper-class neighbourhood, worried he might like me or judge me for all the wrong reasons. As I entered, nervous yet excited, I spotted this stunning man at the end of the counter, wearing stylish Levi jeans, a navy V-neck sweater over a white T-shirt, and slightly worn Adidas running shoes. He stood like an athlete and exuded the gentle confidence of someone comfortable in his skin.

He smiled, walked towards me, and hugged me, saying, "You must be Morgan." I couldn't stop staring into his gorgeous blue eyes, thick grey hair pushed back, square jaw, and lovely warm smile, all while he seemed oblivious to his looks. He appeared confident in how he approached me, exuding a self-assuredness that calmed my anticipation. After buying my coffee, we left, and as I walked to my car, I apologized for bringing my dog, which seemed to excite him. We started walking and casually chatting about his two kids, my daughter, and his marriage to a doctor that ended a year earlier. At one point, he tossed our cups into the garbage, and when I glanced at him, I noticed his perfectly athletic butt. He walked like an athlete, with muscular thighs and a well-defined, firm butt in those Levi 501 jeans. As we chatted, he often teased me or responded with quick wit, which I loved. I felt safe sharing my feelings about the loss of my father, my divorce, and my love for Harvey, though not for his alcoholism. He also mentioned he still loved his ex-wife, but her bipolar disorder worsened during menopause. When she was on her medication, life felt steady, but when she went off, he feared for his safety. We discussed feeling unsafe in our marriages and our concerns about the ultimate protection of our children's lives.

After two hours of walking and chasing Phoebe into properties whenever she spotted a cat or rabbit, he mentioned that he was hungry and wondered if we should grab a bite for lunch. After putting the dog in the car, we discovered a charming little Italian place for pizza, and I immediately sensed I wanted to spend more and more time with him. He was kind, gentle, and not someone who boasted about his elite athleticism. He was different from Joey and Harvey, which made me feel relieved. I wasn't sweating with anticipation but felt relatively calm and at peace in his presence. This was new to me.

We planned to meet for dinner next Thursday at one of my favourite Asian fusion restaurants, and he was excited to try it.

As soon as I got home, I googled his full name since all I had was his first name from when we met. He had shared very little about himself, offering only a brief overview of his career path, and he casually mentioned that he spent a lot of time "running," in his words. Edward G. Brooks appeared at the top of my laptop screen. He placed 10th overall in the Western States 100-mile Endurance Race, which starts in Squaw Valley and ends in Auburn, California. He consistently ranked among the top 10 to 15 in his age group across numerous fifty-mile races. The renowned Knee Knacker run, which he founded and participated in many times, crosses three local mountains in Vancouver, from Horseshoe Bay to Deep Cove, and his list of racing accomplishments continues. The next page displayed his three Ironman races in Hawaii, Penticton, British Columbia, and Kalmar, Sweden. I was astonished that he had achieved so much at an elite level and had never mentioned it in conversation.

He also won an award in his profession for creating a new system for

GPs to use to be more efficient, and he received many accolades for his academic achievements and the creative engineering systems he built for large corporations, which I had heard nothing about. I was now in total awe and shocked that none of these enormous accomplishments were mentioned. An Iron Man competition is a stunning achievement with the 2.4-mile swim, the 112-mile bike ride, and a marathon of 26.22 miles. It's inconceivable, and I thought I was great running the Vancouver Seawall in less than an hour. Thank God I didn't mention that, and worse, brag about it like I tend to do. I only mentioned my golf as a junior and becoming a ski instructor...Yikes, I may have boasted a bit. The poor guy. He must have been biting his lip not to hint at his elite accomplishments.

Eddie confirmed dinner at my favourite Asian fusion restaurant, Bao Bei. Given his blue eyes, stunning physique, and calm, steady, and secure demeanour, I was thrilled to spend more time with him.

The conversation flowed effortlessly, our chemistry was powerful, and our curiosity about each other deepened with every new chapter of our lives. I asked him what his "deal breaker" was in a new relationship. The words slipped from my lips before I could think. He looked down at his plate, lost in thought, took a slow sip of his red wine, then looked at me and said firmly, "Drama."

After another sip of wine, he asked, "What is your deal breaker?"

Without hesitation, I replied, "Substance abuse, emotional abuse, physical abuse—any abuse." I maintained eye contact, feeling confident about our boundaries and knowing we would be together. It felt like we had discovered the right person for the rest of our lives. Perhaps we were finally being rewarded for the pain and suffering we had endured in our previous marriages.

As if he sensed my thoughts and feelings, he took my hand and said quietly, "I'll never be that guy."

As we exited the restaurant, an attractive businesswoman at the entrance glanced our way and spontaneously said, "Wow, you are a striking couple. You are beautiful together."

We exchanged glances, laughing and expressing our gratitude, if only she knew it was our first official date. He walked me to my car, embraced me, and whispered, "I want to see you again soon."

Driving home, I realized how alive I felt with someone who saw and appreciated me. The chemistry was so electric that I felt caffeinated and buzzed from the excitement of being with someone incredible and stunningly handsome. I cranked up the One Direction song and sang loudly to the lyrics of "Night Changes." Those words felt so poignant at that moment. When I glanced at the guy beside me in the car at the red light, he smiled, and I nodded, turning the song up even louder. Yes, it's amazing how quickly the night changes and how swiftly one can fall in love, with no doubts or fears, just complete reassurance that he can be trusted with my heart.

As I drifted off to sleep, I thought of Eddie Brooks and wondered if he slept naked. I imagined him naked, and with that last image in my mind, I melted into dreamland.

Chapter Twenty-Six

Cottage Wedding

Things progressed quickly and energetically with Eddie and me. He moved into my home within a month of that prawn and feta dinner, as we discovered that having dinner at my place was far more intimate and private than dining at a restaurant. We had so much to learn about each other, like how he could make me laugh and surprised me with his interests, such as studying wine and becoming a sommelier for fun. When he put his mind to something, like improving his golf game, he took lessons twice a week and read everything he could find on perfecting his swing. He was curious about everything, from other cultures and their food to the political landscapes of various countries. We made a bucket list of places to explore and possibly live in one day. We shared our dreams, no matter how crazy or absurd, waking each other up at two in the morning just because we could.

Within months of living together, he showed me photos of various rings he wanted to buy for me. One Sunday morning, after I had brought our cappuccinos to bed along with the weekend newspaper, a full-page ad featured this magnificent eternity ring sparkling off the page. The glittering diamonds encircling the finger symbolize the eternity of our love and the inescapable joy of knowing we have each other for the rest of our lives. I rolled over him and whispered, biting his ear, "That's the one, you're the one, and now we are one."

We got married the following summer at our family cottage on the St. Lawrence River, surrounded by my family, Eddie's two children, Harper, and my brothers with their kids. I loved seeing all the ages, from three to eighty-five, on the country farm with hay bales and open meadows, where horses roamed the property next to ours. We strolled along a country road early in the morning with our dogs and coffee or after dinner while the sun set across the river. We had a tennis court, a guest house, and a large tree house, aptly named the Bunky, for the kids to play in or sleep. Tied to our dock were two Lasers and a classic Hinckley that my mother insisted on having, as they were the highest quality boats, beautifully designed with their navy-blue hulls and exquisite finishings. We loved taking the Hinckley down the river to the Thousand Islands Theatre for productions every summer, enjoying dinner on the boat at the dock before heading in for Mamma Mia or whatever musical was playing that summer.

We had a white tent, and a caterer set up the buffet after the ceremony. I wore a 1950s-style white strapless wedding dress with a fitted bodice, complemented by a mid-length crinoline beneath the satin A-line skirt. In my white heels, I felt like Doris Day, and I was thrilled to be marrying such an incredible man. Due to the humidity, my hair fell loosely in soft blonde curls, and my bouquet burst with vibrant summer colours of orange, yellow, bright pink, and purple. They reflected my heart, alive with life, love, and the bold assurance of the man I was about to marry. The day was beautiful, with warm air, a light breeze drifting off the water, and stunning aquamarine skies above, dotted with brilliant white, fluffy cumulus clouds. As I made my way down the rocky path from the cottage to the man waiting for me in his navy-blue suit and warm smile, I was accompanied by the distinct trill of a red cardinal, the distant neigh of a horse, and Rascal Flatts playing our song that spoke so sweetly to us. "I will stand by you, see you through, even when you feel lost; I will never let you down."

That was when the tears flowed freely. I paused and turned to gaze into the magic of his soft blue eyes, which sparkled with tears as well. We cherished this moment as if no one else were present. Just the two of us stood together, aware that we had each other to face our struggles, dry one another's tears, and support each other through whatever storms lay ahead.

After exchanging our vows, I hugged him and nestled my face into his neck. I just wanted to breathe him in and never let go. I whispered, "I love you, Edward G. Brooks."

He leaned back and smiled, cradling my face in his hands, and whispered, "Till death do us part," before kissing me and sending a current through my body that only lovers could understand.

Carly, Ben's wife, graciously volunteered to be our photographer, turning the photos into treasures I will cherish forever. My favourite was the one she captured of me nestled into Eddie's neck, reluctant to leave that safe, delightful space. I also adored the photo of me leaping off the dock, bouquet in hand, arms outstretched, with the large white satin bow fluttering behind me and the bride soaring into the sunset.

Chapter Twenty-Seven

Balloon Filled with Rain

The next five years were filled with adventure. We settled into golfing during the summers, skiing at Whistler in the winters, travelling to Scotland to visit Harper at the University of St. Andrews, joining friends for splendid bike trips in France and Portugal, and spending time in Maui golfing and strolling along the expansive sandy beaches. Eddie was a kind, loving man who made life enjoyable and remarkably easy. I wasn't familiar with a relationship where I didn't feel constantly on edge, walking on thin ice, and getting shivers down my spine when the door opened at two in the morning, accompanied by the strong scent of alcohol. I was now in a safe place with a trusting, kind man who gave me the freedom to soar, knowing that if my wings were clipped, he would help me regain my strength—a man who empowers you, rather than one who holds power over you.

Every summer, Harper, Eddie, and I returned to the cottage on the St. Lawrence River to spend time with my mother and stepdad, Alan, whom I adored, my brother's family from New York, and any other relatives who could join us during that week. It was a tradition I genuinely cherished, and I always looked forward to arriving at the little eleven-car ferry that took us from the mainland to Howe Island in just ten minutes. It felt like pure meditation after a five-hour flight and a three-hour drive to the ferry. I would turn off the car, shut down the music, open the windows, and breathe in the humid air as the haunting call of the loons welcomed us back.

After five years of marriage and five summers at the cottage, my stepdad Alan pulled me aside to the sun porch, where most private conversations occurred. He quietly conveyed, with his faltering speech due to a recent dementia diagnosis, that he did not want to live with this illness. Alan had been a highly respected internist at Kingston General Hospital before retiring and becoming a professor of medicine at Queen's University.

He said, "My body will outlive my mind, and that means I will be a burden to your mother and my children. I don't want that to happen."

He was earnest, and I looked up at him, asking, "What will you do since MAiD is not available to people with dementia?"

He took his hand up to his head and held one finger in the shape of a gun to his temple.

Shocked by his response, I asked, "Have you told Mom this?"

"No, and please say nothing. I have talked to my son Cam, and we have decided the best plan." I looked at him, knowing his demented mind was made up, and I supported him, knowing that losing his dignity and his mind would be the worst curse for such a brilliant man. I witnessed that close-up with my father and would never wish that fate on another person I loved so dearly.

Tears welled up, and all I could say was, "I love you and support your decision."

My mother stepped into the sunroom with an iced tea for Alan. I wondered if she had overheard our conversation, but she cheerfully said, "I think it's Rosé time for us, don't you, Mugs?" I realized she hadn't heard a thing.

"By all means," I attempted to rally, though my voice cracked, betraying my shock and sadness over Alan's plan. It unsettled me how resolute he was and how he didn't want to discuss his impending death with the woman with whom he had just shared 35 years of his life.

This time, I felt so sad for my mother, knowing what horrific heartache she would be subjected to in the not-too-distant future. She and Alan had thirty-five incredible years together, filled with travel, adventure, big family gatherings, intense chemistry, ballroom dancing where people stood back to watch their magic, and constant love and laughter. They had been a formidable team.

I knew my mother would look after Alan until the day he died, even if he did not know her anymore. She was a trained nurse who went to visit a friend with Alzheimer's for years, knowing her friend did not know who she was. Her loyalty to the ones she loved, taking the same photos with every visit, astounded me. I wanted to protect her, but I gave my word to Alan and did not feel it was my place to interfere with his plan to end his beautiful, remarkable life.

When we left that summer and gathered in the driveway to say goodbye, Alan gave me the longest, warmest hug ever. I whispered so no one could hear me, "I'll miss you very much."

Luckily, I was wearing my sunglasses, so when I hugged Mom, she did not notice the tears welling up in my eyes, hoping they would not roll down my cheek.

My heart ached, knowing I may not see Alan again. The strength of his presence around our family was powerful; the tea towel was over his left shoulder when he did the dishes as soon as he finished dinner to avoid our family discussions on religion or politics. It never ended well. I loved our evening walks on the country road when he would tell me my mother was driving him crazy, trying to control him since his retirement, losing his identity as a doctor, or his daughter taking too long getting her PhD in London, England. We had such wonderful, meaningful conversations that I cherished every summer, and I turned to him with whatever male issues I was having at the time, and I always seemed to be having them each summer.

Driving slowly down the long dirt road, under the shade of the enormous oak trees acting like sentries, sunlight dappling through, I glanced in my rearview mirror to see everyone heading back to the cottage except Alan, with one hand over his heart and the other high in the air waving. I thrust my hand out of the sunroof and clenched my hand into a fist to honour his courage, and then I wept until we reached the ferry. Saying goodbye to someone you love so dearly is beyond heart-crushing.

Two weeks later, on the August 1st long weekend, I had friends over for a summer dinner party in the courtyard. The music was loud, our conversation energetic and interspersed with much laughter, and Eddie walked by, handing me my cell phone, saying, "It keeps ringing. I'm not sure who is trying to reach you."

I saw three missed calls from the cottage, which seemed strange on a Saturday evening at nine p.m. their time. I was about to bring the salads and salmon for Eddie to BBQ but went into our bedroom to call the cottage, expecting my mother's voice on the other end.

Henry answered on the first ring, "Mugs, Alan has drowned. The paramedics are down on the dock with Mom, and she is in shock. I don't understand it. Alan was a good swimmer, and they were just by the dock when he drowned. I don't get it. Do you think he had a heart attack?"

My heart sank, knowing this was how he decided to end his life in the water in front of the cottage with his wife of thirty-five years next to him. All I could say to Henry was, "He did this on purpose, Henry, and chose to end his life by drowning. He no longer wanted to live with dementia and knew his body would outlive his mind. I'm so sorry for Mom, as it has shocked her, I'm sure. Thank you for calling and letting me know. Please ask Mom to call me no matter what time. She will want to contact his children to let them know."

"I can't believe he killed himself," mumbled Henry, and then the phone goes dead.

I closed my eyes, put one hand over my heart and the other straight into the air, clenching my hand in a fist, and quietly whispered, "Alan, you are a courageous man, and I will love you forever. Rest in peace."

My mother couldn't accept that it was suicide, that he hadn't warned her, that he hadn't left her a note, that there were no signs of his intentions, and that she no longer had control. She could only question why he didn't take a towel to the dock for their nightly swim together before dinner. "I won't need it," he told her. My poor mother didn't believe me until she spoke to his son Cam, a doctor. He met her at the cottage the next day and explained how he and his father had sat at the end of the dock one day, discussing whether drowning is painful and how one would orchestrate it. Cam reassured my mother that he didn't want to be a burden to his children or her, and he felt incapable of writing a note that could encapsulate his pain and his final decision to end his life. They hugged and cried, and Cam comforted her, confirming that this was what he wanted; no matter how much he loved her and his family, he could not endure losing what he valued most: his mind.

Two weeks later, we held Alan Coval's Celebration of a Remarkable

Life, featuring heartfelt tributes and beautiful stories about a life lived with honour and integrity, just as he wished. For the first time in her life, my mother appeared frail, barely able to communicate with the friends who came to pay their respects. She was a proud woman and had been with a man since her teens. Alan appeared very quickly after my father passed away, just as he had predicted. One month after my father's death, he left his wife to be with my mother. This was not her plan; she would have cared for him and controlled the outcome if she could, but he took that control away from her. I wonder if that shocked her more than the sudden loss of her loving husband. Was there a hint of "Fuck you" in his goodbye? We will never know, but I suspect there may have been, especially since he didn't leave his wife a farewell message.

After gathering for a reception, the family headed to the cottage for our traditional bonfire on the beach. Mom picked handfuls of fresh mint from the garden for peppermint tea, I grabbed bottles of wine, and we made our way down to the dock, accompanied by the soft murmurs of the grandchildren who had experienced their first loss. As s'mores were prepared with brown, often charred marshmallows, milk chocolate squares, and graham wafers, we reminisced about Alan; the grandchildren shared their favourite stories of their cherished mentor and most trusted advisor. Harper and I picked up sixteen red heart-shaped balloons, allowing each person to say their goodbyes at the end of the dock. While everyone continued sharing their warm memories, I quietly walked to the car and brought them down, offering a cheerful break from the gloom.

Each family member, from the eight-year-old to the eighty-five-year-old, had their moment at the end of the dock to say goodbye and let the balloon fly free into the air.

When it was Harper's turn, she paused and glanced back at us, her finger pressed to her lips, "Shhhhh. Listen!" In the distance, we heard the haunting, wavering call of the loon echoing across the rippled water.

My mother's weak, cracked voice shattered our trance at that distinct call, "That's Alan, that's your Pa. The loon appeared the night he died. He's here with us, listening to all your words and feeling all your love."

Harper stood frozen at the end of the dock, bidding farewell to the only grandfather she knew. She lifted the balloon string with her right hand, and as the red heart fluttered in the breeze, she released it.

I handed the last heart-shaped balloon to my mother, who sat in her white Adirondack chair, a Hudson Bay blanket draped over her lap. She cradled her tea with both hands, seemingly lost in thought, as she gazed at the glow of the orange, red, and yellow sunset casting beams across the water.

"Mom, it's your turn to let your balloon go at the end of the dock." I gently brought her back from wherever her mind had wandered.

She slowly looked up at me, tears brimming, and whispered, "I can't, Morgan. My balloon is filled with rain."

Chapter Twenty-Eight

Energetic Vortex

That week in late August blended goodbyes and highs, celebrating remarkable souls. Harper and I attended the last Tragically Hip concert in Kingston, knowing it marked the end of the Hip's performances together, as their lead singer, Gord Downie, had been diagnosed with a glioblastoma brain tumour the year prior. This was his farewell to his fans and his band. The arena was packed, with every fan singing along to each song the band played, interspersed with tears and cheers. I had never witnessed such immense love, with thousands of people singing in unison, fully aware this was the last time they would see their beloved band live and in person. Knowing Gord had only months to live, the band must have felt heartbroken saying goodbye to their brother and bandmate of forty years, acknowledging their careers were coming to a complete stop at the end of this concert. There wasn't a dry eye in the venue, not even Justin Trudeau's. The Canadian Prime Minister, stood gallantly behind me wearing his favourite black Hip T-shirt, singing loudly along to "Ahead by a Century." The fans sang the chorus even louder: "No dress rehearsal, this is our life." Gord Downie was a brilliant, prolific poet, and we are all robbed of the future poems, lyrics, and reflections of the Canadian stories he shared with us, his band acting as the wind beneath his wings. Canadian hearts were one that night—broken but bursting with pride.

Eddie and I returned to work and spent quiet evenings having dinner together, playing Scrabble, watching documentaries, and trying to resume the rhythm of our lives. We spent our weekends skiing, enjoying fresh snow under our skis, and curling up around a fire at night. It was a joyous, carefree feeling, and I kept reminding myself to stay strong and healthy so we could continue skiing. The reminder that without our health, we have nothing resonated with me that winter.

Eddie's 60th was fast approaching, and we were shocked and relieved at how fit and healthy we were. We never took it for granted, eating well and avoiding red meat, too much wine, sugar, and dairy. We joked that 60 must be the new 40.

I loved marking big occasions with celebrations, no matter how small. Eddie loved the idea of driving around Tuscany for his birthday, exploring various vineyards, wine tasting, and taking in all Italy has to offer. I had experienced hiking through Tuscany ten years before, so I suggested marking this big day with a trek from Cusco to Machu Picchu, something significant. I suggested trekking through the mountains and ending up at the top of Macha Picchu on Eddie's birthday.

At first, he was reluctant. Visions of renting a standard Maserati or Alpha Romeo percolated in his dreams, with him at the wheel, sunglasses on, hair blowing, navigating the narrow streets of Montalcino. I got it, but being the passenger in that dream, drinking wine all day, whipping around the corners of little towns, was something other than what I was keen on doing. I know. It wasn't my birthday.

Ultimately, we agreed on the trek ending on his birthday in May at the top of this magical historical site in Peru. Five months later, in October, we would go to Italy and live out his dream—a perfect solution. Eddie and I could always resolve issues with his ex, the children, and friends, as well as challenging work issues that we shared. We ended each day cuddled together, me in that safe, delicious spot nestled into the warmth at the nape of his neck.

May arrived quickly, and I ensured we had all the necessary clothing: hiking boots, gaiters, rain gear, backpacks, bandanas, hats, sunscreen, bug repellent, Diamox for altitude, water bottles with filters, and more. The trek led us over the Salcantay Pass, which rises to 15,300 feet. We needed to be prepared if we didn't adjust well to the altitude. The Mountain Lodges of Peru I reserved were fantastic, as they provided lodges to stay in along the route with hot showers, duvets, and bedding imported from Austria, along with delicious, nutritious meals in the evening and for breakfast, as well as packed lunches during the six to seven-hour hikes each day.

We arrived in Cusco and could hardly walk off the plane as the altitude of 10,000 feet halted us in our tracks. One of the guides on our flight from Lima could be overheard saying, "Slow, slow, slow." It wasn't easy to catch our breath, but we were welcomed with coca tea in the hotel reception area in Cusco. Not many of us enjoyed the taste, but we had heard it was used by the Indigenous people of the Andes for medicinal purposes, including reducing fatigue, acting as a stimulant, and preventing altitude sickness. Eddie and I settled into our room and changed out of our travel clothes into our casual dinner attire to meet the group of people with whom we would be spending the next seven days. It was incredibly exciting to join this group of like-minded individuals with interesting backgrounds from various cultures, bonding over our love for exploring a new country on foot. These people's adventurous spirit, shared curiosity and passion for discovering new cultures, and the challenge of pushing themselves physically and mentally created an instant appreciation and respect.

Every morning, excitement filled the air in anticipation of the upcoming adventure as we gathered around the communal table to discuss our lives, careers, and children. At the table sat an internist from Los Angeles conducting research in genomics, which I found fascinating. He summarized his studies on genome structure, function, evolution, mapping, and editing. A genome represents an organism's complete set of DNA, encompassing all its genes.

I asked him, "What is the one thing you have learned that we should give up for a long, healthy life?"

He looked up from his meal, met my gaze, and replied, "Alcohol." This elicited a gasp from the group who had been so eager for their wine or pisco sour that evening. I felt somewhat vindicated for leaving Harvey and agreed that alcohol had never served me or the people I loved well.

Every day, I made it a point to hike with a new person, listening to a new story of a life lived, traumas suppressed, and proud moments shared. It was truly fascinating to discover that someone you believed to be a quiet, demure housewife who adored her two children and played tennis turned out to be a Supreme Court judge named Patty.

Mai Rutherford was a tall Japanese American woman I was most curious about. She walked with authority, was around forty years old, and had confidence and serenity. One morning, while we were lacing up our hiking boots, gathering our poles, and getting ready for the eight o'clock departure, I looked at Mai and said, "I've been trying to guess what career you are in."

She smiled and walked out the front door, saying, "You have seven hours of hiking to find out."

I learned that Mai Rutherford's father was a neurosurgeon at Mount Sinai who married her Japanese mother, a pediatric oncologist. She graduated from medical school, but she has not revealed her career.

We grabbed our cameras or phones and took photos of the sun peeking between the two snow-covered peaks. The air was so crisp and clear. There was not a town or road for miles and miles. The only access to these lodges we were hiking to each day was by foot, with supplies brought in by horse, donkey or helicopter. I adjusted the red scarf around my neck, tightened the straps on my backpack, and went over to Eddie to take a selfie with the mountains behind us. He loved the trek, the people, and the daily challenge of hiking over mountains to our next lodge. Thank God, I thought, as I had pressured him into spending his 60th trekking to Machu Picchu and not touring Tuscany.

We found our pace with our guide, Alejandro. If anyone tried to pass him, he would extend his pole and gently tap your boot to encourage you to return to the line, reminding us to go slow, slow, slow. We were striving to reach the Salcantay Pass that day, so we knew we needed to pay attention to our guides. The altitude at the peak of the pass was 15,300 feet, and after that, we would spend the next three days hiking toward Machu Picchu at 9,000 feet. I started feeling lightheaded, probably due to my low blood pressure, as we neared the top of the pass. Eddie held back to wait for me and said, "Follow my boots, one step at a time." There was oxygen available if we needed it. Instead, I received a Cliff bar from Eddie, who knew I needed some energy.

We all stood by the Salcantay Pass sign for a group photo, proud of our achievement of climbing for four hours straight up, and we knew we were now heading to a lower altitude for the rest of the trip. The eight of us were giddy with the lack of oxygen, a great sense of accomplishment, and absorbing the magnificence of the range of mountains that took our breaths away. Sharing in that moment created an incredible bond of humanity. No matter where you came from or who you were, we were together on that mountaintop.

We hiked another hour to find an orange tent over a long table. Guides were preparing our hot lunch of potato, leek soup, and pasta primavera, followed by coca brownies, which everyone loved. The spirit was high, and the laughter was more significant than usual, with the group feeling more comfortable and teasing each other, which came naturally, like time spent with family. I gave a toast to all of us getting to the top and to my husband Eddie, who will celebrate his 60th in three days with all of them. I had not mentioned his birthday before, but everyone got very excited that we would all be together on his big day, and that started a whole new flurry of conversations around the table about how young he looked and what a perfect way to celebrate. They all felt honoured and excited to participate in the party on top of Machu Picchu, which was an additional thrill for us to look forward to and another bond for us to share. I made a mental note to order cake when we arrived at the hotel the day before our ascent.

Sipping my coca tea, which tasted like mud blended with marijuana leaves, I glanced down at the far end of the table at Mai and exclaimed, "You're either a surgeon or an investment banker."

Carol, the friend she'd brought from New York, chuckled and said, "Finally, you guessed it. She's an investment banker and Vice President at Solomon."

Mai held her head and looked up with a smile, her toque sitting low over her eyes. She pointed a finger at me and said, "See, we're the same."

Everyone laughed, commenting, "Oh no, now two will be too much."

Eddie remarks, "They'll never be too much; they'll continue entertaining us. Cheers to M&M!"

Eddie tugged my toque down over my eyes and kissed me, prompting laughter from the group. My love for Eddie felt like pure, raw magic at that moment. Trusting someone with your whole heart, not holding back but feeling free to be yourself and love unconditionally, is the most beautiful human experience.

As we put on our packs and quietly descended the mountain, each lost in our private thoughts, I reflected on the poem that captured my love for Eddie. I wanted to write it down tonight and read it to him. It went something like this:

I love you not just for who you are but also for who I become when I'm with you. I love you for the part of me that you bring out, subtly present in my life, and for revealing all the beautiful treasures that no one else has looked deeply enough to find. I love you because you have done more than any creed could to make me good and more than any destiny could bring me happiness. You have achieved this without a touch, a word, or a sign- simply by being yourself. Perhaps that, after all, is what true love really means.

It felt as though Eddie was reading my mind when I saw him glance back with a warm smile, and I responded with a thumbs-up. All good, Eddie! With only two more days of hiking, sweating, and trekking through the mountain trails, we had the time to be alone with our thoughts or engage in conversations about the most fascinating topics, free from distractions and with ample time. It's a beautiful gift to know someone, especially when you suspect you may never see them again. It provides a lot of freedom to express yourself without fear of judgment or consequences for what you did or said when you returned home. I heard about worries concerning their children, retirement years, losses that had torn them apart, health concerns, career stresses, and future bucket list trips. Eddie was becoming good friends with George, a competitive cyclist who had given it up a decade ago. He was a mining engineer, who had travelled around the world with his company and was now beginning to slow down and enjoy himself.

On the morning of May 9th, Eddie woke up to find two presents at the end of his bed, which I had hidden in my backpack to surprise him. I jumped over him in my cozy housecoat and exclaimed, "Happy 60th birthday, Eddie!" As he tried to wake up, I lay on top of him, and he grabbed me, pulling me under the covers.

We checked into the magnificent Sanctuary Lodge, the only hotel near Machu Picchu. This five-star accommodation is nestled in a magical setting, surrounded by diverse trees, a stream, and the calls of exotic birds. Staying at the hotel granted us early access to the Inca citadel at dawn, allowing us to view the ancient ruins while enjoying breakfast at sunrise and relishing its inherent tranquility. The subtropical landscape enveloped us as we drove along the winding road through the rainforest. No tourists are permitted to ascend to the top due to concerns about erosion and preservation. We had the most exceptional guide and storyteller, who led us in wonder, recounting ancient rituals and cultural ceremonies. We learned that it had been abandoned for nearly a century, with dense vegetation obscuring it, and due to its location atop a steep mountain, no one suspected it was there. Hiram Bingham was an academic, explorer, soldier, and American senator credited with the discovery of Machu Picchu by climbing to the top of this steep ridge surrounded by deep valleys, where the small peaks of the ruins peeked through.

Eddie and I sat on a ledge with our feet hanging over the edge, his arm around me, as we watched the sun emerge like massive streams of orange and yellow light behind the steep ridges below. I wished him the happiest birthday and many more to come. He turned to me, quietly saying, "I couldn't be happier than in this moment with you. It's magic, Morgan. I wasn't aware of the spiritual element one feels when sitting on an energetic vortex."

I appeared interested in that term, and he said, "A vortex is thought to be a specific location on the earth where energy is either entering or projecting out of the earth's plane. Vortexes can be found at sacred sites around the world, and this is one of them. No wonder I feel so connected to the Universe right now."

The sun was beginning to warm our faces, and the group was slowly gathering behind us. They started singing, "Happy Birthday to you… Happy birthday, dear Eddie, happy birthday to you!" Eddie wiped a tear from his eye, and at that moment, I could not have loved another human more.

Cheers to Eddie and the Energetic Vortex!!

Chapter Twenty-Nine

The Call of the Loon

The summer, with its longer days and warmer nights, was settling in, and I always wonder how we manage to get through those short, cold days of winter when it's light until almost ten at night, as opposed to losing our daylight at four in the afternoon. Summers always meant returning to the cottage on the St. Lawrence River outside Kingston, but this summer would be difficult without Alan. He was a rock and a mentor, especially to Ben as a teenager. Alan took Ben under his wing after my father passed away and supported him during all the challenging times in his teens and twenties, navigating girlfriends and school. Ben has been living in New York since graduating from university and enjoys raising his two children there with his wife, Carly. This summer marked the first anniversary of a challenging year filled with sadness and grief for my mother. She wanted the entire family to gather at the cottage to honour this anniversary and celebrate her life and the life she once shared with my father. Eddie and I returned a few days before August 1st, the anniversary, so Harper could spend time with us before heading back to work in Vancouver. Eddie brought his son Dax, now fourteen, for the week to hang out with my brother's kids, who were close to Dax's age. Dax, a natural athlete like his father, got along well with everyone but particularly enjoyed competing on the tennis court and in the one-mile run around the country road loop.

The morning of August 1st began with a kiss on my cheek and Eddie whispering, "I love you." I rolled over, hugged him, and whispered, "I love you more." As I brushed my teeth and got ready, I could hear the gentle trill of the red cardinal outside. This unique sound of the family cottage, plus the lapping of the lake against the shore, always made me smile. A distinct bird calls out to me wherever I travel, welcoming me to its home.

Dax walked into the bedroom, excited about the day of cliff jumping at Bob's Lake. Eddie and I were invited to my good friend's lake north of Kingston so the kids could swim, go tubing, and visit the famous cliff jumping spot. We could then return to their island for a BBQ hot dog and picnic lunch. This would keep the kids busy while Mom and Carly prepared dinner for tonight's anniversary.

I drove, knowing the way to Pippa and Alex Henry's Island, while Eddie managed the music and entertained the three kids in the backseat with a car game. "Name the type of car coming toward us first!" Dax, Hailey, and Johnny enjoyed guessing the vehicles, even though Mazdas, Hondas, Jeeps, and Volvos were the most common options on a country road. Johnny was twelve and Hailey just eight, so I knew I had precious cargo in the car and wanted to ensure their safety that day. A Tragically Hip song played on the radio, and Johnny sang every word to "Ahead by a Century." We joined in unison, "You are ahead by a century, no dress rehearsal, this is our life."

Eddie spotted a Tim Horton's and wanted to stop for some Timbits and coffee, prompting the kids to shout, "Tim's donuts, Tim's donuts!" I checked the time and remembered that Pippa would be at the loading dock across from her cottage waiting, and I didn't want to be late, so I said, "No Tim's for you! On the way home, I promise we'll get Tim's!" I think Eddie was more disappointed than the kids were.

We arrived on time to see Pippa waving from her boat at the end of the dock. I have always cherished visiting my university friend during our annual trip, as she radiates remarkable joy and an adventurous spirit. We brought all the towels, a picnic basket, a homemade blueberry pie, a beach bag filled with sunscreen, hats, and a change of clothes. I adored their rustic cabin, which was fully screened-in, where diffused sunlight danced on the cozy beds adorned with quilts and flannelette sheets. The old wood stove warmed the cabin at night, and the antique tables were covered with puzzles, board games, and magazines. Yet, the best part was the signature screen door slam, a crescendo of cottage living, announcing someone's arrival or departure. Their cabin, perched on elevated land, provided views of the lake along with breathtaking sunrises and sunsets, allowing us to immerse ourselves in the tranquillity of the water, interrupted only by the distinct call of the loon. They had running water piped from the lake and an outdoor kitchen boasting a stunning view.

I introduced the kids to Pippa, as Eddie had met her a few times during our cottage visits. There were plenty of hugs on the boat, and then we sped across the lake, making sure the kids wore their life jackets. Pippa shouted above the engine noise that we should do cliff jumping first and take the kids tubing on the way there. Dax smiled and replied, "That sounds perfect."

This kid loved the thrill of mountain biking over hills and tree skiing after fresh snow, always eager to try new things. As we approached their dock on the island, I saw Alex waiting for us with their black lab, Frankie, who was excited when the boat arrived. Alex helped us dock the boat and secured the bow while Eddie tied the ropes at the stern. When Eddie jumped out of the boat to greet Alex, he looked particularly handsome in his blue gingham linen shorts, a white T-shirt, a baseball cap, and flip-flops. His firm, muscular build and legs complemented the shorts perfectly. Although Alex was fifteen years older than Eddie, he had a kind, generous spirit and an adventurous nature that matched Pippa's enthusiasm. We all carried something up the hill to their cottage, changed into our bathing suits, and ensured everyone had sunscreen, sun hats, and towels. I brought the picnic basket with water and snacks for the kids until we returned for lunch—the checklist for a perfect day.

As I rushed back into the bedroom where we had changed, I noticed Eddie's blue gingham shorts lying neatly on the bed, his Tag Heuer watch beside them, and his white T-shirt folded beside the shorts. I grabbed my cover-up to avoid burning while sitting on the boat.

Dax was the first in the inner tube as we set off on the flat, calm lake. Eddie wore a broad smile, watching his son whip back and forth across the wake, trying to go as far as he could, all while knowing that his son had been through a lot with the divorce and the ongoing bitter battle with his mother. I sensed that Eddie viewed this as a cherished moment when he could be a kid, free from adult drama.

Next came Johnny and Hailey, with Pippa at the wheel, trying to ensure that each received equal time tubing. The spirits were high on such a glorious day, with Pippa and me yelling over the sound of the motor, catching up after a year apart. She's a friend for life—the kind you don't check in with for months, and when you do, it's as if no time has passed. A calm, secure feeling sets in, allowing you to be yourself—someone who knows your past without judgment and cheers you on into your future.

We slowed as we neared a secluded area where the cliffs loomed large. Only a few boats drifted nearby—some engaged in fishing, while others transported kids to the cliffs. The scene was serene, interrupted only by the gentle hum of motors, occasionally pierced by excited shouts and the splash of water from someone diving in.

Before we anchored, the three kids had taken off their life jackets and jumped into the water. Pippa yelled as they swam to the shore to wait for us before leaping. Eddie pulled in the inner tube while Pippa lowered the anchor. I jumped into the water, anxious about Hailey trying to keep up with the boys, reminding her to only go to the first ledge. I spotted Dax heading for the highest ledge, at least thirty-five feet up. Johnny stopped at the middle ledge, fifteen feet below, and while they were positioned and ready to jump, I shouted to them, "Don't jump until Eddie gets here."

I needed to ensure we were prepared if one of the kids got hurt. I knew these cliffs, which scared most people, would give Dax an adrenaline rush. Looking back at Eddie, I saw him take off his T-shirt, hat and sunglasses and felt so happy he was having this time with his son. He dove in and swam the competitive crawl he would have used in his Iron Men and triathlons, which was beautiful to watch. When he got next to me, he looked at me with his stunning blue eyes, and I gave him the thumbs-up with, "Nice stroke, Eddie," then looked up at the kids and said, "You can go now; Eddie is here."

While treading water, I looked up at the cliff wall at the three kids, knees bent, hands in front, in position to jump, when Dax took one step to the edge and stopped to yell, "Where's Dad?"

I instantly looked next to me where Eddie was one second ago, and there was no ripple or bubble. The water was flat and calm. He was gone.

I yelled as loud as I could, "He's gone!"

I plunged down, but the lake was filled with green pollen so that I could see nothing. "Goggles! Help! Please!" I shouted at the boaters.

Pippa yelled for everyone to line up to kick together above where he had gone down. I frantically kept diving, but all I saw was green, realizing by now he was slowly dropping to the bottom of the lake, and knowing that was my last sight of his loving blue eyes.

"I can't see!" I shouted and dove down once more.

I surfaced at the same time Dax did, and we stared at each other, and all I could say was, "He's gone, Dax—my God, he's gone."

His face was ashen white, overwhelmed by the reality of never seeing his father again. As I continued treading water, the boaters searching for him gradually gave up, realizing it was too late after a certain point. Pippa swam up to me and said she was taking the children back to Goat Island, where Alex would look after them, and that the police had been notified and were on their way. She assured me she would return as soon as possible. "Morgan, you will get through this."

Treading water, all alone and in shock, a young girl on a jet ski approached me and asked if I wanted to get out of the water and sit at the back of her jet ski until the police boat arrived. I barely had the strength to pull myself out. I sat at the back and asked her not to move so we could let the police know exactly where he went down. My mind felt numb, but I heard a voice whisper, "I'm going to be okay; I'm going to be okay," followed by a deep breath.

A black fishing boat approached us, and the driver asked if I wanted to sit on his boat with a blanket to keep warm until the police boat arrived. I was chattering at that point; even though the air was warm, I was going into shock. As he pulled up next to the jet ski, I stepped onto his boat and sat down. He introduced himself as Gerry from Texas and his son Blake, both speaking with a solid Texan drawl. They wrapped a camouflage coat around me, placed a fishing hat with lures dangling from the brim on my head, and gave me a towel to sit on.

I said, "Thank you. Do you come here every summer?" I try not to dwell on this moment and why I'm sitting on a stranger's boat.

"We love fishing for perch and bass and have owned a cottage on Bob's Lake for a few years now." Then, looking at me quietly, they said, "We are so sorry for your loss."

All I could think about was finding Eddie. It was silent as I sat in the Texan's black boat drifting around Bob's Lake, digesting the reality of Eddie drifting in the green-pollinated lake and what happened to him. What caused him to faint and drop out of sight? No gasp, no sound, no call for help, just gone. He mustn't have felt any pain, and the thrust of that competitive crawl must have sent the blood flowing to his fragile heart or head to burst a vein or artery.

As I sat gazing at the shore, I wondered if Eddy was there, clinging to a rock or scrambling for safety. I wanted to believe in a miracle—that Eddie was still alive.

We need to find Eddie. I must inform his daughter, ex-wife, friends, colleagues, and sisters, but I must stop overthinking and take it one step at a time.

Around the island, we could hear a siren as a massive black police boat with two officers approached us. They slowly navigated toward the black fishing boat from Texas, forcing me to leave behind the comfort of my warm camouflage coat and my hat filled with lures. I hugged the Texans, thanking them for their kindness as I stepped onto the foreboding and much darker police boat.

As the two officers assisted me aboard, I told them, "I need to stay here and show you where he went down. I can't leave my husband until he's found!"

As the engines roared to life, they shouted above the noise, insisting that I go to the mainland for questioning and provide all the details about Eddie.

They offered me a scratchy blanket as I sat in my seat, staring at the last place I had seen Eddie. When that spot faded from view, tears stung my eyes. I felt nauseated at the thought of leaving him alone in the lake, knowing I would never gaze into those blue eyes again or find comfort in the soft, safe space at the nape of his neck. I had to quiet my thoughts as everything felt too overwhelming. As we lost sight of Eddie's spot, I heard a distant yodel and the eerie tremolo of a loon. Was that the loon alerting the police to Eddie's location, or could it be Eddie's spirit saying goodbye, or Alan letting us know he was here with us? I closed my eyes, pulled my knees up, buried my head in the scratchy blanket, and prayed, realizing at that moment that I would never see my sweet husband again.

The police boat docked at a long public pier, flanked by small boats on either side. As I stepped onto the dock, I noticed the flashing lights of an ambulance and two police cars parked at the far end. A crowd had gathered to witness the commotion. I felt exposed, raw, numb, and embarrassed as the onlookers at the end of the dock stared at me in my wet bathing suit, mascara streaking down my cheeks, with nothing else on. The police reclaimed their scratchy blanket, leaving me feeling utterly naked and emotionally vulnerable. For a moment, I was grateful for the one-piece black bathing suit that provided some coverage. My legs felt weak, and my mouth was dry as I slowly walked barefoot down the wooden dock, the hot sun beating down on my face, with one officer beside me as I struggled to cope with my new reality. Another policeman, unfortunately another young male, greeted me halfway up the dock, escorting me to his police car.

As I sat in the front passenger seat, Constable Bobby pulled out his clipboard and forms without so much as a gentle, "I'm sorry for your tragic loss." Instead, I was met with, "What is your name and your husband's name?"

"My name is Morgan Ross, and I'm married to Edward G. Brooks from Vancouver, BC. He's sixty years old and vanished underwater without a ripple or bubble."

After more interrogating questions, like, "What was your relationship like, what do you think caused him to drown, and was he in good health? Did you fight this morning?"

I looked over at this twenty-something man and said, "You are way out of line if you are suggesting I killed my husband in front of his son and with numerous witnesses around."

I asked him if this was his first time speaking with someone who just lost a loved one, and he sheepishly said, "Yes."

I looked at him and said I wouldn't answer another question until he turned down his AC, got me a warm flannelette blanket from that ambulance, and found a nearby bathroom.

While waiting for the flannelette blanket, a woman tapped on my window. I rolled it down, and she said, "I brought you some clothes; I figure you must be uncomfortable in your bathing suit."

I thanked her and inquired if she had a bathroom I could use. After getting out of the police car, I changed into the shorts and top this kind woman had lent me, along with a bucket hat that wasn't really my style. At that moment, I lost all sense of vanity.

Constable Bobby and another policewoman started following me as I trailed behind the woman up a path to her cottage. I waited by the bathroom door while I washed my face and used the toilet. I wondered if I was somehow a suspect or if they thought I might harm myself in this very pink and yellow bathroom.

When I opened the door, I said, "Please take me to Goat Island; I need to see Eddie's son. You have all the information you need right now."

Walking back along the trail to the police cruiser, we all looked up at the massive sound of helicopters, reminiscent of the movie "Apocalypse Now." Loud and flying low, two enormous army helicopters hovered overhead, causing the boats to toss and bang against the dock while people scrambled to shield their eyes from the dust swirling around them.

The policewoman said, "They are here to find your husband. They won't leave until they find him."

The helicopters went beyond us but still in sight to witness four bodies in black wet suits repelling down ropes and into the water. For a moment, I thought Eddie would have loved this scene so much, like his favourite James Bond movies.

Standing in my new attire and refusing to get back into the police car for further interrogation, I noticed Pippa bringing a boat ashore, charging from the water and yelling at Constable Bobby to leave me alone and let me go. "She's in shock, and you had no right to interrogate her like this," she shouted over the rotors of the helicopters, which hovered like monstrous mosquitoes in search of my beautiful husband, now at the bottom of Bob's Lake.

Pippa took charge, and I felt immense relief after bouncing from Ashley's jet ski to the Texan's black fishing boat, then to the even larger and more foreboding police boat, which bore large white letters reading O.P.P. on the side. I had made my walk of shame down the dock to the police car, to the woman's cottage where I was guarded like a suspect in the washroom, all while wearing a checkered shirt and baggy blue shorts, topped off with a muddy gardener's bucket hat. What the hell just happened—in a single heartbeat?

I could see Pippa speaking to the police, saying, "I'm not only her friend, but I'm a doctor, and she needs to get home to her family to deal with this tragedy. If you require further information, here are my contact details. I witnessed Eddie Brooks going underwater, and I can confirm anything Morgan Ross has told you. Now, please take us back to my island so she can see her stepson, who is fourteen years old and has just lost his father."

Pippa wrapped her arm around me and said, "Let's go now."

Two police officers escort us down the dock; this time, I'm dressed in my gardening outfit, glancing back at strangers with sad expressions. An ambulance that may be unnecessary—or will it take Eddie to the hospital for an autopsy if they find him? Oh my God, what if they don't find his beautiful, perfect body?

Pippa and I climb onto the police boat and settle at the front, staring ahead as we wrap the scratchy blanket around ourselves. The boat lurches forward, and we feel the wind whip against our faces, saying nothing and simply trying to process what has happened to us both. I glance at her and say, "There's no one else I want with me now but you and Alex. The universe has orchestrated this, knowing I would need you. The last person to see Eddie go under was his son, Dax, and I was beside him. The two people he loved most were with him when he died. That's the universe, Pippa."

As we roared through the pristine lake toward Goat Island, we also roared away from Eddie, somewhere at the bottom of Bob's Lake.

Chapter Thirty

One Heartbeat

The police boat loomed large and ominous as we slowly approached Pippa's small dock. One of the officers leapt onto the dock with ropes to secure the boat, but they had no intention of staying. As I stepped off the boat and onto the dock, the youthful, kind-faced officer approached me and hesitantly said, "I'm sorry for what happened today. Would you mind giving us the clothing so we can return it to the woman on the mainland?"

As I undid the checkered flannel top and removed my shorts, Pippa took the hat and passed everything to the officer. Once again, I stood in my bathing suit, which was now dry; however, I still felt shy and vulnerable in front of these men who had witnessed me at my most broken state. I said, "Thank you, and please do everything you can to find my husband."

Pippa wrapped her arm around my shoulder, the next best thing to a towel, as we walked toward my first meeting with Eddie's son, Dax. He came running down the hill, his face appearing so young and innocent, much like Eddie's. His eyes, as blue as his father's, were filled with fear and uncertainty about what death meant as he struggled to comprehend such a traumatic loss. As I embraced him, I whispered, barely audible, "I'm so sorry, Dax. They're searching for him now. You were the last one to see him. He loved you so much."

Johnny and little Hailey joined us, looking shell-shocked after witnessing their uncle drown before their eyes. What had started as a day meant for fun, filled with tubing, cliff jumping, and hot dogs, suddenly shifted for all of us in an instant.

Pippa suggested that I change and pack up, and we would head out together in two cars to inform my family. That was the next thought. Oh my God, my stepfather drowned on this very day a year ago, and we are gathering tonight to support my mother after the tragic loss of her husband in that drowning.

I walked into the screened-in bedroom where we had left our clothes, and there was the first of many reminders that he was gone. His blue gingham shorts lay perfectly on the bed, with his watch beside them and his white T-shirt folded on top. He should be putting them back on instead of me folding them up and placing them in my beach bag. While I put on my shorts, I sat on the bed and pulled his white T-shirt to my face; his scent, which lingered at the nape of his neck, was both intoxicating and devastating at once. I will never wash this T-shirt. I returned it to the bag, put a baseball cap over my messy hair, looked up at the ceiling, and thought, "Fuck, here we go."

We drove to the cottage mostly in silence, with Pippa asking the children if they were okay or had any questions. Pippa was a doctor, and I wanted them to feel safe asking questions, no matter how complicated the answers might be.

Hailey sheepishly asked from the back seat, "Where is Uncle Eddie now, and will I ever see him again?" Before I could respond, her older brother Johnny intervened and, with a shaky voice, said, "Uncle Eddie drowned just like Pa did last summer. Maybe they'll be together in heaven."

Hailey replied, "I hope so, but they must find Uncle Eddie in the lake first."

Johnny breaks the long silence by saying, "I'm sorry you have lost your father, Dax. I can't imagine what that must feel like. If there's anything I can do to help, please let me know."

Dax speaks for the first time, saying, "Let's play tennis when we get back to the cottage."

We were all still in shock, and for a fourteen-year-old boy to have witnessed his father slip underwater, never to be seen again, is too much for the brain to comprehend.

Looking ahead, Pippa was driving and said, "Eddie felt no pain, is at peace, and will always be in your hearts. We will soon discover what caused him to drown, but we need to pray that they find his body first."

That ended the conversation until we drove up the long, winding driveway to the cottage. Everyone had been calling, panicking about why they hadn't heard from us, but I couldn't bring myself to share the news over a cell phone. We stumbled out of the car like zombies, overwhelmed by the tragedy we all experienced in one way or another. Hailey ran towards her mother, Carly, who was relieved to see her children, while my mother emerged from the cottage wearing her apron and said, "Where have you been? We've been worried sick about you and trying to reach you."

As she spoke, I could see her trying to register my shocked and blank expression, doing a headcount, wondering why Pippa was there, why Alex was now arriving down the driveway in their car, and finally asking, "Where's Eddie?"

Everyone stopped walking and waited for me to inform her, "Eddie drowned this morning, and the police are still searching for his body."

With that, my mother sunk against the cottage wall and screamed a guttural, gut-wrenching scream, "NOOOOO, Oh My God, NO. Not another drowning."

I sat on the step with Carly's arm around me as my mother slowly stood up. Dax walked past us, opening the screen door that banged shut before disappearing inside. He likely wanted to avoid the drama of others reacting to his father's death today. Part of me wishes I could escape the drama of other people's reactions.

She didn't come to me, but I overheard her on the phone with my brother Ben in New York, saying, "Your children are okay, Ben, but Eddie drowned today; your children witnessed him going under. I suggest you come here as soon as you can." Then I heard her add, "No, from what I understand, they're still looking for his body, and it's the anniversary of Alan's drowning."

As I listen to the phone call, there is no mention of me or how I may be coping with the loss of my husband.

Pippa brought me the first thing I had all day: a glass of water. I didn't realize just how parched, sunburned, and drained I was until then. I knew I needed to sit in the sunporch and make some necessary phone calls. The police had my contact information and would reach out to me when they found Eddie. I told Carly her children were terrific, diving in to save Eddie and being incredibly supportive. I got up and hugged both Johnny and Hailey, thanking them for being so strong and compassionate today, and asked them if they could check on Dax to make sure he was okay. "Please tell him that I'm calling his mom and sister now and that he should come downstairs to chat with them."

There was lots of commotion in the kitchen as my mother and Carly got the update on our day from Pippa and Alex. I would repeat it often in the calls and days to come.

I took out my red journal and began jotting down the names of people to call, the police officer's contact information I had received, and the details as I recalled them.

Then, the first phone call was made. "Hi, Whitney, it's Morgan." I took a deep breath. "Dax is fine, but Eddie isn't. He drowned today." I could hear my voice shaking as I said those words out loud.

"What? Oh my God, no! Where is Dax?" Whitney cried out.

"Your son was the last to witness him go underwater. He seems to have shut down, but I'll have you speak with him when he's ready. Please inform your daughter. The police are still searching for him at Bob's Lake, where we went cliff jumping with friends. It was a beautiful summer day, and Eddie never complained about any issues."

Whitney, his ex-wife and a doctor, gasped when I told her. I could hear her sniffling and holding back tears, as Eddie was the father of her children. She said, "Oh my God, I can't believe it. Eddie was always afraid of water when competing or putting his head underwater. I wonder if it was a premonition. Should Dax fly home tomorrow to be with me?"

"I'll ask him, but with the kids around and the cottage full of family and friends, maybe he should stay here until we find his father and then let him decide."

With that, Dax arrived at my side and handed him my cell phone.

"Hi, Mom, I'm okay. I was the last to see him. (Pause.) No, I don't want to come home. I want to stay with Morgan and Dad. I'll call you when we find out what happened and when they find him. I'm going to play tennis now. Bye."

After she handed me the cell phone, I said goodbye to Whitney, knowing she had to tell her daughter this unbearable news.

Then I knew I had to deliver this gut-wrenching news to my daughter, Harper, who loved and adored Eddie. She would be devastated, especially since she had just been here with us two days ago when the world felt cheerful and ordinary. With a three-hour time difference, Harper would be finishing work at Lululemon. I called her closest friend and asked if she could meet Harper at her apartment. I wanted someone to be with her when she received the news. Shortly after, I got a text confirming they were together at Harper's place, so I dialled my daughter's cell number with trembling hands.

"Harper, please sit down. I have some sad news." Another deep breath. "Eddie drowned today while we were cliff jumping at Bob's Lake with the kids."

A primal scream turned into sobbing and crying over the phone. "No, not Eddie. I loved him so much. Oh, Mom, no!" The sobbing softened, and I heard a barely audible voice, "I'm getting on the next flight. You can't do this alone."

That was the moment I broke down for the first time that day. The pain in Harper's voice, that gut-wrenching cry, pulled me out of the protective cone of shock that freezes us from our ability to express emotions. This protective bubble allows us to carry on with the necessary tasks of death, evading reality, all the while knowing that, eventually, the bubble will dissolve, and the pain will take over. Only after attending to the business of death can one cry. You can grieve, and then you can fall apart.

Still wearing her apron, my mother stepped out from the bustling kitchen crowd onto the sun porch. She brought me a glass of much-needed Rosé and Pippa, as well as a gin and tonic.

As she handed me the chilled glass of pink sedation, she quietly murmured, "I was alone when Alan drowned."

I looked up at her, and that was the moment I realized that Eddie drowning today, on the anniversary of her husband's death, had stolen the attention away from her grief and her moment to celebrate Alan with us. Did I steal her thunder again? There was still no comforting hug from my mother as she turned around, wiped her hands on her apron, and stepped back to her role as the family matriarch.

Sipping my Rosé, distanced from the chaos in the kitchen and still numb, I swirl in the bold thought that my mother is jealous of me. Has she always felt this way? Jealous that her late husband Alan constantly remarked on how good I looked in my bathing suit, how her male friends flirted with me, envious of my youth, accomplishments, career, lifestyle, and personality? Can a mother truly be jealous of her daughter, or is jealousy merely a form of control? Toxic emotional jealousy manifests as anxiety, threatening her love, yet it feels destructive, leaving me feeling helpless as her child. Perhaps it's rooted in my father's unconditional love for me, but her inability to show love in this most intense moment is shockingly hurtful.

I made the calls with the same flat, emotionless directness to his sisters, colleagues, and a friend whom I asked to inform the other friends about the news of Eddie's death. I could still barely comprehend the words coming out of my mouth.

Eddie drowned today, but what led this elite athlete to such a fate? Was it his heart or his brain? Still no news of the police recovering his body. All I could visualize were the men in black wetsuits rappelling from the massive army helicopters, plunging into the murky green water, searching for a perfectly fit body clad in his favourite purple Vilebrequin turtle swimsuit, still with dreams yet to be realized, graduations and weddings to attend, a body still to embrace adventure, love, and laughter, not death at the bottom of Bob's Lake.

I heard Dax and Johnny fly through the screen door, which always announced someone's arrival or departure. They were chatting about swimming while my mother fed the people coming and going. She had to change her plans for a nice sit-down dinner to commemorate and celebrate her man. I asked Dax to come in for a moment. It felt like I was holding court in the sunporch, with people leaving me to tend to the business of death while they carried on with the business of life.

"Dax, I want you to know that I'm here for you. We're both in shock, so let me know if you'd like to go home and be with your mom. I can take you to the airport, but if you'd prefer to stay with me and come home with

Harper and me, I can arrange that. Also, would you like to hear all the details I've learned about your dad?"

Without hesitation, he looked straight at me and said, "I want to stay at the cottage, go home with you, and learn everything that has happened and will happen to my father. Thank you, Morgan. I'm so sorry for you, as I know how much you both loved each other."

We hugged, and my heart broke free from its protective bubble, aching for that boy. He wasn't aware that this had become his life story. On the day his father died, when he was just fourteen years old, cliff jumping on a beautiful summer day at Bob's Lake, he vanished without a ripple or a bubble.

Pippa and Alex joined me, bringing their favourite gin and tonics. Alex asked how I was doing, and I replied that I was all right. My voice was nearly gone from talking too much or from exhaustion.

Pippa looked equally drained, and while these two remarkable individuals were doctors, they were also dear friends, emotionally exhausted from losing a friend that day on their lake.

It was 8:20 p.m. when my cell phone rang. Not recognizing the number, I answered it, putting it on speaker so we could all hear any news.

"Hello, Mrs. Brooks, this is Constable Tim Roberts. We have located your husband and are transporting him by ambulance to Kingston General Hospital, where they will be prepared for his arrival. An autopsy will be performed to establish the cause of death, and you will be notified once that process is complete. The time of death was 11:10 am, and it took the team eight hours to find his body. I am deeply sorry for your loss. Do you have any questions for me?"

"Thank you very much for letting me know, and please express my gratitude to the divers for ensuring they found him. I don't believe I have any questions at this moment." I glanced at the family gathered in the sun porch, looking to see if anyone had questions for the officer. Yet, everyone remained silent, absorbing the finality of the news regarding his discovery.

I hung up and whispered, "I suppose he didn't swim to shore."

Alex and Pippa hugged me goodnight. I told them I would reach out tomorrow when I received the autopsy results and thanked them for being there. I couldn't imagine two better people to have been by my side when this tragedy occurred. The Universe placed Dax and me next to Eddie and positioned Alex and Pippa beside me—the strange and beautiful world of chance.

After booking a flight for Harper from Vancouver and a train ticket from Toronto, I called her to check in and expressed my relief that she was coming back.

"See you at the train station tomorrow, Harper. I love you so much."

Harper was in shock and packing the clothes that she had just unpacked.

Her life story has now changed.

Slowly, people started heading to bed, and I bid goodnight to everyone as I climbed upstairs to my pink room, where Eddie's suitcase and toiletry bag were in the bathroom. My beautiful Eddie lies on a cold steel table, about to be cut open. What must he look like after lying at the bottom of a lake for eight hours? I couldn't bring myself to visualize that, but somehow, my mind kept drifting there.

I was brushing my teeth, wondering if Eddie had any idea that when he got up this morning and said he loved me, it could be his last morning, his last cappuccino, his last chance to play the car game with his son, his last day to breathe in summer, laugh, and embrace life. Did he know?

As I curled up in bed, hugging Eddie's pillow and hoping to sleep while knowing there was so much to do tomorrow, I heard a gentle knock on the door. My mother often came into my room, sitting at the end of the bed after a busy day at the cottage to chat when it was just the two of us.

She didn't stay this time but handed me a book by Elizabeth Kübler-Ross titled "On Grief and Grieving," along with a warm glass of milk. That was always her go-to, but never mine. Standing at the side of my bed, the little bedside lamp illuminating her tired face in the floral bathrobe I'd given her, she said, "This little book helped me through some tough days."

I looked up at her and said, "We now have husbands who drowned on the same day, one year apart. What are the odds of that happening?"

Without a response, she slipped out of my room, and I soon fell asleep, comforted by the news that my daughter would be arriving tomorrow.

Chapter Thirty-One

Purple Lupins

It's day one without Eddie, following a sleepless night filled with waking in a sweat and reaching for him, hoping I had merely emerged from a terrible nightmare. I grabbed a coffee and headed out to pick up Harper at the train station after her red-eye flight to Toronto and then the train to Kingston. The poor girl will feel dreadful—an emotional hell without any sleep. If only I could shield her from the heartache and pain of losing someone you love.

When she came out of the station, her eyes were hidden behind sunglasses, but her face was red and raw from the tears. She ran into my arms and repeated, "I can't believe he's gone; I can't believe he's gone."

I needed to take her back to the cottage to rest, or she risked getting sick. She had countless questions, and I recounted every detail of each memory from the previous day. By that point, we still didn't know what had happened to Eddie, only that he had gone underwater and drowned. Harper received a warm welcome from everyone, especially her Nan, who adored her as the first grandchild and nurtured a playful bond that my mother had fostered from a very young age. I felt relieved and happy that my daughter and mother share a beautiful bond, uncomplicated by years of power struggles—simple and free.

The cousins gathered around her, and she broke down when Dax came off the tennis court to greet her. All she could do was hug him and express how sorry she was. "I can't imagine, Dax. I will miss your dad so much."

After settling Harper into the same bedroom as mine, I left her to nap while I headed downstairs to greet a friend who had driven from Toronto with a car full of flowers and food. Millie Michaels and I grew up together, our mothers having served as each other's Maids of Honour. Millie was like my little sister, and I loved her unconditionally. Her arms were overflowing with flowers, and the boys went to her car to help unload all the groceries and food she had brought for us. It was wonderful to see her; like Pippa, she is a friend for life. She had endured trauma from her time living in New York, where her husband's company was in one of the World Trade Towers.

My cell phone rang, so I excused myself, as the number displayed was KGH. Millie and my mother were quite close, and they gathered at the kitchen counter to discuss the bizarre coincidence of both husbands drowning on the same day, one year apart, in a manner she couldn't share with me.

On the other end of the call, in the sunporch, my reprieve, a man said in a comforting voice, "Hello, Morgan Ross. This is Dr. Paul Dungey, the coroner from Kingston General Hospital. We have completed your husband's autopsy. Do you have a minute to go over it with me?"

"Of course, I'm just processing those words right now."

"I understand. Your husband had severe coronary artery disease, which led to a heart attack while he was swimming vigorously. When blood was pumped into the heart, the arteries blocked it, likely causing Eddie to lose consciousness. This condition is often referred to as a Widow's Maker. Since he lost consciousness in the water, the cause of death was classified as drowning, even though the fainting originated from his heart issues. He had a very muscular heart, indicating that he must have been an elite athlete at some point. He suffered from significant hardening of the arteries, with 75% blockage in the right artery, and the main artery was 80% occluded, showing signs of fibrosis, suggesting he had likely experienced a silent heart attack in the past. He may have been experiencing heartburn or symptoms related to this blockage but chose to ignore them."

"Thank you for letting me know. Could this have been avoided with stents or a strict diet?"

I started to feel guilty for not ensuring Eddie had a stress test or for getting his cholesterol checked. I continued, "Even though I didn't eat red meat, he was fond of cheese and red meat. Over the past month, he had been taking Tums regularly, and I thought it was due to the spicy food he enjoyed at lunch with his colleagues. The issue is that Eddie was an elite athlete who seemed healthy, so his doctor didn't prioritize cholesterol screening or a stress test."

The doctor said, "This is a classic case with athletes. It's based on the assumption that they are healthy, and most have a high pain threshold."

"He hesitated to go into the water the day before he died. Do you believe people have premonitions about their death?"

Dr. Dungey made the time to answer all my questions. He spoke in layman's terms and reassured me that there was nothing I could have done. He provided his contact information and asked if I would like to visit Eddie before he was cremated.

I couldn't speak. I could only say, "Will that help or re-traumatize me?"

"This is your decision; perhaps discuss it with your loved ones."

"I know my decision, Dr. Dungey. I don't want my final memory of my beautiful husband to be of him lifeless on a cold metal table after being cut open; I wish to remember him alive and happy. Thank you for asking, but I can't bear to see him that way."

"We will send his body to John Reid Funeral Home for cremation, and they will contact you when his ashes are ready for pickup."

I waited for Harper to wake up and then asked everyone at the cottage to gather so I wouldn't have to repeat myself with all the information.

Two days later, Harper, Dax, and I entered the John Reid Funeral Home, characterized by its solemn atmosphere, quiet surroundings, dark wood accents, and burgundy leather furniture—a stark and disheartening place with inappropriate music playing softly in the background. We inquired about Penny Smith, who had called me earlier. She led us into a room with a round table, and as we settled in, she left but soon returned with a black box and an envelope. We sat in silence, stunned by the harsh reality that Eddie was in that box; my beautiful Eddie, the father, husband, and stepfather to us all—the man we loved to the moon and back was now reduced to ashes in a simple black container.

Carrying Eddie out of the funeral home and back to the cottage felt surreal and was impossible to comprehend, especially for a fourteen-year-old boy who loved and idolized his father. No words could make that easier or right.

After a few more days at the cottage, swimming and playing tennis with family and catching up with friends who stopped by, it was time to head home and return Dax to his mother and sister. I hesitated to go back to our home, which was filled with Eddie's presence and everything he loved, from his golf clubs to his skis to his treasured racing bikes. This would be brutal.

Harper, only twenty-five years old, looked at me after bringing a glass of Rosé following yet another emotionally charged and overwhelming day grappling with this loss. We sat on wicker chairs adorned with pink floral pillows, inhaling the aroma of the lake alongside the shrill calls of the purple martins, whose throaty, rich songs filled the air around us. They seemed particularly chatty that afternoon as we attempted to absorb the moment. A beautiful sailboat, its enormous rainbow spinnaker billowing, drifted peacefully down the river, propelled by the gentle breeze. How lovely it must be to be free from pain and to lead such an easy life. I suppose we once felt carefree, revelling in the everyday tapestry of living and loving. Harper mentioned she would move in with me for a month or however long I needed her. She will go to work but will stay with me at night until I adjust. As I gazed at my only daughter, my miracle child, I saw such inner strength and compassion in her eyes. I couldn't have been more grateful for this incredible blessing.

The following day, the entire family gathered to bid farewell. I embraced my mother for the first time, feeling overwhelmed by the complexity of our emotions. I held Johnny and Tegan close, reassuring them that if they ever wanted to discuss Uncle Eddie and the events of that day, they could call me anytime. I love them and admire their strength and remarkable maturity.

Harper and I drove to Toronto, listening to the British Open on the radio while Dax was engrossed in his iPhone. We had run out of things to talk about.

As we passed through security, we had to show the documents detailing the contents of the black box. I blurted out, without thinking, "It's my husband."

The three of us sat together, taking turns glancing up at the overhead compartment where Eddie was, in his black box, inside Harper's backpack. The idea of Eddie being in the overhead compartment was incomprehensible on every level, but strangely, knowing he was with us was reassuring.

Harper was listening to her country music and gazing out the window when she handed me an AirPod, inviting me to listen. "It's Thomas Rhett, 'Die a Happy Man.'"

"Eddie died a happy man." I smiled as I held my daughter's hand.

As we arrived home and were greeted in the driveway by wonderful friends, my golden retriever Phoebe, the dog walker, and some home-cooked food, the garage door slowly opened to another kick in the heart. Eddie would never use those three Cervélo speed bikes hanging from large hooks, the new PING golf clubs in that beautiful black and red PING bag, or those Völkl skis he so effortlessly turned through the deep snow at Whistler. I imagined him in the garage, tinkering with his bike or cleaning his golf clubs while we drove slowly into the parking spot beside his black Maserati.

Harper slept on the side that Eddie once occupied, which felt more comforting than I had realized. She helped me sort through the clothes on one side of the closet, the toothbrush and shaving kit in the bathroom, along with all of Eddie's favourite books, his Apple computer, and his sports gear. We loaded both cars, with my bike rack carrying all three bikes, and I took everything I thought Dax would need to his place. We unloaded the items from my garage and returned them to the garage Eddie had left a decade ago. Ten days after Eddie vanished underwater, Dax, Harper, and I drove to Whistler to scatter Eddie's ashes in the perfect spot.

I couldn't bear the thought of Eddie stuck in our closet, trapped in a black box any longer. He was a free spirit who cherished the outdoors. I instructed Harper and Dax to look for purple lupins and a freshwater creek as soon as we stepped off the gondola at Whistler on a stunning summer day, with crisp mountain air and patches of snow scattered across the peaks against a deep blue sky. They looked at me as if I were crazy, but I reassured them that we'd find the perfect spot to release Eddie. After hiking across the mountain for nearly two hours, we spotted purple lupins near a small lake in the distance, and Dax cheered that we had finally discovered what he had feared might remain elusive. We settled by the little freshwater creek, unfolded the blanket from the backpack, and Harper brought out the heavy black box as we all took a deep breath. This moment felt incredibly charged, and I knew I had to stay composed for Eddie's son.

Harper slowly lifted the lid off the box, revealing dark grey ashes. I wasn't sure what I had expected, but Dax dove in, scooping up his father's ashes to toss into the air, unaware that some might land back on us. We laughed, as it was the only emotion we could muster. Then, Harper carefully placed her handfuls of ashes into the stream, watching the water carry them down the mountain, though some ashes sank to the rocks below. I couldn't hear her words, but this was her private moment with someone she cherished, who cherished her in return.

When it was my turn, I was startled to feel shards of bone among the ashes, a stark reminder that this was Eddie's body. I scattered his ashes around the lupins, saying, "I will always love you, Eddie. You are free now to fly with the angels."

Chapter Thirty-Two

Higher Ground

The celebration of Eddie's life occurred at the charming English-style country church, St. Francis-in-the-Wood, which overlooks the Pacific Ocean, with seagulls soaring above the parked cars. Harper and the family gathered in the back room while friends and relatives filled the pews. I wanted this day to honour Eddie Brooks and his impact on people through powerful music, poetry, and heartfelt dedications from friends. I asked everyone to wear colours instead of black, as it was a celebration of joy, and I wanted to see vibrant hues that day. Although I chose to wear black like a widow on a day of mourning, complete with a black fascinator adorned with a delicate veil that flowed over my face as I walked down the aisle of the church, it shielded my eyes, diverting them from the sadness reflected on so many faces. Once seated, Reverend Janice Lovett began the service with a prayer and invited us all to stand and sing Cat Stevens' 'Morning Has Broken.

Planning this beautiful service filled me with purpose, uniting people from my world and Eddie's beneath one sacred roof in the heart of the woods. We sang as one and reflected on a life lived, our mortality, and our fragility while light danced through the stained-glass windows, symbolizing hope, truth, love, and life. If there is a God, I felt her presence in that quaint little church at that moment, believing in her with all my soul.

I asked Harper if she could read a reading after the minister's introduction and Eddie's friend's tributes. Although she felt nervous, I reminded her that we only had one chance to show up, and I didn't want her ever to regret not saying a few words for someone who touched her heart like Eddie did.

She looked stunning that day in her black polka-dot dress and long blonde hair. She was a natural beauty, blissfully unaware of her youthful charm. After I squeezed her hand, she stood up.

Broken Chain
We little knew that morning,
that God was going to call your name.
In life, we loved you dearly,
in death, we do the same.
It broke our hearts to lose you,
you did not go alone
for part of us went with you,
the day God called you Home.
You left us with peaceful memories,
Your love is still our guide.
and though we cannot see you,
you are always at our side.
Our family chain is broken,
and nothing seems the same.
But as God calls us one by one,
the chain will link again.
By Ron Tranmer

She did everything she could to hold back her tears until she returned to her seat beside me, at which point she allowed herself to cry. Her good friend Jess, with a voice as beautiful and powerful as Adele's, stood up and walked to the front of the church in a lovely pink floral dress. The pianist glanced up and nodded to her as she positioned herself by the microphone. Then, this angelic voice emerged, filling the church with "Make You Feel My Love" by Bob Dylan. I could hear people gasping behind me at the beauty of her voice—rich, deep, and full of colour, with soulful depth. We were united in the congregation, breathing in this intoxicating moment together as she elevated us to higher ground.

It was my turn to take the mic and read the poem I had written for

Eddie. I lifted my small veil and stood before the microphone, gazing at the faces filled with empathy and encouraging me onward with their love and support.

Dear Eddie,
There's so much to say,
Did you know you were with Dax and me on your last day?
You didn't get your Timbits and coffee to go,
I said, "No Tim's for you, we'll go tomorrow."
The water was warm, we were all having fun,
A perfect summer day in the midday sun.
Pippa, you and I were watching the kid's cliff jumping,
When suddenly, your heart stopped thumping.
Not a bubble, a ripple, not a sign of life,
It was peaceful until the silence was broken by your wife.
"He's gone," was echoed across the lake,
The panic to find you was more than I could take.
Someone named Gerry lifted me into his boat,
He gave me his camouflaged hat and an oversized green coat.
He was from Texas, a Trump supporter and kind,
Gerry kept looking for you until we were all…resigned.
The next few hours were like your favourite double O Seven,
I was hoping you saw the divers repelling from choppers in heaven.
In typical fashion, you left quietly, without ego or drama,
Harper, Dax, family and friends need to deal with the trauma.
You will never know the number of people who showed up today
All the beautiful words your friends needed to say
You will never know just how much you are missed.
And how much I cherish the last time we kissed.
You will never know whether Trump gets impeached,
Or whether Dax goes to Queens like I've preached.
You will never know how your son was so strong,
Or that your daughter showed up today to sing along.
Maybe you do know and will be our guiding light.

Your gentle, strong, loving spirit, I embrace every night.
You at least know something that none of us know
What happens to us when we die, and where do we go?
Please let me know by any number of signs.
I love you, Eddie, and believe in Universal designs.
Love Morgan

As I stepped down from the pew, Luciano Pavarotti's voice slowly captivated the congregation with Puccini's Nessun Dorma, the most spectacular aria, causing most of us to close our eyes and soar with his stirring voice.

As Reverend Janice Lovett read The Commendation, we were softly reminded of sitting in church pews and singing one final hymn together: "Joyful, Joyful, We Adore Thee."

On the back of the program given to everyone as they entered the church, along with a photo of Eddie with his sunglasses and bike helmet, were words that resonated with me and that I believed he would want us to feel.

I'M FREE
Don't grieve for me; for now, I'm free.
I'm following the path God laid for me.
I took His hand when I heard Him call,
I turned my back and left it all.
I could not stay another day,
To laugh, to love, to work, or to play.
Tasks left undone must stay that way.
I found that place in the middle of the day.
If my parting has left a void,
Then, fill it with remembered joy.
A friendship shared, a laugh, a kiss,
Ah yes, these things I, too, shall miss.
Be not burdened with times of sorrow.
I wish you the sunshine of tomorrow.

My life's been full, I've savoured much.
Good friends, good times,
A loved one's touch.
Perhaps my time seemed all too brief.
Don't lengthen it now with undue grief.
Lift your heart and share with me…
God wanted me now,
He set me free.
By Anne Lindgren Davison

I was the first to stand and walk down the aisle behind the minister, smiling and glancing at faces, moved by the music, the words, and the profound emotion. As the oak doors of St. Francis-in-the-Wood swung open, beams of light streamed in. I embraced and thanked everyone for coming, reciprocating the love from the service and the spiritual connection we shared in that quaint little church in the woods. I bid farewell to a man we cherished.

Chapter Thirty-Three

Base Camp

The business and busyness of death began to slow down by September; the closets were emptied of any remaining reminders of my life with Eddie. Yet, memories lingered in wedding photos, and my phone stored thousands of reminders from the past. From the moment I woke up—my hand reaching for his side in search of him—to the Nespresso machine with his cherished mug, to Keith Urban's "Blue Ain't Your Colour" playing on the radio. Will my mind remain locked in the past, gripping my heart and head, insisting, "Don't forget me, remember who I was, remember our love, remember!" When someone we love passes away, there is no looking forward, only backward. One can merely glance back at the past, for there is nothing to anticipate with that person ever again. Someone once said that's why we have a small rearview mirror and a large front windshield: to glance occasionally in the rearview mirror but to keep our eyes firmly focused on the road ahead.

My therapy became my daily walks alone in the forest, accompanied by the sounds of chirping birds and the shrill, high-pitched call of an eagle. I breathed in the nurturing health benefits offered by the enormous Douglas firs and ancient red cedars, standing tall against the constant motion of the wind and saltwater from the ocean. I felt my body melt as it absorbed the strength and wisdom of these stoic survivors and protectors of humanity, allowing me to be. They whispered, "Welcome back, stay awhile, breathe us into your fragile soul. We have weathered many storms and much abuse from humans, but we persist." As I saw rays of sunshine filtering through their branches, I realized I had two choices: survivor or victim. The survivor felt strong, resilient, tenacious, and capable of moving forward without getting stuck in grief, trauma, or sadness. It would be easy to slip into victimhood; many people felt sorry for me, and I could linger in that zone for a while, but it felt like hell on earth. I wanted to fight for the future, and Eddie would want me to live a life full of adventure and new love, continuing to make people laugh.

Now sitting alone at home, curled up with Phoebe on the couch, I decided to find something that would challenge, excite, and motivate me to get out of bed, looking forward to this adventure. While watching a documentary on Mount Everest, they showed the climb to Base Camp, which led me to Google treks to Everest Base Camp and discover that G Adventures had some available in April the following year. I read through all the details and verified the best time of year to climb. April was when the 200-year-old rhododendrons bloomed alongside the cherry blossoms. Many expeditions took place in April to acclimatize for six to eight days before attempting their ascent of the world's highest mountain at 29,000 feet. Base Camp sits at 17,300 feet, and I felt comfortable at 15,300 feet, so I should be able to manage this over the seven days it takes to acclimatize. You trek through Nepalese villages, and the Himalayan mountains appear stunningly majestic in the photos.

That night, I booked with G Adventures for the first two weeks of April and then searched for flights through Hong Kong connecting to Kathmandu. It would take seven days to trek up to Base Camp and seven days to return to Lukla, from where I would take the plane back to Kathmandu.

I went to bed that night, no longer sad and lonely but excited and thrilled about my decision to go alone to Nepal and join a group of young adventure seekers who wanted to share this experience.

From that point onward, I placed one foot on the floor every morning and said, "Base," then brought down the other foot flat while exclaiming, "Camp!" It's time to get into shape and be my best self for this trip.

It forced me to look forward, which felt much better than looking back with painful reflections. Dealing with my grief one step at a time, climbing to the base of the largest mountain on this planet, kept my eye on the future of living and the present of getting in shape and organized for this trek.

After a nine-hour flight to Hong Kong and a six-hour layover, I arrived at Kathmandu airport five hours later, surrounded by a whirlwind of people colliding with one another, unique smells, unfamiliar languages, and chaos, ready to start my new adventure. I was to be met by one of the G Adventures guides, so all I needed to do was look for a sign with my name in this sea of humanity. It was overwhelming yet exhilarating at the same time. I hoped my duffle bag had made it from Vancouver, and surprisingly, it did, once I found my way to the baggage claim area.

Out on the streets, it was an even crazier madness with no apparent traffic flows, just everyone moving in whatever direction they wanted to go, horns blaring just to be blaring, only impacted by the thousands of mopeds weaving in and out of the cars, with sometimes a family of four holding onto each other. Luckily, I caught sight of a van with G Adventures on the outside, and as it pulled up to me, a guy jumped out, introduced himself as Miguel, and said, "Hop in, Miss Morgan, and I will get you to the hotel."

My room was sparse but had a clean washroom and bed, so I had to lower my standards quickly. I reminded myself that this was the start of an adventure and that our living quarters would become increasingly limited as we ascended to Base Camp. After changing and washing up, I was eager to explore the city of Kathmandu and grab something to eat. Leaving the quaint hotel, I narrowly avoided being hit by a moped. I had to stay focused and alert, yet I was incredibly excited to immerse myself in a new culture, experience life in its rawest form, and witness the true struggle of poverty. The dogs lying on the sidewalks didn't appear healthy or clean, but they looked friendly and content. Walking the streets of Kathmandu was chaotic and wild, yet I never felt threatened or unsafe as the locals hurried by, allowing tourists to blend into their lives and culture. I found a place serving a delicious bowl of vegetarian curry and rice, which was lovely. While I checked my phone, I took a few bites of the coleslaw before realizing I should have eaten everything cooked. Whoops. Oh well, I'm sure I'll be fine.

We met at the hotel at five with the group we would spend the next two weeks with. As we gathered around a large table, I counted ten of us, which seemed like a good number. A mix of women and men, mostly in their thirties and forties, with one older man around seventy, appeared

American. When we started introducing ourselves at the table, I discovered we had two guys from Germany, two from Sweden, four young women from England, myself from Canada, and the rest from the United States. When it was my turn to introduce myself, a sudden knot formed in my stomach, soon followed by a stronger urge to throw up. I signalled that I needed to leave and dashed to my room, barely making it in time to vomit all over the door of my bedroom. Damn that coleslaw. I spent the next twelve hours in that cramped bathroom, not even bothering to turn down the bed sheets, but determined to rally once I hoped all the E. coli had exploded out of my gut. I took some Imodium tablets and packed my duffel bag, hoping I wouldn't vomit on the bus ride to the airport, where I would catch the tiny 12-seater plane to Lukla. At 5:00 am, there was a knock at my door, and Miguel asked if I could travel. I told him I hadn't slept a wink and had thrown up all night, but I had to go. He looked at me and probably thought, this isn't good. I'm sure he was anticipating a guest who might throw up on the bus or small plane and be incapable of hiking the first day of five long hours.

I picked up a small bag from the kitchen table that contained granola bars for our bus ride, hoping the worst was behind me. Fortunately, I had added electrolytes to my bottle of purified water, but I still felt lightheaded and weak. The anxious person seated next to me on the small prop plane said, "Hi, I'm Kate, and I'm so sorry to hear you were unwell all night," in a polished English accent. "It was brave of you to come after such a miserable start."

I smiled at her and said, "It's not as brave as you sitting next to me."

She laughed and asked me if I would like an English digestive biscuit that might be good for my stomach. I realized I had eaten nothing since the coleslaw, and my stomach was so painful that this may help.

As the plane taxied down the runway and into the sky with mountains surrounding us, I was stunned and in awe of these peaks that jutted three times higher than the Rocky Mountains or Whistler Mountain. They were pure and potent, awe-inspiring for miles and miles to see from our little plane in the sky. Everyone was snapping photos, and the buzz of excitement got me out of the nightmarish night of my body ejecting those two bites of coleslaw as violently as it could. I was impressed with how our bodies try to protect us and save us from ourselves.

Lukla Airport is considered one of the most dangerous airports for landing due to its short runway. The plane must land swiftly, ascend a hill, and stop before tumbling off the 2,000-foot cliff. At that moment, after Eddie's death and my near-death experience from the previous night, I was leaving it to fate. If this was my time, they could say, "She died at the most dangerous airport in the world instead of in a small hotel in Kathmandu after eating coleslaw."

As the plane receded, every head was turned to make sure it stopped before the end, and then when it stopped, everyone screamed with joy and shot their hands in the air and clapped. Okay, let's go!! The digestive biscuits and the Immodium somehow held things together, and I was relieved to make it.

After we put on our day packs and wandered through Lukla, with cows and yaks meandering through the streets like pets, I spotted a small hut advertising 'Yak Milk Lattés'. I was tempted to grab a caffeine boost for the five-hour hike ahead, but my stomach warned, "Don't you dare!"

We began our hike out of Lukla on a well-trodden trail, and even though I was exhausted and my stomach ached from the wicked contractions, I was exhilarated by the anticipation of climbing to the base of Mt. Everest. With each step, I would say, "Stay strong," while breathing in the crisp mountain air. I needed every ounce of energy to get through the next five hours. Still, the conversations with Kate and Libby from England, George from Germany, and Elsa from Sweden were so engaging that I became lost in their stories and the thrill of gazing up at the majesty of the Himalayan mountains against the brilliant bluebird sky. I felt giddy and childlike, experiencing the natural high of discovering something breathtakingly beautiful and humbling in their presence. The immense power of these Himalayan mountains loomed like kings over their subjects, with nine of the world's ten highest peaks in this range. They soar into the sky with steep, jagged peaks blanketed in pillows of snow. At the same time, alpine glaciers slowly melt through deep river gorges into the valleys, nourishing the rich vegetation with diverse flora and fauna. Their ancient history, world dominance, and fascinating existence for thousands of years before me and for thousands more to come magnified this magical moment.

I gazed down at my hiking boots, taking one step at a time and allowing myself the luxury of space to reflect, enveloping and embracing moments from my past that triggered a tidal wave of emotion. These moments remain alive and vivid with colour, movement, and sound, representing a place I can visit as a ghost floating above, examining the reality of each little scene as an impartial critic. I hover above with a compassionate, unemotional gaze that allows for a clearer understanding of all the cast members in the film. Humanity surges with uncontrollable passion and is tumultuous with ungoverned grief, tossed about by anxiety and doubt. Only the person at peace, whose thoughts are controlled and purified, can make the soul's winds and storms obey her. Our thoughts can prevent suffering, and I choose not to suffer.

After losing myself in meditation for a few hours, I returned to my dusty hiking boots, filled with forgiveness and love. The act of forgiveness liberates me to embrace today, this magnificent moment, as I release the pain associated with these memories. My heart is grateful for the challenges I have faced and overcome, and I recognize that they are my most cherished blessings. Returning to the earth, I pause to inhale the overwhelming power of nature in all its spectacular glory. This must be heaven.

As I joined my group, we gathered at metal tables adorned with red and white checkered tablecloths outside a small cement house draped in strings of prayer flags, surrounded by vibrant purple and soft pink rhododendrons, served by the kindest Nepalese people offering us steaming noodles in hot broth. No fresh vegetables would be available on the trek, as Sherpas deliver everything on foot or by yak. For once, I felt relieved not to have fresh produce, just primarily carbs. The noodles were exactly what I craved, knowing it was time to get something somewhat nourishing into my poor stomach, aside from digestive biscuits. The group was getting along wonderfully, with everyone already teasing each other, featuring an equal number of women and men, mostly young and in their thirties. I chose not to share the news of my husband's recent death, as I wanted to experience liberation from grief, a chance to feel alive, and a moment to be free from the pain. My story will be told when I'm ready to share it. For now, I am not a widow but an enthusiastic Canadian woman who spent all night vomiting, embracing the joy of trekking with strangers in the Himalayas.

The Nepalese people in the small villages we passed through were friendly, kind, and generous hosts, considering how little they had. Their children wore uniforms and attended the Sir Edmund Hillary schools established by him and his foundation. Despite living in harsh conditions, the children appeared happy, clean, well-fed, and never begged. This made me think of a quote by Rudyard Kipling: "Do not pay too much attention to fame, power, or money. Someday, you will meet someone who cares for none of these, and then you'll know how poor you are."

Every night, I slept with a toque pulled over my head because the air in the tea houses was cold, as they were only heated by the fireplace and stoves used for cooking. Luckily, I had a warm sleeping bag and plenty of clothes, nestling my face into the one luxury I packed in my duffle bag: my down pillow. Each day brought a new adventure, starting with hot coffee, yak milk, eggs, toast, and Miguel's route rap for the day ahead. He checked our blood oxygen levels each morning using a small device clipped onto our index finger called a pulse oximeter to ensure our bodies acclimatized to the lower oxygen levels. We were going from sea level to 17,300 feet, and most of us had Diamox to assist with the adjustment.

The days got progressively more challenging as we approached Base Camp, with colder nights, moving more slowly each day with less oxygen, some struggling more than others, cold showers, and more primitive living quarters. The toilets were now replaced with holes in the ground, which you had to squat over, and dreams of flush toilets and hot showers were dancing in my head as I attempted to sleep.

This was our last day to reach Base Camp at 17,300 feet, and everyone was excited despite their sleep deprivation and oxygen deficiency, causing some of the group to suffer miserable headaches. I knew we were getting over the daily grind of hiking with little oxygen and eating the same pasta or noodle soup when the topic of conversation was what we were most looking forward to at the end of this trek.

The list included hot bubble baths, cell reception, freshly squeezed orange juice, an In-and-Out burger, fresh clothes, heat, shampooed hair, a warm, cozy bed, breathing at sea level, a large vegetable salad, sushi, and a steak and kidney pie.

One said, "When we have those things, we will dream of being here, in the majesty of the Himalayan mountains, squatting over a hole in the ground."

After seven days of trekking together, someone finally asked me if I was single or had left my husband at home. I explained that my husband had recently passed away suddenly from a heart attack while swimming beside me, and this was my chosen form of therapy. I chuckled and remarked, "I can sum up my life as three weddings and a funeral."

The faces around the table appeared shocked as they tried to understand what it meant, and then they joined me in laughter.

"Do you think that's a good line for the next guy I meet? I suppose it's better than the movie, Four Weddings and a Funeral."

With a sweet smile, Kate added, "You have something to strive for now."

My new friends were kind and understanding, and they were impressed that I embarked on this journey alone, bringing my broken heart to be healed in the Himalayan mountains.

We gathered for a photo shoot beside the large yellow sign that read, "Way to Mt. Everest B.C.," marked by a red arrow. Thrilled, we felt a sense of achievement and anticipation for warmer weather and more oxygen. As I looked up at Mount Everest, I inhaled deeply and closed my eyes, overwhelmed with gratitude and a deep sense of joy and peace.

The night before, I had chatted with Miguel about the possibility of leaving once we saw Base Camp, a sea of yellow, red, and orange tents scattered in a small village adorned with prayer flags, all resting on glacial silt from the tallest mountain looming above them. Everyone gathered with a shared goal and mission: to conquer the tallest mountain and survive the climb without succumbing to the potential demise from numerous unforeseen circumstances. Depending on the weather, they would stay in that small village of tents for four to five days or weeks before ascending to

Camp 1, which is halfway up the Khumbu Glacier. After reaching Camp 1, climbers acclimatized for a few more days before continuing their ascent, reliant on finding a good weather window.

As we gathered, proud of our accomplishments and taking numerous selfies while absorbing it all, the sound of a helicopter's propeller echoed in the distance. Someone wondered if it was delivering supplies to the climbers or if someone was hurt on the mountain. Just then, a tiny red bug appeared, growing larger and louder as it approached, eventually touching down on a flat area fifty yards away from us.

Miguel glanced at the group and said, "We are losing one of our members. She has decided to leave us today for a hot bath in Kathmandu this evening."

Everyone looked around, and then I hugged Kate and Libby. "I'm sorry I can't climb down with you, but I'll be thinking of all of you. I loved sharing this adventure with you. Please send me photos."

Kate and Libby began to cry, and Libby shouted above the noise of the rotors, "You can't leave us now; we had seven more days to get to know you."

As Miguel grabbed my duffle bag from the yak carrying our gear, he headed towards the bright red helicopter, with everyone following him to take a photo in front of it. As I stepped into the helicopter and took the seat next to the pilot, who handed me a headset, I yelled out to the group, now moving away as the propellers started up, "So long, suckers!" They laughed in unison and began waving like the Munchkins, shouting goodbye to Glinda, the good witch from The Wizard of Oz. We lifted off, and I told the pilot in my headphones that I wanted to fly over Base Camp and the Khumbu Icefield. The Nepalese pilot looked at me and replied through our headphones that we could only go up to 21,000 feet. I smiled and gave him a thumbs-up. He slowly lifted off as I gazed below at the propellers stirring up dirt and dust, some hands shielding faces, and many others waving as we banked over Base Camp and up the mountain to the massive Khumbu Icefall. Soaring like an eagle in that little helicopter around the Himalayan mountains was pure magic, and I couldn't wipe the smile off my face.

We soared over climbers clad in bright yellow jackets against the white snow, their hefty packs gradually ascending, and the pilot noted they were headed for Camp Three at 23,000 feet. He banked suddenly, descending into the valley towards Lukla, where I needed to catch a flight to Kathmandu, hoping to find a hotel with a bathtub and room service. Absorbing the aerial view of the Himalayan mountains was overwhelmingly emotional, being so close to those majestic peaks in all their power and glory. The thirty-minute journey through the valley allowed me time to reflect on my trek with my new friends, feeling proud that I managed it without falling ill and impressed by my body's stamina for six to seven hours of daily hiking. A wave of excitement washed over me as I looked forward to my new life, rejuvenated by the belief that life is meant to be lived and that even as a single woman, one can experience the thrill of adventure, joy, and an exhilarating sense of fulfillment and peace.

Namaste, Nepal, Namaste.

Chapter Thirty-Four

Saluti

Landing back in Vancouver after my whirlwind trip to Nepal took more out of me than I realized. I needed to restore and replenish myself with a healthy diet of fresh vegetables and fruit, my morning boost of Nespresso coffee and freshly squeezed orange juice, and breathing in sea-level air along with a good night's sleep. Harper looked shocked when she met me at the airport, unsure if my mascara was smudged across my face from the overnight flight or if my hair was a big, tangled mess, but her mouth remained open for an unusually long time.

"Welcome home, Mom. Thank goodness you made it back safely. You look a little thin. Didn't you eat?"

"I'll share all about my coleslaw mishap the night before my trek, and my stomach still hasn't fully recovered. Maybe I look thin in these baggy hiking pants. I'm so happy to be home, and I can't wait to indulge in a bubble bath and crawl into bed. Harper, I cherished every breathless minute I spent there. It truly was the trip of a lifetime! I would love to return but wouldn't eat the coleslaw."

As I opened the door to my home, an unexpected wave of memories washed over me; everywhere I looked, there were reminders, scents, and echoes of Eddie not being alive, not being here to hear about my incredible trek, not being here, never to be here again. Our minds strive to comprehend where our loved ones' spirits reside. All I know for sure is that they remain in our hearts until our hearts stop beating, part of every heartbeat, every touch of pain or joy, never to be gone or forgotten.

Grief is very sneaky. A sound. A scent. A song. A smile becomes tears.

Two months later, golfing felt impossible. Eddie and I loved golfing together so much that I would find myself putting on the third green with tears streaming down my cheeks beneath my Maui Jim sunglasses. As I walked down the fairway, about to take my club out of the bag, I would see the blue Cookie Monster headcover Eddie gave me and break down. I inevitably encountered people who didn't know Eddie had passed away the summer before, commenting on how they hadn't seen him around the club. It became torturous to drive into the golf club parking lot, visit the driving range, and tee off, as that was our routine weekly during the summer. That's when I realized I needed to get away on my own again and honour Eddie for the birthday we were supposed to celebrate in Tuscany. It might be a year later, but I decided I needed to rent that Alfa Romeo, zip through the narrow Italian streets, and fulfill Eddie's 60th birthday wish. Being at home hurt more; getting away hurt less. Being in a new culture, living in the moment, and meeting new people who didn't know me was my therapy. Fly to wherever it doesn't hurt so much. Home hurts: travel heals.

Driving to Montalcino in my red Alfa Romeo sports car from Florence Airport was exhilarating, as I felt Eddie was with me in some way and loved it. I arrived at a stunning vineyard estate featuring large, romantic rooms and enormous wooden doors that opened onto patios overlooking the rolling hills blanketed in vines. As I unpacked and admired the exquisite, rich textures of the Italian fabrics, the antique armoire, and the charming walnut desk, I was filled with joy and relief, knowing that coming to Tuscany was the right choice. I needed to be here.

A beautiful courtyard, surrounded by purple wisteria and overlooking the vineyards, was next to the dining area. I poured myself a glass of my favourite Super Tuscan wine, and as I admired its deep burgundy hue and inhaled its earthy aroma, I took in the rolling hills blanketed with vines and olive trees. Nestled in a large, comfy chair in the courtyard, adorned with vines entwined around the trellis, I reflected on the highlights of my life to the soft sound of Pavarotti playing in the background. As the lush pink roses blended into the backdrop of the blood-orange sunset filling the sky, nature's expansive light embraced my spirit, wrapping around me like a warm blanket. The delightful sip of wine and the gentle warmth of the breeze brushing against me brought a profound sense of calm and gratitude for the immense power of the universe—the universe that grants me my three wishes: to find peace with my aching heart and soul, to be supported and loved by family and friends, and to achieve financial security and freedom.

At that moment, I felt a surge of energy to connect with the sun's glow, the vineyard, and the sweet, ripe scent of the earth as I stood up and opened my arms as if I were at the bow of the Titanic.

"Buonasera," a man's voice whispered.

With my arms still raised in the air, I turned in surprise, my cheeks flushing, and responded, "Buonasera, Signore," captivated by the magic of his eyes—dirty, dark, stunning magic.

With a slight smirk, a thick head of curly brown hair, and eyes reflecting the sunset, I hear him say, "Sono l'enologo di questo vigneto. I am the winemaker of this vineyard; welcome," he reiterates in English.

I read about Nico Ricasoli, the legendary winemaker acclaimed as the best in Tuscany. He is the grandson of the founder of Ricasoli Wines. In person, he was even more striking than he appeared in the photo on the website of this prolific vineyard.

Without hesitation, I blurted, "Would you care to join me for some pasta? You can share all about this delightful wine."

"Mi Piace unirmi a te, love to join you."

As the sun sets, we gently clink our glasses together and smile, knowing that the chemistry is undeniable.

"Saluti Nico Ricasoli."

"Saluti, Morgan Ross."

After a delicious dinner of seafood linguine and exquisite red wines, playing bocce until midnight and enjoying some delightful flirting, I kissed Nico goodnight, irresistibly drawn to his charm. As I wandered back under the moonlight to my lovely little villa, uplifted by the evening and proud of my ability to walk away, I breathed in the tranquil peace of the night.

Waking to the crowing of a rooster was a perfect way to start a new day. Sipping my cappuccino and packing my bag, I hopped into my little red Alfa Romeo and drove down the Cypress tree-lined driveway before the others were awake. I felt as though I was escaping yet again from another dangerous romance, and the thrill of that excitement while driving down the Italian road made me yell, "Start the car!"

Giggling joyfully to myself, proud of my courage to live independently, I shifted into fourth gear and merged into the fast lane towards Florence and my future.

Acknowledgements

This book would not have been written without the unwavering encouragement and support of my remarkable daughter, Courtney Gordon. She was also why I hesitated to share my story: to protect her from aspects I wasn't proud of. Shame dissipates when stories are shared in safe spaces, and this book became my safe space.

Thank you to all the men I have loved and lost, as well as those I chose to walk away from. My heart still holds a special place of love and light for each of you, free from lingering pain or blame.

Thank you to my mother, the matriarch, for all the love and guidance she provided. She revelled in laughter and embraced life wholeheartedly. I am eternally grateful to have had her as my mother, and I miss her terribly. Her recent passing also gave me the freedom to share my story.

Thank you to my wonderful, loving, and generous friends who let me live freely without judgment and who joyfully laugh or cry at my stories. You are the reason I feel courageous and willing to take risks. You create a safe space for me when I return home.

Thank you to all the ancient trees and eagles in Lighthouse Park for your constant, attentive presence. You are my steadfast support.

Author Bio

Holly Gordon narrates her story through the eyes of Morgan Ross, drawing on memories of her life's tumultuous yet remarkable events. She grew up in Kingston, Ontario, enjoying a privileged upbringing but one marked by heartache, ambition, and trauma. Her journey has taken her from a passion for sports to teaching, to a fulfilling career in the investment industry, and now to her role as an author.

Holly lives in West Vancouver, B.C.